LAWS AND LEGISLATION

RELIGIOUS LIBERTY AND PUBLIC ACCOMMODATION LAWS

CONSTITUTIONAL RIGHTS VERSUS STATUTORY OBLIGATIONS

LAWS AND LEGISLATION

Additional books and e-books in this series can be found on Nova's website under the Series tab.

LAWS AND LEGISLATION

RELIGIOUS LIBERTY AND PUBLIC ACCOMMODATION LAWS

CONSTITUTIONAL RIGHTS VERSUS STATUTORY OBLIGATIONS

ANTHONY WALSH

nova science publishers
New York

Library of Congress Cataloging-in-Publication Data

ISBN: 978-1-53619-578-1

Published by Nova Science Publishers, Inc. † New York

CONTENTS

Preface		**vii**
Acknowledgments		**xi**
Chapter 1	The United States Constitution: Originalism v. Living Document	**1**
Chapter 2	The Establishment Clause: Ally or Adversary of Religious Liberty?	**19**
Chapter 3	Religious Liberty: The Free Exercise Clause	**35**
Chapter 4	Religious Freedom as Freedom of Speech	**53**
Chapter 5	Religious Liberty and the Legalization of Same-Sex Marriage	**71**
Chapter 6	Religious Liberty in the Age of LGBTQ Rights	**89**
Chapter 7	Freedom, Equality, Discrimination, and Involuntary Servitude	**107**
Chapter 8	Two Iconic Religious Liberty v. Anti-Discrimination Cases	**125**
Chapter 9	Photographs, Cakes, and Pizzas	**141**
Chapter 10	Federal Government Animus Toward Religion	**157**

Chapter 11 Some Important Victories for Religious Liberty **175**

Chapter 12 Big Government and Freedom **191**

Chapter 13 Concluding Remarks on the Battle for Religious Liberty **209**

References **227**

Author Contact Information **253**

Index **255**

PREFACE

The issue of LGBTQ rights versus religious liberty is a fiery one in Western societies at present, particularly in the United States which has a strong history of religious freedom coupled with a cultural undercurrent of distrust of big government. Numerous cases in which these rights clash have inched their way through the courts for three decades. After the legalization of homosexual behavior in 2003 and same-sex marriage in 2015, LGBTQ activists embarked on a crusade against religious liberty whenever it ran afoul of their agenda. We may celebrate the newly found rights of an historically persecuted group while at the same time soundly condemning attacks on people of faith who refuse to endorse same-sex marriage with their labor. LGBTQ rights are important, but not at the expense of religious liberty. Religious dissenters should be accommodated and not marginalized and pushed out of the public square.

The foundational principle of this work is the sacred rights enumerated in the United States Constitution, specifically, in the First and Thirteenth Amendments. These amendments have frequently been violated by the state when, in the name of public accommodation laws, attempts to force Christian business owners and religious entities to facilitate events, provide services, express opinions, change attitudes, or to enter into associations that violate their religious consciences. The book explores what it means to have free exercise of religion, free speech, and to be free of involuntary servitude in the context of LGBTQ rights. LGBTQ rights are neither denied nor disparaged, but I argue that the constitutional rights of religious dissenters should not be denied or disparaged either. I thus take an accommodationist perspective.

Religion was so important to the Founding Fathers that they enshrined it in the very first words of the Bill of Rights as the first freedom. The accommodationist view of the Establishment Clause is that it is a means of ensuring the free expression of religion by forbidding the establishment of a preferred religion: A Church of the United States. On the other hand, a strict separatism view is the belief that it implies a ban on any government support for religious organizations whatsoever, even when aid is based on neutral criteria. Justice Joseph Story, a man intimately acquainted with many of the founding fathers and their views on the place of religion in society, viewed the Establishment Clause as a tool in the service of the rights of religious conscience guaranteed by the Free Exercise Clause. However, the Establishment Clause it has been used in ways hostile to the Free Exercise Clause, and as though the two clauses were conflicting rather than complementary.

The Free Speech Clause of the First Amendment is also involved in LGBTQ v. religious liberty cases. Religious business people are not only being forced to endorse the LGBTQ message on pain of draconian legal penalties, they are actually being forced to create the very messages to which they object. United States Supreme Court jurisprudence has come down against the practice of forcing a person to endorse a message created by others; how much more repugnant is it to force one to create the message as well? The Free Speech Clause is a tool that enables people to pursue their own paths in life, set their own goals, and to defy the orthodoxies of society. If a person cannot dissent from the general will, society is not truly free. If one group can be denied free speech rights, then so can all others. Christians who believe in traditional marriage are gagged today; whose turn may it be tomorrow?

The Thirteenth Amendment's prohibition of involuntary servitude at issue as well. One person being forced by law to labor for the benefit of another is the essence of involuntary servitude. This is constitutionally forbidden, as well as forbidden by federal and state legal codes. In the name of public accommodation laws, however, various states have told devout Christian business owners that they must provide services to facilitate practices that their consciences will not allow. These people face the tragic choice of either obeying state laws or face financial ruin. Indeed, many have already been forced out of business because they cannot violate what they see as God's law. Having to make such a choice is precisely what the First Amendment is there to prevent.

History reminds us of the dangers of unconstrained government, thus the struggle for limited government; one powerful enough to protect inalienable rights, but not powerful enough to take them away. Ever since the French Revolution, the political left has been at war with religion, and with the emergence of LGBTQ rights they have been provided with a modern rallying cry. Karl Marx knew that for socialism (the quintessence of big government) to be successful in the West it must first spiritually disarm the people by destroying Christianity and the traditional family. As the government's role in our lives continues to expand, an increasingly important question is: "Does a person's life belong to his or herself or to the state"? By definition, the socialist is a believer in collectivism; the notion that the individual's life belongs to the state, and that individuals have no rights except those the state permits.

The book is not just a legal monograph. It engages political, philosophical, and sociological issues such as freedom v. equality, socialism v. republicanism, the liberal-progressive agenda in higher education, and the many benefits Christianity has bestowed on Western civilization. The underlying theme, however, remains, and that theme is that if we lose the freedom of religious conscience which the founding fathers made the "first freedom", we will lose all freedom.

ACKNOWLEDGMENTS

I would first like to thank acquisitions editor Aleksandra Bator for her faith in this project, and the rest of the Nova Science team for expertly seeing it to fruition. The copyeditor spotted every stray comma, dangling participle, and missing reference in the manuscript. I would especially like to thank my old buddy Rich Stamper, the Midwest's Mr. Karate. Rich read the entire manuscript and caught several grammatical errors. I didn't want to argue the point with him since he is a 7th degree black belt. Thanks also to the reviewers of the manuscript. Finally, as always, I reserve my greatest appreciation for my lovely wife, Grace Jean, for 30 years of love and support. She is a real treasure, the nicest of persons, candy for the eye, and the center of my universe.

Chapter 1

THE UNITED STATES CONSTITUTION: ORIGINALISM V. LIVING DOCUMENT

FOUNDATIONAL PRINCIPLES

Every book requires a foundational idea or principle to structure its content. Nathanial Hawthorn's *The Scarlet Letter,* first published in 1850, illustrates this. The first sentence in Hawthorn's book reads: "The founders of a new colony, whatever Utopia of human virtue and happiness they might originally project, have invariably recognized it among their earliest practical necessities to allot a portion of the virgin soil as a cemetery, and another portion as the site of a prison" (2003, p.1). Hawthorne is reminding us of two things we cannot avoid—death and human corruption—and that we must make provisions for both. The remainder of Hawthorn's book centers around the formal and informal methods of social control considered necessary for social cohesion exercised by the Massachusetts Bay Colony. The foundational principle undergirding the present book is the sacred rights enumerated in the United States Constitution, specifically, in the First and Thirteenth Amendments. These amendments frequently have been violated by the state when, in the name of public accommodation laws, it attempts to force Christian business owners and religious institutions to facilitate events, provide services, express opinions, change attitudes, or to enter into associations that violate their religious consciences.

Nineteenth century British Prime Minister William Gladstone once said that: "The American Constitution is, so far as I can see, the most wonderful work ever struck off at a given time by the brain and purpose of man" (in Matthew, 1997, p. 267). Prior to the liberal/progressive capture of higher education, and prior to the United States Supreme Court's slow erosion of our religious freedom, most Americans shared this view. The erosion started slowly with the removal of school prayer in 1962, gathered speed during the sexual revolution, and became a whirlwind following the legalization of homosexual behavior in 2003 and of same-sex marriage in 2015. These cases emboldened radical lesbian, gay, bisexual, transsexual, and queer or questioning (LGBTQ) activists to embark on a crusade against religious liberty whenever it runs afoul of their agenda. We may celebrate the newly found rights of an historically persecuted group, but we must at the same time soundly condemn attacks on people of faith who refuse to endorse same-sex marriage with their labor.

The United States Constitution was ratified at the Constitutional Convention in Philadelphia, on September 17, 1787. It presented a radically new theory of government based on timeless principles cemented by an underlying presumption of individual liberty. The United States is the only nation in the world founded on the truth that God created man to be free, and which acknowledges that there is a power that transcends that of the state. The Constitution is the supreme law of the United States, and is the longest lasting constitution in human history.

A constitution of any nation is a document that creates (formally constitutes) a government by laying out the mode in which a government is organized, and the way power is distributed to its various branches. It enumerates national goals and aspirations according to a system of beliefs and values, regulates institutional and social behavior, and sets forth the rights of individuals living under it. The radical nature of the United States Constitution is apparent in the fact that it actually limits the power of the government to the protection the inalienable rights of its citizens, and makes plain that these rights are not granted by government but rather by God. Sir

Edward Coke, Chief Justice of England in the early 17th century, and the father of Anglo/American common law, viewed the law of England as "written with the finger of God in the human heart," and that God is "the fountain and founder of all good laws and constitutions" (in Zimmerman, 2013, p. 92). Americans traditionally viewed the United States Constitution in this manner.

The United States Constitution sets forth a government under the rule of law and not of men. The meaning of the rule of law is captured well by James Otis in his 1774 pamphlet, *The Rights of the British Colonies Asserted and Proved,* in which he wrote:

> Parliaments are in all cases to declare what is good of the whole; but it is not the declaration of parliament that makes it so: There must be in every instance, a higher authority, viz. GOD. Should an act of Parliament be against any of his natural laws, which are immutably true, their declaration would be contrary to eternal truth, equity and justice, and consequently void" (in Beitzinger, 2011, p. 122).

Since the natural law is given by God, any law passed by either the federal government or by a state government that violates it is impermissible. Yet, public accommodation laws have been passed by many states that violate the First Amendment liberties of religious exercise, speech, and association, and the Thirteenth Amendment's injunction against involuntary servitude. As a general rule, public accommodation laws are socially desirable because they are designed to prevent any business that offers goods and services to the general public from discriminating against any group of people based on their ascribed status such as race or sex. These laws, however, have failed to differentiate between the sale of everyday goods and services and services that require business owners to actively participate in events that offend their religious beliefs. If the state forces anyone to violate their conscience on pain of legal sanctions and financial ruin, it tramples on the Constitution. Liberal progressives support these laws in the name of antidiscrimination, while conservatives and libertarian view them as serious attacks on religious liberty, and liberty in general.

Although the Constitution's timeless principles have made America the freest and most prosperous nation on earth, it stands in the way of liberal/progressive notions of social perfection, something that intellectuals on the left have yearned for down the centuries. To achieve their vision of social perfection, there must be a radical and immediate fundamental transformation of society. In such a society, it is necessary to make every citizen bend to state orthodoxy. Unfortunately for them, the Constitution has a built-in bias for evolutionary change rather than the revolutionary change. The idea of gradual change recognizes that the art of governing requires the exercise of experience and caution. Change cannot be based on abstract ideas, no matter how well they may commend themselves to emotion or to the wisdom of ignorance. The great British philosopher Edmund Burke recognized this when he wrote in 1790:

> The science of government being therefore so practical in itself, and intended for such practical purposes, a matter which requires experience, and even more experience than any person can gain in his whole life, however sagacious and observing he may be, it is with infinite caution that any man ought to venture upon pulling down an edifice, which has answered in any tolerable degree for ages the common purposes of society, or on building it up again, without having models and patterns of approved utility before his eyes. ...The nature of man is intricate; the objects of society are of the greatest possible complexity; and therefore no simple disposition or direction of power can be suitable either to man's nature, or to the quality of his affairs...When ancient opinions of life are taken away, the loss cannot possibly be estimated. From that moment we have no compass to govern us; nor can we know distinctly to what port we steer (1841, p. 404).

This is a profoundly conservative position, but conservatives do not oppose change. Burke also wrote that "a state without the means of some change is without means of its own conservation." (1841, p. 405). Conservatives distrust big government and have a preference for what James Madison called "auxiliary precautions"—a set of absolute restraints the Constitution places on what the government can or cannot do. Conservatives and libertarians revere the Constitution for this reason. Liberal progressives have a profound distaste for such constraints and favor big government rushing in to impose its will on whatever is the *cause de jour*. Because it thwarts their will, many leftists consider the Constitution an irrelevant and even dangerous document: “For many modern-day liberals, the Constitution is, at best, a piece of quaint, even irrelevant, parchment” (Wehner, 2016, np). Leftist professors and administrators at elite universities have been caught on tape shredding copies of the “flawed, oppressive, and racist” Constitution at the request of an undercover student working for Project Veritas (2015) who complained that someone was passing out copies of the Constitution on the quad and the sight of it made her physically sick.

Even the late Supreme Court Justice Ruth Ginsberg called the document that was supposed to guide her judicial decisions as outdated and inferior to other national constitutions. Ginsberg said in a radio interview: “I would not look to the U.S. Constitution, if I were drafting a Constitution in the year 2012. I might look at the Constitution of South Africa. That was a deliberate attempt to have a fundamental instrument of government that embraced basic human rights” (in Keating, 2012, np). But South Africa’s constitution is merely cosmetic; it permitted President Ramaphosa to simply ask for and implement an amendment to allow for state expropriation of land owned by white farmers without compensation.

Viewing South African democracy as a miserable failure, political scientist Richard Pithouse notes that its people are “subject to institutional contempt and terrifying rates of criminal violence, governed with increasing state violence and at risk of serious repression, including, in some parts of the country, assassination, if they have the temerity to organise outside the governing party” (2019, np). The basic human rights Ginsberg lauds do not exist in South Africa, especially for white farmers. Although the South African constitution was only adopted in 1996, it has been amended an average of once a year since then. The U.S. Constitution has been amended only 27 times in its 230-plus years, with the first 10 amendments (the Bill of Rights) being adopted as an integral part of the original document. A constitution is just lofty words on paper unless the state actually respects it and lives by it.

Constitutional Originalism or "Living, Breathing" Document?

We rely on the Supreme Court to read the Constitution's plain words as they are written, and not on each justice's idiosyncratic interpretation of it that bears little resemblance to the words in the document. A strict interpretation of the Constitution implies restraints on the individual power of judges to read into it anything they want. The issue of judicial restraint is the battle line drawn between the conservative and libertarian preference for originalism and the liberal progressive belief that the Constitution should be a "living" document to be contemporaneously and not historically interpreted. Originalism asserts that judges must not place their own interpretations on the Constitution, even if by adhering to it would be personally abhorrent.

Originalism mandates that judges must read the document as it *is*. This does not mean according to the Framers' unknowable subjective intentions, but rather according to the exact words in it that they all signed off on. This is the rule of *law*. The goal of originalists is not to venerate the founding fathers long gone to their glory, but rather to restrain living judges from imposing their values on the whole country by interpreting in idiosyncratic ways what the Constitution plainly says. A living interpretation is a reading of the Constitution as how it *ought* to be according to the subjective political opinions of a majority of the nine unelected Justices sitting on the Supreme Court. This is the rule of *man*. If ambiguity arises in a given case, then constructionists look for original intent by perusing relevant material in an effort to try to discover the collective intention of the framers. There certainly is ambiguity in parts of the Constitution, but there is no ambiguity in the First Amendment because it lays out inalienable rights in plain language:

> "Congress shall make no law respecting an establishment of religion, or prohibiting the free exercise thereof; or abridging the freedom of speech, or of the press; or the right of the people peaceably to assemble, and to petition the Government for a redress of grievances."

Supporters of a living Constitution see originalism as imprisoning American law and values, in eighteenth century thinking and legal rigidity. They may have a point, but as Winston Churchill wrote: "It may well be that this very quality of rigidity, which is today thought to be so galling, has been a prime factor in founding the greatness of the United States. In the shelter of the Constitution nature has been conquered, a mighty continent has been brought under the sway of man, and an economic entity established, unrivalled in the whole history of the globe" (2012, p. 743). The rigidity of the Constitution is imposed by the timeless principles that it embodies. If a novel new social, political, or economic issue arises that requires Constitutional guidance, its timeless principles of liberty should guide the issue; they should not be perverted to justify a desired outcome of the issue as seen by the majority of the Supreme Court. Churchill saw the Constitution as an enduring source of strength for America, and considered it a bulwark, while modern liberal progressives view it as a fetter to be loosened in their frazzled search for change in the name of "social justice." Witness the insanity of Representative Alexandria Ocasio-Cortez's agenda, warmly embraced by DNC Chairman Tom Perez as "the future of our party" (in Morton, 2018, np). Churchill warned us of the folly of change implemented without due regard for the past: "The onus must lie always upon those who propose a change, and the process of change is hardly ever beneficial unless it considers what is due to the past as well as what is claimed for the future" (2012, p. 740).

A favorite argument of the adherents of a living constitution is that an originalist Supreme Court put its stamp of approval on slavery in *Dred Scott v. Sandford* (1857). They argue that because originalists take the Constitution as they find it, they fear that slavery could linger into perpetuity. This is absurd, and an indication of a serious misunderstand the scaffolding of American law. Issues of justice such as slavery are the proper domain of Congress, not the Supreme Court. Congress can amend the Constitution in ways that accord with contemporary views of morality, but until it does so, the Justices are bound to find in the Constitution only that which is there. Chief Justice Roger Taney put it this way in *Scott*: "If any of its provisions are deemed unjust, there is a mode described in the instrument itself by which it may be amended; but while it remains unaltered, it must be construed now as it was understood at the time of its adoption." The blot of slavery on America's soul was not removed by the Supreme Court. It was removed in 1865 with the passage of the Thirteenth Amendment which legally cemented President Lincoln's Emancipation Proclamation of 1863.

The Supreme Court has significantly departed from originalism in its rulings since the middle of the 20th century. It no longer abides by Taney's pronouncement that if some provision of the Constitution is deemed unjust it may be amended by ratification by three-fourths of the states. Amending the Constitution is a long and arduous process, as it should be. Yet, in effect, the Supreme Court amends the Constitution every time it rules something previously constitutionally acceptable (e.g., school prayer and public displays of religious icons) to be unconstitutional, or something previously constitutionally unacceptable (e.g., abortion and same-sex marriage) to be constitutional. Although this practice is not nominally an amendment, what else can it be if it changes what is constitutionally permissible or impermissible? This practice of changing the Constitution's meaning is unconstitutional according to Article V of the document. Article V plainly states that a constitutional amendment is the sole duty of the legislatures of the "several states;" that is, the power to do so should come from the people. When the Court takes this power for itself it deprives the people of a fundamental liberty. In the words of Antonin Scalia, one of the greatest legal minds to have sat on the Court: "In practice, the Living Constitution would better be called a Dead Democracy" (Scalia, & Garner, 2012, p 410).

A living Constitution conforms with former Chief Justice Charles Hughes' famous dictum that the Constitution is "what the Supreme Court says it is". If this is the case, we have a Court that rules the Constitution rather than a Constitution that rules the Court. We are thus stuck with the rule of the majority of nine unelected lawyers who have told us that the Constitution means one thing at one time and quite another thing at another time. Thomas Jefferson warned that if the Constitution means whatever judges want it to mean, it would be like "a mere thing of wax, that they could twist and shape it into any form they please" (1819, np). A Court that views the Constitution as a political tool presents us with a body of constitutional law which is derived from the actual Constitution only when it suits the majority of Justices. As Justice Scalia has remarked in his dissent in *Wabaunsee County, Kansas v. Umbehr* (1996):

> What secret knowledge, one must wonder, is breathed into lawyers when they become Justices of this Court that enables them to discern that a practice which the text of the Constitution does not clearly proscribe, and which our people have regarded as constitutional for 200 years, is in fact unconstitutional... The Court must be living in another world. Day by day, case by case, it is busy designing a Constitution for a country I do not recognize.

If the Constitution is a "living" document to be interpreted in any way a majority of the Court sees fit, why have a Constitution at all? If the Constitution is "living" in the sense that it can mean just about anything, then the Constitution as drafted by the framers is dead, or at least in dire straits. If it does die, the left will dig it up, polish its bones, and declare it living again and useful to their agenda, because: "The living Constitution is a weapon of ideological war when wielded by legal elites who view constitutional law as the means of imposing their view of the good life on everyone else through the supreme law of the land" (Duncan, 2016, p. 23). The living constitution argument is, at bottom, an argument for not being bound by a written constitution at all, and thus an argument against the principle of constitutional government.

Natural Law and Positive versus Negative Rights

Many conservatives and libertarians view the Constitution as a sacred document that instantiates natural law in its parchment, while many liberals view it as mere words on paper that can mean anything they want. Conservatives and libertarians believe that there are natural laws governing human conduct just as there are physical laws governing the physical world. Immanuel Kant spoke of the two things he could be absolutely sure of: "The starry heavens above and the moral law within" (in Thomas, 1962, p. 255). And Alexander Hamilton wrote: "The sacred rights of mankind are not to be rummaged for, among old parchments, or musty records. They are written, as with a sun beam, in the whole volume of human nature, by the hand of the divinity itself; and can never be erased or obscured by mortal power" (1775, pp. 97-98). Hamilton saw the rights laid out in the First Amendment as rights demanded by our God-given human nature. Natural law means that all humans should be treated with dignity and respect and viewed as intrinsically valuable ends-in-themselves, not as means to some other end. This is the idea behind the Golden Rule: "Do unto others as you would have them do unto you" (Luke 6:31), or Shabbat 31a in the Talmud: "What is hateful to you, do not do to your fellow man."

The writings of the founding fathers reveal that they believed that absolute moral standards of right and wrong exist that transcend time and culture. Natural law may be considered "law within the law"; a set of moral precepts that tempers positivist law with concerns of fairness and justice that are absolutist principles and morally binding. The ringing passage of the Declaration of Independence: "We hold these truths to be self-evident, that all men are created equal; they are endowed by their Creator with certain inalienable rights" invokes natural law. These words make it clear that the Constitution does not *grant* rights to the people, but rather it established a government of laws in order to *secure* their preexisting rights to life, liberty, and property "to which the laws of Nature and Nature's God entitle them". The function of law is thus not to create justice; rather it is to prevent injustice by guarding natural rights that existed pre-constitutionally. Leftists reject moral absolutes and believe that what is morally acceptable or unacceptable depends on time, place, or person.

What Does the Left Want from the Constitution and Why?

The pillar of American conservatism is belief in Divine Providence and Christian faith. Conservative belief is tethered to the idea that although we must render unto Caesar what is his, there is an authority greater than the secular state that commands our behavior through a natural moral code. No state can rightly demand our absolute obedience or attempt to control every aspect of our lives, especially if it attempts to prevent us from rendering unto God what is His. Liberty is a gift of God that must be protected by the rule of law. To the atheistic left this is pious twaddle; there is no God and the state is the highest authority. Leftists preach that we must discard the "superstitions" of religion and the constrictions of the traditional family. It is this idolization of the state that leads the left to discount constitutional originalism and to savage any Supreme Court nominee who practices it. They fear the originalist nominees because the fear the Constitution, and they fear the Constitution because is places limits on government power.

The left views the Declaration of Independence's "Life, Liberty, and the pursuit of Happiness" as a guarantee of endless positive rights, and are miffed that the Constitution provides only negative rights. Negative rights imply restraints on state power; a constitutional framework by which government non-interference is guaranteed. Negative rights include the right not to be subjected to wants and demands of others. This obliges only government inaction unless another's negative rights are infringed. Positive rights include demands that some must provide others with goods and services, despite conscientious objections, which obliges government action to secure them. The left believes that it is legitimate to force others into living their lives subordinate to state orthodoxy in all matters.

Barack Obama considers that the Constitution should have provided for strong positive rights. He considers himself to be wiser than the framers, who foisted a "flawed" document on America. In a 2001 interview on a Chicago radio station, he revealed exactly what he tried to do as president: scrap the Constitution and spread the wealth. Obama bemoaned the fact that although the civil rights movement succeeded in gaining civil rights for all citizens:

> The Supreme Court never ventured into the issues of *redistribution of wealth*, and of more basic issues such as political and economic justice in society. To that extent, as radical as I think people try to characterize the

> Warren Court, it wasn't that radical. It didn't *break free from the essential constraints that were placed by the founding fathers in the Constitution,* at least as it's been interpreted and Warren Court interpreted in the same way, that generally the Constitution is a charter of negative liberties. Says what the states can't do to you. Says what the Federal government can't do to you, but doesn't say what the Federal government or State government must do on your behalf (in *American Thinker*, 2012, np; emphasis added).

So, our pesky Constitution sets inconvenient boundaries on government. Obama is not alone in this opinion; former Chief Justice of the U.S. Court of Appeals for the 7th Circuit, Richard Posner, trashed the Constitution as outdated and incapable of guiding modern society. He sees no value in studying the Constitution because: "Eighteenth-century guys, however smart, could not foresee the culture, technology, etc., of the 21st century. Which means that the original Constitution, the Bill of Rights, and the post–Civil War amendments (including the 14th), do not speak to us today" (in DePlato, 2019, p. 70). Posner views the freedoms of religion, speech, assembly, and the press, the rights that most irk the radical left, as outmoded concepts because they were articulated by 18th century white guys who rode astride horses on their appointed rounds and lacked smartphones and computers! The world is undeniably immensely more complicated today than when the immortal words of the Constitution were penned, but the words still speak to us because they are timeless. The document is based on eternal principles of human liberty and on a firm understanding of unchanging human nature and its demands, and thus they transcend whatever cultural and technological changes that occur.

When the Constitution does not speak to an issue undreamt of by the framers, the people of each state should decide it via the legislative process guided by the Constitution's principles of liberty; it should not be decided by judicial fiat. According to our system of federalism, it is within the enumerated power of the Congress to pass valid laws to address the needs and requirements of changing times as long as said laws do not violate the Constitution's fundamental rights. The Ninth Amendment: "The enumeration in the Constitution of certain rights, shall not be construed or deny or disparage others retained by the people," makes it plain that the enumerated rights in that document do not exhaust all rights that citizens may claim. The Constitution thus lives in this sense, but the point is that any new right granted must not infringe on the more fundamental rights enumerated in the First Amendment. Many of the other amendments of the Bill of Rights contain moderating language that makes them subject to broad "living" interpretations, but the First Amendment is singularly absolute in what it forbids the state to do. The freedoms of religion, speech, press, and association are natural rights that protect the autonomy and dignity of the individual. Other *unenumerated* rights hiding in the Constitution's shadows such as abortion and same-sex marriage rights, may be granted, but these are not natural rights, so if they clash with the fully visible *enumerated* rights, the former must yield to the latter. We shall see that this has rarely been so in cases involving LGBTQ issues.

The different views of the Constitution held by liberals and conservatives may rest with what psychologists call the "locus of control." Locus of control is the degree to which individuals believe that they have control over their lives as opposed to external forces beyond their control. Conservatives and libertarians tend to attribute the locus of control to dispositional factors such as conscientiousness and self-control: "I am in control of my own destiny and can go as far as my talents and ambition allow." Liberals, on the other hand, tend to attribute the locus of control to external factors such as sociocultural forces: "My life is under the control of others, and I can go only as far as outside circumstances allow." The reality of this is revealed in a Cato Institute nationwide poll which found that strong liberals believe that the top reasons for people's level of wealth are family connections (48%), inheritance (40%), and getting lucky (31%); strong conservatives say top reasons are hard work (62%), ambition (47%), self-discipline (45%). Likewise, strong liberals say the top causes of poverty are discrimination (51%), an unfair economic system (48%), and lack of educational opportunities (48%), while strong conservatives say that the problems are poor life choices (60%), lack of work ethic (52%), breakdown of families (47%), and drugs and alcohol (47%) (Ekins, 2019). Outside forces doubtless impact our lives, but in a free society, the attitudes one holds about them—one's locus of control—is a major factor in determining what one gets out of life.

There is voluminous literature on the locus of control, and there is not a single study that disputes this liberal-conservative difference. One article noted that: "The results indicate supporters for the two major parties are wired differently, in line with previous findings about ideology. Democrats were driven by an external locus of control and Republicans by an internal locus" (Sweetser, 2014, p. 1183). Another article linked locus of control to motivation and belief in free will: "Evidence from three studies reveals a critical difference in self-control as a function of political ideology. Specifically, greater endorsement of political conservatism (versus liberalism) was associated with greater attention regulation and task persistence…this relationship is shown to stem from varying beliefs in freewill [conservative belief stronger]" (Clarkson, et al., 2015, p. 8250). For those who believe that they have little control over their lives it may make sense to appeal to a political party that promises to use the power of government to make society a better place for them since they can't manage it themselves.

WHY SUCH DIFFERENT MODES OF THOUGHT?

Modes of thought are formed raw from each person's genetically driven temperament. The two founding giants of Western philosophy—Plato and Aristotle—illustrate this. A well-known fresco in the Vatican's Apostolic Palace painted by Raphael known as *The School of Athens* depicts a number of famous ancient philosophers, with the central figures being Plato and Aristotle. These two men represent the archetypes of two very different modes of thought representing the left and the right wings of the political spectrum. In the fresco, Plato is depicted as gesturing with pointed finger upwards toward the heavens, and Aristotle with palm downwards gesturing toward the earth. These gestures symbolize the central aspects of their respective temperaments that guide their philosophies; Plato the dreamer of the "ought," and Aristotle the practical empiricist of the "is". The 18th

century English poet and philosopher, Samuel Taylor Coleridge believed that all humans are temperamentally destined to follow the path of one or the other of these two pillars of Western thought:

> Every man is born an Aristotelian or a Platonist. I do not think it possible that anyone born an Aristotelian can become a Platonist; and I am sure that no born Platonist can ever change into an Aristotelian. They are two classes of man, beside which it is next to impossible to conceive a third. The one considers reason a quality or attribute; the other considers it a power (Porteous, 1934, p. 97).

Reason as a "quality or attribute" implies that Plato considered reason to be constitutive; that is, reason itself can constitute existence—create new forms of reality. Knowledge is made in the mind rather than discovered by the senses. As his theory of the Forms attests, Plato was a lover of abstractions, and his notion of reason led him to rationalize what "could be" without need of evidence from experience, which leads to radical subjectivism and relativism. This culminated in his theory of the ideal city-state outlined in his *Republic,* which he called Kallipolis. Kallipolis was to be under the absolute control of enlightened leaders ("philosopher kings") who knew what is best for everyone else, and who were to make sure that everyone was subservient to their orthodoxy.

Aristotle was an empiricist who considered reason as "a power," which means that he considered it to be regulative; that is, reason regulates a pre-existing reality with pre-existing constitutive rules. Aristotle did not dismiss Plato's Forms, but he did not see them as abstractions independent of real things—every form is the form of something. Nor did he have any illusions about social or individual perfection. Rather than imagining perfection in a society newly constituted, Aristotle counseled tinkering with deficiencies in the existing one. He saw the state as springing naturally and spontaneously from the human needs for sustenance, cooperation, friendship, and stability, and not as something dreamt up in a chair in the British Museum, as Karl Marx did. In Aristotle's state, each individual decides his or her own function, and not assigned some function according to the demands of elites. As for Plato's communistic notion of common ownership of life's necessities, Aristotle pointed out the obvious: "What is common to the greatest number gets the least amount of care. Men pay most attention to what is their own; they care less for what is common; or at any rate they care for it only to the extent to which each is individually concerned" (in Pederson, 2010, p. 143).

A.T. D. Porteous's analysis of the works of Plato and Aristotle led him to view emotion as the primary guide of Platonists, and "dispassionate analysis" as the primary guide of Aristotelians. He describes Plato's thought as "challenging and revolutionary" that brings to the table an "emotional quality" which he finds lacking in "Aristotle's dispassionate analysis … Aristotle is the master of those who know, as Plato is of those who dream" (1934, p. 105). Porteous also noted that it is the reliance on the dispassionate analysis of experience that prevents conservatives from appreciating leftist emotional dreams of perfection in an earthly utopia under the centralized rule of enlightened despots.

American conservatism is Aristotelian, and is a disposition, not an ideology. It is a tradition sustained by a body of values which describes a way of evaluating social, economic, and political issues in the light of the experience of the ages. It does not possess a holy writ like the left's *Das Kapita* to guide it; it rests instead in the belief in a timeless moral order, God's providence, the dignity of all human beings, ordered freedom, love of family, and sociopolitical permanence and ordered progression. Conservatism is the realization that a good state is one that respects individual freedom, which is difficult to create but easily destroyed. Conservatives believe Abraham Lincoln's words in his 1838 *Address Before the Young Men's Lyceum of Springfield, Illinois,* that the country our forefathers have bequeathed us will never be destroyed from without, and ask with Lincoln: "At what point then is the approach of danger to be expected? I answer, if it ever reach us, it must spring up amongst us. It cannot come from abroad. If destruction be our lot, we must ourselves be its author and finisher. As a nation of freemen, we must live through all time, or die by suicide" (1838, np). Conservatives want a government limited to the powers clearly laid out in the Constitution and to be left alone in matters of conscience. On the other hand, liberal progressives want an expansive government with tentacles reaching out to micromanage everyone's life supported by a living constitution that can be interpreted in ways that grant them whenever suits their purpose. Should this, now trending in that direction, be further realized, we are at the point when Lincoln's "approach of danger" is "to be expected."

Chapter 2

The Establishment Clause: Ally or Adversary of Religious Liberty?

The Establishment Clause and Its Meaning

Religion was so important to the Founding Fathers that they enshrined it in the very first words of the Bill of Rights as the first freedom: "*Congress shall make no law respecting an establishment of religion, or prohibiting the free exercise thereof.*" The Establishment Clause refers to the non-institutionalization of religion, and the Free Exercise Clause refers to non-interference in matters of conscience. Non-establishment of religion is the necessary foundation in the service of religious free exercise because it protects the rights of those who may dissent from coerced conformity with an established religion. The founding fathers knew that religious freedom is the foundation stone of all other freedoms, and that a community cannot prosper without freedom.

The Establishment Clause prohibits the United States Congress from one thing only: creating an official Church of the United States. This straightforward interpretation has evolved into a philosophy known as non-preferentialism. Non-preferentialism maintains that the Framers meant to forbid government policies and actions that prefer one religion over another. This view believes that government should give aid and comfort to religion, since it is the font of social morality, if it does so in a non-preferential manner. Non-preferentialism is essentially an accommodationist view. That is, the United States would privilege no one religion, and likewise it would dispense with theological support for the state. This being said, adherents of the accommodationist view believe that the government should accommodate religion non-preferentially when it performs the same functions that secular institutions perform. That is, whenever government supports a secular institution such as public schools, charities, or hospitals it should support an analogous religious institution equally and allow them to function according to the tenets of their faith. In the accommodationist view, the prohibition against religious establishment was a means of ensuring the free expression of religion, and certainly not as a mandate for the establishment of secularism.

This view stands in stark contrast to strict separatism; that is, the belief that the Establishment Claus implies a ban on any government support for religious organizations whatsoever, even when aid is based on neutral (non-preferential) criteria. This is the belief of secularists and atheists, who want to remove religion completely from the public square, and to create a thoroughly secularized society. Contrary to popular belief, the phrase "separation of church and state" does not appear anywhere in the Constitution, and is merely shorthand for mutual non-interference. There is no historic evidence at all that the framers intended strict separation of church and state or envisioned a secular society shorn of its Christian roots. The separation of church and state merely assumes a division of labor, with the church doing its job, and the state doing its job, without either trespassing in the domain of the other; it does not mean the separation of state and God. In every state constitution in force after the United States won its independence that mentioned "establishment", the term was always used in conjunction with "preference", and never in terms of a strict separation or the secularization of society (Antieau, Downey, & Roberts, 1964). Separation of church and state is a legal, not a moral separation. It was never meant as a tool for silencing religion or removing it from the public square, but the very clause the founders meant to be an ally of religious liberty has been slickly turned into an adversary by this notion.

ESTABLISHMENT AS THE FOUNDERS MEANT IT

Justice Joseph Story provides the most authoritative view available of the meaning of the Establishment Clause as the founders meant it. Justice Story served on the Supreme Court from 1811 to 1845, and was acquainted with many of the men who penned the Constitution and the Bill of Rights. He had an encyclopedic knowledge of the historical, philosophical, and religious foundations of the Constitution, and wrote 12 books on law, including his magisterial *Commentaries on the Constitution of the United States* (three volumes). Justice Story first tells us the purpose of the Establishment Clause of the First Amendment as he knew it to be meant by the founders:

> The real object of the First Amendment was, not to countenance, much less to advance Mahometanism, or Judaism, or infidelity, by prostrating Christianity; but to exclude all rivalry among Christian sects, and to prevent any national ecclesiastical establishment, which should give to a hierarchy the exclusive patronage of the national government. It thus cut off the means of religious persecution, (the vice and pest of former ages) and of the subversion of the rights of conscience in matters of religion, which had been trampled upon almost from the days of the Apostles to the present age (1833, p. 728).

Notice that Justice Story viewed non-establishment of religion as a tool in the service of the rights of religious conscience. Indeed, he considered this to be the singular function of the Establishment Clause. Story fervently believed that religion should be respected, accommodated, encouraged, and supported as long as this was done in a non-preferential manner. He would have been outraged by today's grotesquely distorted Establishment Clause jurisprudence that denies religious believers the liberty of exercising their faith in the public square. Story and his contemporaries saw the sole purpose of both Religious Clauses was to deny the state any power whatsoever to limit religious freedom, and he provides a hierarchy of three variations of the meaning of "establishment" from the weakest to the strongest.

The first level is a minimalist version of establishment in which support is given to a preferred religion and not to others, but there is no interference with the religious conscience of members of other denominations and the preferred religion is not officially established as such. In the second instance, the state officially establishes a particular set of religious doctrines, but does not infringe on the beliefs or practices of dissenters. The third is the strong meaning of establishment in which an official national church is established to which all citizens either belong or suffer disabilities. Saying voluntary prayers in schools and at football games, or Christian icons displayed in the public square, does not even approach the level of weak establishment in Story's hierarchy. However, all such exercises of religion have been considered by a number of recent Supreme Court Justices to equate to religious establishment.

A strong established religion verges on a theocracy in which the marriage of religion and the state is absolute, and in which the ruler enjoys both secular and spiritual authority. Saudi Arabia is an example of such a theocracy. The *Qur'an* serves as its constitution, and religious courts govern all aspects of life. Non-Muslims living in Saudi Arabia cannot become citizens, and any Muslim converting to another religion, or any one blaspheming Islam, may be put to death. Most modern states with established religions retain them mainly for traditional and ceremonial reasons—a weak kind of religious establishment that is weaker even than Story's minimalist level. For instance, although the Church of England is England's established religion, its role is purely symbolic and ceremonial. It has no more power to influence the government than any other religion, nor does it receive special supporting funds or special privileges from it. The establishment of the Church of England does not preclude the free worship of the multitude of religions that exist there, and all but the monarch can be of any religion, or no religion at all.

Depending on how strongly one defines establishment, nine or eleven of the thirteen American colonies had established religions at the time of the

American Revolution. The Establishment Clause was written into the Constitution with the recognition that a plurality of denominations made an established national church politically unsupportable, for it would have endangered efforts to forge national unity. If Congress had established the Episcopal Church, for instance, on the grounds that it was the most numerous and influential denomination in the United States, it would have simultaneously disestablished churches in other states, thus angering members of the other denominations. The Establishment Clause was thus a device for securing national unity and keeping religious passion out of American politics; in no way was it a declaration of hostility to religion or an excuse to interfere with the "free exercise thereof." Most states disestablished their religions within 25 years after the Revolution. Massachusetts was the last state to disestablish its religion, not doing so until 1834 (Kaminski, 2002).

The Supreme Court has in piecemeal fashion applied the Bill of Rights to the states over many years and in many cases. This process of applying constitutional provisions to the states that previously applied only to the federal government is known as incorporation. The Establishment Clause of the First Amendment was not incorporated until 1947 in *Everson v. Board of Education* (discussed below), and in doing so has placed an interpretation on the clause that its authors would not recognize. Entirely separate spheres can lead to tragic choices if certain features of each sphere clash. If the secular always prevails, there is no religious liberty. When political issues clash with spiritual considerations, a person's religious conscience must be sacrosanct except in the most extreme cases. Government should have no part in imposing its will on that conscience by demanding conformity with social practices that violate it. As James Madison declared: "There is not a shadow of right in the general government to intermeddle with religion. Its least interference with it would be a most flagrant usurpation" (in Cogan, 2015, p. 66). Yet, the state grants itself the right to meddle with religious conscience under the canopy of the Establishment Clause, which was meant to prevent exactly that.

THOMAS JEFFERSON'S "WALL OF SEPARATION"

The radical notion of a complete and hostile separation of church and state gained its first toe-hold in *Everson v. Board of Education* (1947). The Supreme Court incorporated the Establishment Clause in this case, thus opening the door to federal litigation in state matters involving religious freedom claims, and set the legal ambience for cases involving it from then on. *Everson* involved a New Jersey district school board using public funds to reimburse parents for bus fares to and from both public and parochial schools. The Court introduced a novel interpretation of the Establishment Clause, one that did not accord with either its wording or its spirit. In essence, it precipitated the notion that any state accommodation of religion at all amounts to an unconstitutional establishment of religion. Justice Hugo Black wrote:

> Neither a state nor the Federal Government can, openly or secretly, participate in the affairs of any religious organizations or groups and vice versa. In the words of Jefferson, the clause against establishment of religion by law was intended to erect "a wall of separation between Church and State'... The First Amendment has erected a wall between church and state. That wall must be kept high and impregnable. We could not approve the slightest breach. ... In the words of Jefferson, the clause against establishment of religion by law was intended to erect "a wall of separation between church and State."

These words represent a radical change from a negative limit on federal power ("Congress shall make no law") to a positive federal mandate to wall off religion from public life. Referring to the last sentence of the quote, Patrick Garry writes that it "has proved to be the curse of Establishment Clause jurisprudence over the past half-century, for it is anything but indicative of the Framers' intentions regarding the constitutional treatment of religion. Not only did the Framers not believe in a wall of separation between church and state, but they never even once used such a phrase during the debates on the First Amendment" (2004, p. 495). Nevertheless, Black's use of Jefferson's metaphor weaponized the Establishment Clause, once positively linked to the Free Exercise Clause as a protective, to purge religious opinion from political and legal discourse. It is as if Black magically found a contradiction between the two Clauses. The Religious Clauses should be read together like any English sentence not linked by a conjunction such as "but," which is used to introduce a clause that contrasts with the previous one. The entire case for the strict separation of church and state notion rests on the "wall of separation" metaphor. The metaphor is clearly extra-constitutional since Jefferson took no part in crafting the First amendment, although Black erroneously claimed that he had a "leading" role. Jefferson returned from his duties as minister to France more than a decade after it had been approved by Congress and sent to the states for ratification (Natelson, 2005). This constitutional re-interpretation was taken from Jefferson's private correspondence, but it has been used to transform explicit Constitutional language into something Jefferson would never have approved.

Although the majority of the Court ruled that the New Jersey schoolboard's action *did not* violate the Establishment Claus because reimbursements were made to parents, and not to a religious institution, the four dissenting Justices pointed out that if Black's logic was to be the Court's guide, the board's actions should have been ruled unconstitutional. But surely it is a giant leap to say that a state helping parents to defray the costs of transporting children of all faiths, or no faith, to school is tantamount to the United States, or at least New Jersey, establishing a state religion. Thus, while the *result* in *Everson* is consistent with the obvious meaning of the Establishment Clause, Black's *reasoning,* with which four other Justices concurred, relies upon the extra-constitutional "wall of separation" notion that became precedent in subsequent cases involving the Clause.

Not only is Jefferson's "wall of separation" metaphor non-constitutional, the metaphor as currently interpreted is inconsistent with Jefferson's actual practices and beliefs. Jefferson's infamous metaphor is contained in a letter written in 1802 to the Danbury Baptist Association of Connecticut. The Danbury Baptists wrote complaining to President Jefferson about the infringement of their religious liberty by the Connecticut state legislature that supported the established Congregational Church.

Citizens of Connecticut of all faiths paid taxes to support the established church, and Congregationalists were privileged by state and local governments in a number of ways (Muñoz, 2009). In his response Jefferson voiced sympathy for the Baptists in their opposition to the state's established religion and expressed support for the First Amendment's religious clauses. In his letter, Jefferson wrote:

> Believing with you that religion is a matter which lies solely between Man & his God, that he owes account to none other for his faith or his worship, that the legitimate powers of government reach actions only, & not opinions, I contemplate with sovereign reverence that act of the whole American people which declared that their legislature should "make no law respecting an establishment of religion, or prohibiting the free exercise thereof," thus building a wall of separation between Church & State (1998).

The letter says absolutely nothing about limiting public religious expression; it only addressed Connecticut's interference with the public expression of faith, and is more sensibly read as "keep your hands off our religion". Jefferson was plainly not advancing the view that religion should be excluded from the public square. He did, after all, sign off in his capacity of President of the United States with the words: "I reciprocate your kind prayers for the protection & blessing of the common father and creator of man." What is more, during his two terms as President, he pursued policies and performed actions totally at odds with Black's "high and impregnable" wall notion. Jefferson approved of the use of federal funds to build churches and to support Christian missionaries, so Jefferson was either a hypocrite for routinely violating his beliefs or his use of the "wall of separation" metaphor has been grossly and purposely misinterpreted. Jefferson's wall was meant only to rip apart the cozy relationship that church and state had enjoyed in Europe (and the American colonies and states) which had caused such strife.

Jefferson's wall trope was not meant to imprison the free exercise of religion but to positively affirm it. Neither does the metaphor mean that Jefferson was an enemy of religion, as some think. Professors Paul Butler and Alfred Scanlan highlight the high esteem in which Jefferson held religion: "Jefferson has written that religion was 'a supplement of law in the government of man,' and 'the alpha and omega of the moral law'" (1961, p. 219). This hardly reveals a man who was so hostile to religion that he wanted to wall it off from all other social institutions. Jefferson merely believed that the various denominations must stand on their own two feet, with their survival and success depending on the force of their message and the faith and good example of their members, not on preferential state aid. Such preferential aid would be *de facto*, if not *de jure*, establishing that favored denomination as the religion of the United States. This is the proscription of the Establishment Claus; there is no prescription of religious hostility to be found in it.

Although hundreds of individuals participated in some manner in the drafting of the Constitution and its first 10 amendments contained in the Bill of Rights, James Madison was their main architect. Like Jefferson, Madison was deeply committed to the inviolability of private conscience, religious liberty, and to the notion that religion was a necessary and valuable institution. In his *Memorial and Remonstrance against Religious Assessments* given before the General Assembly of the Commonwealth of Virginia, he said:

> Because we hold it for a fundamental and undeniable truth, "that Religion or the duty which we owe to our Creator and the manner of discharging it, can be directed only by reason and conviction, not by force or violence." The Religion then of every man must be left to the conviction and conscience of every man; and it is the right of every man to exercise it as these may dictate. This right is in its nature an unalienable right...It is unalienable also, because what is here a right towards men, is a duty towards the Creator... *This duty is precedent, both in order of time and in degree of obligation, to the claims of Civil Society*. Before any man can be considered as a member of Civil Society, he must be considered as a subject of the Governour of the Universe (Muñoz, 2009, p. 223).

The Supreme Court and the Wall of Separation

Despite the countless statements favoring accommodation of religion and its importance to civil life made by the men who crafted the Constitution and the Bill of Rights, the Supreme Court has seen fit to focus on Jefferson's "wall of separation" metaphor and has used it to create a hostile interpretation of the Free Exercise Clause. Although the majority of the Court has read the Establishment Clause as if Jefferson's metaphor is written into it, some Justices have maintained the original plain meaning of the Establishment Clause. For instance, in *Zorach v. Clauson* (*1952*) Justice William Douglas noted the growing hostility to religion in government and wrote: "But we find no constitutional requirement which makes it necessary for government to be hostile to religion and to throw its weight against efforts to widen the effective scope of religious influence... We cannot read into the Bill of Rights such a philosophy of hostility to religion." Likewise, Justice Warren Burger in *Lynch v. Donnelly* (1984) wrote:

> The concept of a 'wall' of separation between church and state is a useful metaphor but is not an accurate description of the practical aspects of the relationship that in fact exists. The Constitution does not require complete separation of church and state; it affirmatively mandates accommodation, not merely tolerance, of all religions, and forbids hostility toward any. Anything less would require the 'callous indifference' that was never intended by the Establishment Clause.

Chief Justice William Rehnquist perhaps voiced best how wrong Black's reading of Jefferson's metaphor was and how injurious to religious liberty it has proved to be. In his dissent in *Wallace v. Jaffree* (1985) in which the Court used a strict separationist interpretation of the Establishment Clause to rule that silent prayer or "moment of meditation" in school violated it and was therefore unconstitutional. Rehnquist's memorable words are reproduced below:

> It is impossible to build sound constitutional doctrine upon a mistaken understanding of constitutional history, but unfortunately the

> Establishment Clause has been expressly freighted with Jefferson's misleading metaphor for nearly 40 years... But the greatest injury of the "wall" notion is its mischievous diversion of judges from the actual intentions of the drafters of the Bill of Rights. The "crucible of litigation" is well adapted to adjudicating factual disputes on the basis of testimony presented in court, but no amount of repetition of historical errors in judicial opinions can make the errors true. The "wall of separation between church and State" is a metaphor based on bad history, a metaphor which has proved useless as a guide to judging. It should be frankly and explicitly abandoned.

Whether due to its lack of historical support or its practical unworkability, the *Everson* "wall" has proved all but useless as a guide to sound constitutional adjudication. It illustrates only too well the wisdom of Benjamin Cardozo's observation that "Metaphors in law are to be narrowly watched, for starting as devices to liberate thought, they end often by enslaving it."

Rather than being "frankly and explicitly abandoned," the wall of separation was built higher and stoutly reinforced in *Lemon v. Kurtzman* (1971). In *Lemon*, the Supreme Court ruled unconstitutional a Pennsylvania act allowing the state to partially reimburse parochial schools for the salaries of teachers, and a Rhode Island act that used state funds to supplement salaries at parochial elementary schools. This case established the so-called "Lemon test." The Lemon test lays out a three-pronged test detailing the constitutional requirements for state legislation as it may relate to religion:

1. The statute must have a secular legislative purpose.
2. The principal or primary effect of the statute must not advance nor inhibit religious practice.
3. The statute must not result in an "excessive government entanglement" with religious affairs.

If any of these prongs are violated, the legislation is deemed unconstitutional under the Establishment Clause. The Lemon test's bitterness can be tasted even in the ruling in the case that gave the test its name. In terms of the first prong; surely the legislative acts under scrutiny in *Lemon* had a secular purpose; that of educating children while removing some of the financial burden from the tax payer, since the families of children who attend parochial schools bear most of the financial burden. As a byproduct, the legislation also had an unavoidable religious purpose; that of adding spiritual and moral dimensions to the curriculum. This also serves a valuable secular purpose, since moral people make better citizens.

As for the second prong stating that the legislation must not advance or inhibit religion, the Court's ruling violated its own principle because it assuredly inhibited religion by negatively impacting parochial schools' ability to function. Catholic schools (the principle victims of this ruling) have been far more effective in educating disadvantaged minority students than public schools that have frequently failed them. Anthony and Renee Setari have pointed out that the benefits of attending Catholic schools for minority children have been demonstrated repeatedly, such as getting better grades and having fewer behavioral problems. The Setaris add: "the closing of Catholic schools has impacted the educational outcomes of minority students and the overall social quality of the neighborhoods in which these schools were located." (2016, p. 5).

How does the closing of parochial schools serve any secular purpose other than that of advancing the cause of atheism? It burdened the parents of children attending those schools because they must pay tuition fees while simultaneously supporting public schools with their taxes. The only way that they can avoid this unfair double cost is to withdraw their children and place them in public schools, thus depriving their children of the moral compass they desire for them. The state discriminates against all religious schools because none can avail themselves of the public funding available to their secular counterparts.

Legal scholar Arnold Loewy points out that: "No serious scholar has ever contended that the Establishment Clause was intended to bespeak hostility towards religion. Yet that is exactly what happens in a regime that allows the State to pay a student's tuition or an English teacher's salary at a private nonreligious school, but denies the same to students and teachers at a private religious school" (2002, p. 539). This is a direct violation of the second prong of the Lemon test against the inhibition of religion, and would be a legally actionable case of discrimination if it involved any group other than religious groups. Imagine an all-black school or a sex-segregated school being so treated based on race or sex status. The third prong is addressed in the next chapter dealing with how the Court has dealt with cases involving the Free Exercise Clause in schools.

The Coercion test is another device that the Supreme Court has used to remove God from American public life. The test ironically arose from Justice Anthony Kennedy's accommodationist view expressed in *Allegheny County v. Greater Pittsburgh ACLU* (1989), in which the Supreme Court ruled against the city of Pittsburgh's Christmas holiday display containing a crèche and a menorah. Kennedy proposed that the concept of "coercion" explains the limitations imposed on the states by the Establishment Clause. This test appears to be fully in accordance with the original and plain meaning of "establishment;" that is, forcing people to conform to a state-sanctioned religion. The coercion test proclaims that the government violates the Establishment Clause if it (1) provides direct aid to religion in a way that tends to establish a state church, or (2) coerces people to support or participate in religion against their will.

Even this reasonable test has been used against religious practice by a very broad interpretation of coercion. Using the coercion test the Court has ruled against school prayers and singing Christmas carols, as well as Pittsburgh's display because they "offend" some delicate atheist claiming coercion. Coercion is typically defined as the use of force or intimidation to obtain compliance with some demand. In no case was anyone coerced into praying, listening, or viewing religious icons, but the Court has seen fit to interpret individuals who are accidently or incidentally exposed to anything religious as being forced or intimidated into participating a religious ritual. This is an indication that the Court can redefine a word or phrase any way it pleases as if they are privy to a living dictionary as well as a living Constitution. In his dissenting opinion in *Allegheny County*, Justice Kennedy wrote:

> Government policies of accommodation, acknowledgment, and support for religion are an accepted part of our political and cultural heritage. Rather than requiring government to avoid any action that acknowledges or aids religion, the Establishment Clause permits government some latitude in recognizing and accommodating the central role religion plays in our society. Any approach less sensitive to our heritage would border on latent hostility toward religion, as it would require government in all its multifaceted roles to acknowledge only the secular, to the exclusion and so to the detriment of the religious.

In short, the Supreme Court has created a number of conflicting Establishment Clause tests resulting in a confusing labyrinth that both contradicts the text of the Constitution and the cultural history of the United States. The Court appears to be operating from a stance that "No one must be offended by someone's public affirmation of religious faith", and tends to rule accordingly. In this republic of free citizens, every moral opinion and aspiration should have access to the public square. If the religion of our forefathers is somehow a blight on society rather than a blessing as the foundation of public morality, the people of each state should deliberate on it and fight it out at that level, as Thomas Jefferson said that they should. The doctrines of republicanism are violated when such matters are left to an elitist and unelected federal judiciary, many of whom have on a number of occasions demonstrated hostility to Christianity, make those decisions for us by legal fiat. It is tragic that the Supreme Court cannot fathom, or will not heed, the considered opinions of the founding fathers. Robert Natelson, one of America's leading constitutional scholars, speaks for them:

> As was true of other foundational values, such as liberty and republicanism, the sides disagreed on the application—but not on the basic principle: Government should, directly or indirectly, foster religion. In this climate of public opinion, no Establishment Clause erecting a "wall of separation" between religion and state ever would have been adopted or even seriously proposed... For them, the relationship between good government and religion was interactive and symbiotic, rather than rigid and distant (2005, p. 119).

The fact is that ever since *Everson*, the Supreme Court taking an overly expansive view of the Establishment Clause and an overly restrictive view of the Free Exercise Clause, both to the detriment of religious liberty. In *Walz v. Tax Commission of the City of New York* (1970), Justice Warren Burger perceived conflict rather than cohesion between them, which he says has caused the Court to "struggle to find a neutral course between the two Religion Clauses, both of which are cast in absolute terms, and either of which, if expanded to a logical extreme, would tend to clash with the other." The Religious Clauses are indeed stated in absolute terms, but if read as the founders meant them, there can be no clash. The "logical extreme" of the Establishment Clause is already contained in its wording: "*Congress shall make no law respecting an establishment of religion,*" that's it; no Church of the United States, period. Burger also noted that: "for the men who wrote the Religion Clauses of the First Amendment the 'establishment' of a religion connoted sponsorship; financial support, and active involvement of the sovereign in religious activity." Doing this would mean that the United States had a de facto, perhaps even a de jure, established religion. Of course, it does not, but the various courts act as if there would be if the state accommodates religion even minimally.

The courts often fail to see that the Free Exercise Clause is likewise cast in absolute terms: "*or prohibiting the free exercise thereof*". Taken to its "logical extreme", the government can engage in no action at all that would have the effect of preventing the free exercise of religion. There are legitimate reasonable restrictions on free exercise, as we shall see in the next chapter, but an expansive Establishment Clause evidently has no reasonable restrictions as to what it may mean. For instance, in *Committee for Public Education & Religious Liberty v. Nyquist* (1973) the issue was the state of New York's establishment of financial aid programs for "maintenance and repair" of facilities and equipment to ensure the "health, welfare and safety" of students attending parochial schools. The state established tuition reimbursement for parents of children attending those schools for low-income families, and provided tax relief to parents failing to qualify for tuition reimbursement. All three plans were struck down by the Supreme Court as violating the Establishment Clause "because their inevitable effect is to subsidize and advance the religious mission of sectarian schools." This ruling restricted free exercise of religion by denying low-income children access to religious schools as well as compromising their "health, welfare and safety". As Justice Byron White wrote in his dissenting opinion: "No one contends that he can discern from the sparse language of the Establishment Clause that a State is forbidden to aid religion in any manner whatsoever". The ruling lays waste to Justice Kennedy's coercion formula for determining if the Establishment Clause has been violated; to wit: The government violates the Establishment Clause if it (1) provides direct aid to religion in a way that tends to establish a state church, or (2) coerces people to support or participate in religion against their will. New York State did neither.

But many of Justice White's colleagues have discovered in the Establishment Clause all sorts of restrictions on religious liberty. Of course, we may still believe what we will, and attend the worship centers of own choosing without state interference. Nevertheless, because the Court has turned the Establishment Clause against the Free Exercise Clause to render it almost impotent, we may be required to violate those beliefs and be forced to labor on the demand of others in this age of same-sex marriage and other newly minted LGBTQ rights.

The stalwart Christians who drafted the Constitution could not have imagined an America so debased as to have the law openly attacking the very values and practices that informed its drafting. Perhaps we should scrap the Constitution and write a new one, as has been seriously suggested in left-wing articles, books, and blogs. This time we can leave Christian morality out of it altogether and infuse it with the immorality of the hard left. It is ironic that Thomas Jefferson, a champion of free speech and religious freedom, who, because of his unfortunate "wall of separation" trope, has become a folk hero to leftists who would deprive us of these precious rights. The new constitution could be drafted by a committee of former Obama czars with a postmodernist professor or two hired to put their ideas in fuzzy prose so that it is entirely open to any and all interpretations. In short, it will be in all regards the opposite of the Constitution that made his nation great.

Chapter 3

RELIGIOUS LIBERTY: THE FREE EXERCISE CLAUSE

THE RELIGIOUS CLAUSES: CONFLICT OR COHERENCE?

Although annoyed by the Quaker's pacifism during the American Revolution, in September of 1789, George Washington wrote to the annual meeting of the Quakers promising not just tolerance, but full liberty of conscience no matter what one's religious beliefs happen to be. He was paving the way for the Religious Clauses of the First Amendment, which would be added to the Constitution on December 15, 1791. Washington's letter read:

> Government being, among other purposes, instituted to protect the persons and consciences of men from oppression, it certainly is the duty of rulers, not only to abstain from it themselves, but, according to their stations, to prevent it in others.
>
> The liberty enjoyed by the people of these states of worshiping Almighty God agreeably to their consciences, is not only among the choicest of their *blessings*, but also of their *rights*. While men perform their social duties faithfully, they do all that society or the state can with

> propriety demand or expect; and remain responsible only to their Maker for their religion, or modes of faith, which they may prefer or profess.
>
> Your principles and conduct are well known to me; and it is doing the people called Quakers no more than justice to say, that (except their declining to share with others the burden of the common defense) there is no denomination among us, who are more exemplary and useful citizens.
>
> I assure you very explicitly, that in my opinion the conscientious scruples of all men should be treated with great delicacy and tenderness; and it is my wish and desire, that the laws may always be as extensively accommodated to them, as a due regard to the protection and essential interests of the nation may justify and permit (1789, np).

The Free Exercise Clause of the First Amendment forbidding the United States Congress to make any law prohibiting the free exercise of religion was a product of religious pluralism in America. The founders yoked the Establishment Clause to it for this very reason. The two clauses depend on one another for their effectiveness in guaranteeing "essential rights and liberties." Michael Paulsen views both clauses as complementary protections of religious liberty: "As I have written elsewhere, the two clauses protect a single central value, religious liberty, from two different angles. The Establishment Clause forbids government *prescription* in matters of religious exercise. The Free Exercise Clause forbids government *proscription* in matters of religious exercise" (2014, p. 1607).

Yet, the Supreme Court has managed to decouple the Clauses, and has used the Establishment Clause to eviscerate the Free Exercise Clause. In effect, the Establishment Clause has morphed into an ideology that institutionalizes atheism. This is the result of Justices on the Court discovering a so-called "tension" between the two clauses; a tension that the founders who wrote them would not recognize. The Court has shown a tendency to interpret the Free Exercise Clause such that any "entanglement" of state and religion, even of the most trivial sort, is a violation of the Establishment Clause. The situation now is that if individuals and institutions dare to take the Free Exercise Clause seriously and act upon its guarantees in the public square, their actions amount to an establishment of religion. The entanglement claim is effectively turned against free exercise claims as if the Free Exercise Clause is itself unconstitutional.

Despite assurance from the authors of the Religious Clauses that their words can be taken at face value, the Supreme Court has pored over them as if they were the ladies of Bletchley Park trying to decipher the Enigma Code. Justices on the Court behave as if the founders were so unlettered as to be unable to put a sentence together that does not contradict itself. The clauses mean exactly what they say and contain no cryptic meaning. Stephen Pepper notes that many provisions of the Bill of Rights contain buffering language that moderates their impact, and thus making them subject to different interpretations, such as the right to be free of unreasonable searches (what is "unreasonable?"), or that excessive bail (what is "excessive"?) or cruel and unusual punishment (what exactly does that mean?) be imposed. Compared to these rights, he points out that the Free Exercise Clause is "singularly absolute: 'Congress shall make no law... prohibiting the free exercise [of religion]'" (1986, p. 300).

Vincent Bonventre also wonders why the justices cannot find the plain meaning of the Free Exercise Clause when he writes: "The significance of this provision is exceptionally clear. It was not buried deep in the Constitution where it would be difficult to find. This dual protection of religious liberty is the very first provision in the Bill of Rights—the very first guarantee enumerated in the very first amendment made to the Constitution" (2018, p. 650). Another constitutional scholar writes of the Court's magical discovery of conflict between the clauses: "If they appear to be in conflict, then at least one of the clauses is being judicially misapplied. Imagining these two denials of government power as frequently in 'tension' and having to be judicially 'balanced', is deeply at odds with the central reason that Americans demanded the addition of a bill of rights to the 1787 Constitution" (Esbeck, 2011, p. 608).

Likewise, the Office of Legal Policy notes how reading the Religious Clauses in the current manner implies different meanings of religion, which makes no sense when the term is used in a single sentence: "Grammatically and structurally, there is no justification whatsoever for supposing that 'religion' should mean one thing in Free Exercise cases and another in

Establishment cases. In fact, to do so would seem to violate principles of construction so basic as to be beyond dispute" (1986, p. 24). The Office of Legal Policy also remarks on the how this illogical separation of the Religious Clauses constitutes a real danger: "Such an approach is unjustified because it ignores the text of the Constitution; and the exercise of judicial power unrestrained by the text is an open invitation to rewrite the First Amendment. (1986, p. 25).

There is no logical conflict between saying that Congress must not prohibit the free exercise of religion, and saying that it must not establish a state church. We might even argue that there is but one religious clause in the First Amendment viz: "Congress shall make no law," and the rest of consisting of modifiers stipulating what laws Congress must not make. Conflict arises only when the Justices, unrestrained by the text of the Constitution, read their biases into them. Both clauses are clearly negative restraints on the government, so they are pulling in the same direction and thus there can be no tension between them. The negative in the Establishment Clause bars Congress from establishing an official state religion, and the Free Exercise Clause restrains Congress from inhibiting the "free exercise thereof". Both Clauses are restraints on government, and it is logically impossible for these two overlapping and complementary negatives on state power to be in conflict. Likewise, Carl Esbeck notes that:

> Free Exercise Clause and the Establishment Clause overlap and thereby doubly restrict the field of permissible action by the national government concerning religion, but they cannot conflict. Again, it is impossible for two overlapping negatives on the government's power to conflict. To be sure, the religion clauses, each in its own way, work to protect religious freedom. But when circumstances are such that the scope of the clauses overlap, they necessarily complement, rather than conflict with, each other (2011, p. 607).

Even if there is conflict between the Clauses, the Constitution contains no formula for deciding which should prevail, but I agree with Robert Natelson opinion that: "If the Establishment Clause exists to serve the Free Exercise Clause, then in the event of conflict, the former must yield" (2005,

p. 90). The Establishment Clause is the easiest clause for the state to comply with, if plainly read, because it can be violated in just one way—Congress establishing a Church of the United States—whereas the Free Exercise Clause can be violated in numerous ways. Thus, if there is to be a hierarchy of the clauses, the Free Exercise Clause should have priority. Mark Noll declares that it was never the intention of the Founders to be hostile to the public expression of religion: "the founders' desire for the separation of the institutions of church and state reflected a desire to respect not only religion but also the moral choice of citizens. It was not a provision to remove religion as such from public life" (1988, p. 67). The free exercise of religion is not called the "first liberty" for nothing. As Justice Rutledge remarked in is dissenting opinion in *Everson v. Board of Education* (1947): "No provision of the Constitution is more closely tied to or given content by its generating history than the religious clause of the First Amendment." The Free Exercise Clause was designed to shield religious people from state persecution; it is a fortress of conscience against all assaults, and necessarily entails the right to conscientiously object to public accommodation laws that require the faithful to engage in conduct they consider sinful. Take away this most fundamental of liberties or water it down to mean only freedom of private belief and worship, and we no longer have a free society.

Jefferson's "Wall of Separation" and the Erosion of Religious Liberty

The Supreme Court incorporated the due process clause of the Fourteenth Amendment in *Cantwell v. Connecticut* (1940). The Fourteenth Amendment adds extra layers to the free exercise of religion in its liberty clause. The relevant section of the Fourteenth Amendment reads: "No state shall make or enforce any law which shall abridge the privileges and immunities of citizens of the United States; nor shall any State deprive any person of life, liberty, or property, without due process of law; nor deny any person within its jurisdiction the equal protection of the laws". Above all, the liberty clause was designed to protect liberties deemed fundamental, which are those rights enumerated in the First Amendment—freedom of religion, speech, association, press, and petition. The Free Exercise Clause prevailed in *Cantwell*, but it has subsequently been eroded.

Cantwell involved Jehovah's Witnesses Newton Cantwell and his two sons going door-to-door handing out pamphlets containing messages hostile to the Catholic Church in a largely Catholic neighborhood. The Cantwells were arrested and charged with failure to obtain a required solicitor's certificate and inciting a breach of the peace. Cantwell responded that the government had no right to interfere with their free exercise of religion. The Supreme Court agreed, and stated that citizens had a right of free expression as well as freedom of belief. Justice Owen Roberts wrote in a unanimous opinion something that many later Justices have ignored—people actually have the inalienable right to *act* on their faith, even if it offends others:

> The constitutional inhibition of legislation on the subject of religion has a double aspect. On the one hand, it forestalls compulsion by law of the acceptance of any creed or the practice of any form of worship. Freedom of conscience and freedom to adhere to such religious organization or form of worship as the individual may choose cannot be restricted by law. On the other hand, it safeguards the free exercise of the chosen form of religion. Thus the Amendment embraces two concepts—freedom to believe and freedom to act.

Unlike Roberts, there are many today that think that the Free Exercise Clause should be limited to freedom of belief. But the Free Exercise Clause guarantees not just private beliefs, it explicitly says "exercise." What good is the right to believe if it can't be publicly expressed in action? As Roger Trigg says: "Totalitarian governments are no doubt quite satisfied for religious believers to think what they want as long as it is never manifested. ... religion is public, not private, communal, not just individual, and a matter of action and not just propositional belief" (2011, p.118). Freedom of worship is just a part of the free exercise of religion. Mere freedom of worship means that you can worship where and when you please, but leave the message behind in church; the free exercise of religion means that you are free to act on that message in the public square without fear of reprisal. The Constitution proclaims that Americans are both free to believe what they like and to act on those beliefs as long as such actions do not cause tangible harm to others. Austin Rogers reminds us that: "Free Exercise Clause is not a misnomer. That is, it was not intended to be consigned to the realm of thought, but was designed to protect practices" (Rogers, 2019, p.170). The right to believe in God and His commands is enfeebled without a corresponding right to exercise it publicly by saying "No!" to petty government bureaucrats who want to force Christians to deny God's commandments.

As a private right of conscience, the free exercise of religion is a pre-constitutional inalienable right, and as Thomas Jefferson said, the state can only have authority over natural rights to the extent that we have submitted to it, but "The rights of conscience we never submitted, we could not submit. We are answerable for them to our God" (1784, np). The state plays God and acts unconstitutionally when it seeks to command people's thoughts and behavior in matters of religious conscience. Jefferson has stated that "no provision in our Constitution ought to be dearer to man than that which protects the rights of conscience against the enterprises of civil authority" (1809, np). That protection is dear to us, but the clauses that guarantee it must be respected and acted upon by the state if they are to be more than mere words on parchment.

Federal or state governments act unconstitutionally when they enact laws that would prohibit a religious practice or that command an act that would prevent the fulfilling of a religious duty. Governments do this when they try to prevent religious believers from fulfilling their duty to God by requiring them to participate in acts contrary to His commands. As constitutional law professor Michael Paulsen forcefully states: "The Establishment Clause of the First Amendment does not in any way authorize, and the Free Speech and Free Exercise Clauses do not permit, direct government discrimination against religion, religious persons, religious groups, or religious expression in government programs, policies, benefits, or forums. Ever" (2015, np).

Secularists who embrace government discrimination should note the words of the *Universal Declaration of Human Rights*, a document dear to them. Article 18: 1 of the *Declaration* reads: "Everyone shall have the right to freedom of thought, conscience and religion. This right shall include freedom to have or to adopt a religion or belief of his choice, and freedom, either individually or in community with others and *in public or private, to manifest his religion or belief in worship, observance, practice and teaching*" (United Nations, 2015, p. 38; emphasis added). The article declares that the religious person should be able to "manifest" (exercise) his or her religious beliefs in the public square if it causes no tangible harm to others, and not just in private worship. This contradicts the former Obama administration's attempt to redefine the Free Exercise Clause as mere freedom of worship.

As noted in the previous chapter, the erosion of religious liberty began slowly in 1947 with Justice Black's "wall of separation" reasoning in *Everson v. Board of Education,* so few people noticed. James Madison warned us about such a strategy in his Speech in the Virginia *Ratifying Convention on Control of the Military* long before the wall of separation trope saw daylight: "There are more instances of the abridgement of the freedom of the people by gradual and silent encroachments of those in power than by violent and sudden usurpations" (Nowlan, 2012, p. 171). The erosion gained speed with the sexual revolution and emerged as a serious threat during the Obama administration. The Obama administration actively worked to intimidate religious believers in church charities and small businesses with mandates that they violate their consciences, making it "increasingly difficult for them to run a business or operate in the public square in accordance with their convictions" (Levin, 2016, p. 30).

The threat from the Obama administration is over, but the threat of the American Civil Liberties Union (ACLU) remains. The ACLU wraps itself in the legal rhetoric of freedom to fill their financial coffers, but Ralph De Toledano reminds us that: "the aims and principles of its founder, Roger Baldwin, who wrote in 1935 that 'Communism is the goal'. In its early days, the ACLU was not shy about making known its agenda" (2002, p. 48). The ACLU has gone to the mat on religious freedom issues defending peyote-smoking Native Americans, the right of turban-wearing Sikhs to join the army, Muslim prisoners to keep their beards, and the Santeria cult's right to ritualistically slaughter animals. However, when Christians decline involvement in private commercial activities on religious grounds, for the ACLU religious freedom no longer applies.

The ACLU involved itself in almost all cases arguing against the religious liberty of Christians when it butts heads with LGBTQ rights. Long before the emergence of LGBTQ activism, William Donohue wrote that: "Removing religion from the womb of culture has become the practiced virtue of the ACLU over the past several decades" (1985, p. 51). He goes on to say that: "Separationist groups such as the ACLU, People for the American Way, and Americans United for Separation of Church and State are doing all they can to sweep religion's influence out of every nook and cranny of Americans' public life" (1985, p. 62). Donohue wrote this in 1985 when few perceived that the threat would become such that in today's morally degraded culture where "the core of religious exercise gets no more protection than the practice of throwing rice at church weddings" (Laycock, 1990, p. 108).

Alexander Hamilton warned that if there are no constraints on the judiciary, judges will engage in judicial lawmaking of the sort that has been used to attack religious liberty. In *Federalist Paper No. 78,* he wrote: "To avoid an arbitrary discretion in the courts, it is indispensable that they should be bound down by strict rules and precedents, which serve to define and point out their duty in every particular case that comes before them" (1788, np). Precedence is a common law principle stating that courts should adhere to principles established by decisions in earlier cases, and not to be overlooked by the Court's desire to suit its preferred result.

Precedence becomes problematic if it is not firmly grounded in Constitutional principles. When constitutional principles and precedent are one and the same, all is well in the legal world. When they are not, we have a body of law that is nominally constitutional but may bear little resemblance to the principles embedded in the document. That is, once the Supreme Court hands down a ruling based on extra-constitutional grounds, such as the "wall of separation" trope, it magically became constitutional. As Roger Pilon puts it: "It requires but a casual acquaintance with our constitutional history, however, to appreciate that many of today's constitutional precedents are derived from the Constitution by only the most strained reasoning" (2013-2014, p. vii). This is the "living Constitution," or judge-made "constitutional law," at work.

If some Justices cannot understand the plain words of the religious clauses, perhaps they should go to the source. In his first inaugural address in 1809, President James Madison stated exactly what they mean, to wit: "to avoid the *slightest interference* with the right of conscience or the functions of religion, so wisely *exempted from civil jurisdiction*" (Madison, 1809, np; emphasis added). It is a mystery why the high priests of the Supreme Court cannot heed the plain words of the author of the clauses instead of twisting their meanings beyond recognition as if they were postmodernist academics. We would still have freedom of religion as Madison understood it if the Constitution was still read in a sense most obvious to the common understanding at the time of its adoption Furthermore, far from any hint of approval of government hostility to Christianity, Madison closed his inaugural address with these reverent words: "We have all been encouraged to feel in the guardianship and guidance of that Almighty Being whose power regulates the destiny of nations, whose blessings have been so conspicuously dispensed to this rising Republic, and to whom we are bound to address our devout gratitude for the past, as well as our fervent supplications and best hopes for the future" (1809, np).

Does Religious Liberty Deserve Special Treatment?

Under the Establishment Clause, religion is treated differently from secular ethical and moral views. Congress can "establish" almost anything constitutionally permitted, but it cannot establish an official religion of the United States. This was wisely meant, because an established religion implies that the state knows what religious truth is. The Establishment Clause recognizes that the state is not competent to judge such matters. Under the Free Exercise Clause, on the other hand, religion is treated more favorably than any secular system of belief. This Clause recognizes that religious liberty is an inalienable right and has traditionally been granted more favorable treatment, but this "first liberty" has increasingly been trampled on as our society becomes more secular. In a free society, one can be a theist, atheist, agnostic, postmodernist, feminist, socialist, or anything else. The difference between secular systems of thought and theism is that they can be taught, promoted, and exalted in the classroom and in the public square, but theism cannot. This does not seem like something uniquely privileged, but rather something uniquely burdened.

Nevertheless, the Free Exercise Clause singles out religion as deserving of special protection not offered to secular systems of belief, which upsets the atheistic avant-garde that asks "What's so special about religion to warrant this heightened protection"? The short answer is that the founding fathers considered it to be so valuable to a moral society that they found its private and public practice to be crucial, and made that plain in the absolutist wording of the Religious Clauses. However, the argument that there is nothing special about religion that warrants special protection requires addressing because that view has been seriously argued. For example, Micah Schwartzman purports to show that "religion cannot be distinguished from many other beliefs and practices as warranting special constitutional treatment. As a normative matter, religion is *not* special" (2012, p.1353). Given that premise, he maintains that the Religious Clauses "should be rejected as morally deficient" (p. 1403), or they should be reconciled by "expand[ing] the definition of religion to encompass secular doctrines" (p.1415).

That the Religious Clauses should be called "morally deficient" and rejected or reduced to the level of mere secular beliefs would shock the founding fathers who considered religious liberty to be the paramount liberty. No secular belief system can function as a moral basis for society. An organized religion is a belief system rooted in centuries of history and tradition that binds together a community of believers sharing a collective conscience. A religious conscience is of special significance to believers; it is at the center of their self-understanding, and of the understanding of a transcendental reality beyond themselves. Religious people want to live a life connected to, and in accordance with, their transcendental truths. This alone makes it more special than secular systems that do not make intelligible claims about the human condition in terms of ultimate reality.

A conscience is not simply an individual matter. To the extent it is premised on the doctrine of a religious community, an attack on any individual's conscience is an attack on the collective conscience of that community and thereby marginalizes it. After all, freedom of the press is not respected out of respect for a particular journalist or publisher, but out of respect for the whole community of journalists and publishers because a free press is important to our freedom. A conscience derived from a nonreligious source, however virtuous, does not possess the same compelling force as one derived from religion because a religious conscience is qualitatively different from any secular conscience. A religious conscience provides transcendent values and a moral legitimacy not provided by secular systems, and recognizes a domain for the conscience beyond the control of the state. Violating the commands of God is taken far more seriously than violating the precepts of any secular worldview. Religious believer does not want to be forced to make the tragic choice of having to pledge their allegiance to the state or to God. For the religious believer, the source of religious conscience is both prior and superior to the proscriptions and prescriptions of civil society, and must take precedence as long as they cause no manifest danger to the peace and safety of the state.

Professor Schwartzman does not agree. He believes that: "Instead of disabling or protecting only religious beliefs and practices, the law ought to provide similar treatment for comparable secular ethical, moral, and philosophical views" (2012, p. 1355), and that the: "Religion Clauses do not protect secular claims of conscience" (p. 1405). *Wisconsin v Yoder* (1972) proves Schwartzman correct in his claim that religion has been afforded special protection. In this case, the Supreme Court articulated the special nature of religion when, based on the Free Exercise Clause, it granted Amish children a religious exemption from mandatory school attendance after age 16. The Court stated that it would not have exempted others with merely "philosophical and personal" views because "such belief does not rise to the demands of the Religion Clauses". In other words, secular claims do not fall within the domain of the Free Exercise Clause. Schwartzman is not correct, however, when he claims that the Free Exercise Clause does not protect secular claims of conscience. It provided the underpinning to secular claims of conscience in *United States v Seeger* (1965). In this case, the Court held that a conscience objection to a generally applicable law—a conscientious objection to the military draft during the Vietnam war—is satisfied by any sincerely held belief that "occupies a place in the life of its possessor parallel to that filled by the orthodox belief in God."

Although the Free Exercise Clause may be extended to satisfy secular conscientious objections, a purely secular conscience cannot be "parallel to that filled by the orthodox belief in God." Belief in the divine and the behavior that flows from it is ontologically different from all secular world views. Religion plays a wider variety of roles in a sincere believer's life than can be said of any secular system of beliefs because it provides a comprehensive worldview that offers answers to questions of ultimate reality. Religious faith is at the center of a believer's identity, and is the Alpha and Omega that provides believers with a moral guide to living their lives. No other worldview is so all-encompassing. Secular worldviews might, in watered down fashion, provide its followers with a sense of community and a source of personal identity. However, we may ask if proponents of any secular worldview would be willing to defy the state if it were to tell them that they cannot freely exercise their worldview on pain of financial ruin and vile public ostracism the way many Christian small business owners have. In light of this, it is be more important to maintain the vitality and independence of religion against the incursions of the regulatory state into private conscience than it was at the time of the founders.

Another reason for protecting religion is pointed out by Professor Michael McConnell. He opines that protecting religion is important because the state relies on its citizen's voluntary compliance with the law, and thus the state has pragmatic reasons for deferring to principled religious values: "Since some persons, otherwise good and law-abiding citizens, will view religious claims as higher authority than civil law, it may be preferable to accommodate them than to provoke confrontation and disobedience" (1985, p. 16). However, Professor Paulson believes that social peace may have been a part of the founder's objective of protecting the free exercise of religion, but adds: "Isn't it more plausible that the founding generation chose to protect religious freedom primarily because of its perceived importance, and not merely to forestall the secondary effects, as it were, of the fact that people viewed it as important? (2014, p. 1609).

Social and political peace was the animating principle behind the adoption of the Establishment Clause, not the Free Exercise Clause. Religious freedom cannot thrive in the absence of a vibrant religious community, but that freedom requires that government policies and actions should not prefer one religion over another. Founders Jefferson and Madison were well-versed in history. They were thus aware of how governments with an established religion crush human freedom and how religious rivalries had prompted numerous wars. Not favoring any one religion is the basis of religious freedom and social peace. They were very much cognizant of Voltaire's 1733 *Letters Concerning the English Nation*. The most famous quotation from those letters reads: "If there were only one religion in England, there would be danger of tyranny; if there were two, they would cut each other's throats; but there are thirty, and they live happily together in peace" (Durant & Durant, 1965, p. 119).

The free expression of religion is thus important, not primarily to ensure peace in the land, but rather the idea that religious conscience is a cherished inalienable possession to which people will cling, even under threat of death. God created the mind free, and all attempts to bend it to the state's will by threats of punishment or civil incapacitation depart from His plan. God chose not to propagate His plan by coercion, although it is in His power to do, because He wants us to freely choose His way. It is therefore an impious presumption of civil legislators to attempt to do what God will not. A reading of the history of the reasoning behind the drafting of the Free Exercise Clause reveals that the founding fathers knew and respected this.

The Religious Freedom Restoration Act

In 1993 Congress passed the Religious Freedom Restoration Act (RFRA) to protect religion following a notorious 1990 Supreme Court case (discussed in the next chapter) that rendered the Free Exercise Clause almost impotent. The RFRA recognizes that religiously neutral laws can burden the free exercise of religion as much as laws that intend to do so, and thus requires the courts to apply strict scrutiny to laws burdening religion, and reads in part: "Government may substantially burden a person's exercise of religion only if it demonstrates that application of the burden to the person (1) is in furtherance of a compelling governmental interest; and (2) is the least restrictive means of furthering that compelling governmental interest." The RFRA was passed by a unanimous vote in the House, and only three senators voted against it in the Senate. On signing the act into law, President Bill Clinton remarked:

> We all have a shared desire here to protect perhaps the most precious of all American liberties, religious freedom. Usually the signing of legislation by a President is a ministerial act, often a quiet ending to a turbulent legislative process. Today this event assumes a more majestic quality because of our ability together to affirm the historic role that people of faith have played in the history of this country and the constitutional protections those who profess and express their faith have always demanded and cherished.[18]

Despite the overwhelming support for the RFRA by Congress and the President, the Supreme Court struck it down as applied to state and local governments in *City of Boerne v. Flores* (1997). The issue before the Court in *Boerne* was simply the denial of a building permit to a church's application to build in a defined historical district of Boerne, Texas, but it had far-reaching consequences for religious liberty. The Court ruled that Congress overstepped its authority by requiring the states to provide protection of religious liberty, and ruled that: "This is a considerable congressional intrusion into the States' traditional prerogatives and general authority to regulate for the health and welfare of their citizens." In other words, Congress acted constitutionally by enacting the RFRA, but it may not determine the manner in which states enforce the substance of their legislation. The federal RFRA does not apply to the states, and thus claims of violation of religious liberty cannot be brought against the states under it. In response to this ruling, several states enacted their own RFRA's but many did not, leaving it to state statues to determine the scope of its intrusion on free exercise. Justice O'Connor's dissent in *City of Boerne* points to the centrality of the Free Exercise Clause as the framers saw it:

> Our Nation's Founders conceived of a Republic receptive to voluntary religious expression, not of a secular society in which religious expression is tolerated only when it does not conflict with a generally applicable law... the Free Exercise Clause is properly understood as an affirmative guarantee of the right to participate in religious activities without impermissible governmental interference, even where a believer's conduct is in tension with a law of general application. Certainly, it is in no way anomalous to accord heightened protection to a right identified in the text of the First Amendment. For example, it has long been the Court's position that freedom of speech—a right enumerated only a few words after the right to free exercise—has special constitutional status. Given the centrality of freedom of speech and religion to the American concept of personal liberty, it is altogether reasonable to conclude that both should be treated with the highest degree of respect.

THE ATHEIST ARGUMENT FROM SCIENCE

A favorite atheist argument against affording religion any special protection is that religion does not mesh with current understanding of science, and is therefore just an irrational belief system. In his book *Why Tolerate Religion?,* Brian Leiter disparages religion as consisting of intrinsically irrational beliefs "unhinged from reason." He claims that religion is insulated from "reason and evidence" which he defines as "believing in something notwithstanding the evidence and reasons that fail to support it or even contradict it" (2014, p. 39). Atheists like Leiter are of the opinion that God has been given His walking papers by reason and science, and uses this assertion to push their idea that religious conscience deserves no special protection. But as science has progressed it has resurrected a belief in God among many prominent scientists. Nobel Prize winning physicist Max Planck, who can hardly be called irrational, once remarked in a lecture:

> There can never be any real opposition between religion and science; for the one is the complement of the other. Every serious and reflective person realizes, I think, that the religious element in his nature must be recognized and cultivated if all the powers of the human soul are to act together in perfect balance and harmony. And indeed it was not by accident that the greatest thinkers of all ages were deeply religious souls (I949, p. 184).

Many people such as Leiter believe that scientists are mostly atheists, but a national study of 1,400 scientists found that only a piddling 9.8% so described themselves. Of the remainder, 34.9% believed in God and held no doubts, 16.6% believed in God but had doubts, 19.2% believed in a higher power, 4.4% believed "some of the time," and 13.1% were agnostics (Gross & Simmons, 2009). The rate of religious belief among scientists is below that of the general American public, but the rate is higher than the general public's among physicians, with 76% of a national sample of them affirming their belief in God (Easton, 2005). With almost two-thirds of scientists and just over three-quarters of physicians reporting some degree of belief in a divine Creator, it is patently false that science and reason are on the side of atheism—science and reason are on the side of God.

It is doubtless true that exposure to education in modern secular universities may push one in the direction of atheism, but the problem is not education, it is insufficient education. Among all Nobel Prize-winning physicists—the brightest folks on the planet—from 1901 to 2000 only 4.7% described themselves as an atheist, agnostic, or freethinker (Shalev, 2003). Perhaps this is why prize-wining quantum physicist Robert Griffiths has said: "If we need an atheist for a debate, we go to the philosophy department. The physics department isn't much use" (in Kainz, 2010, p. 21). The process of belief to atheism and back again is described in Francis Bacon: “A little philosophy inclineth man’s mind to atheism, but depth in philosophy bringeth men’s minds about to religion” (1889, p. 57). Or as more recently stated by Nobel laureate physicist Werner Heisenberg: “The first gulp from the glass of natural sciences will turn you into an atheist, but at the bottom of the glass God is waiting for you” (in Walsh, 2020, p.1).

So, in light of everything, why should we protect religious liberty in the way the Constitution demands that we should? Perhaps the best short answer is given by constitutional law professor Michael Paulson:

> We protect freedom of religion because knowledge and worship of God, and obedience to God’s will, are of the first importance. These things must take precedence over the contrary commands of all mere human authority. We protect religious liberty because we recognize that, as a matter of first principle, true religious beliefs necessarily take precedence over the commands of the state and because we recognize, as a matter of widely-shared faith, the possibility of religious truth. We also recognize the reality of human error, and especially of governmental error, in matters of religion, and so we do not trust the state to tell us the proper way to know, worship, or obey God (2014, p. 1610).

In short, religion is deserving of special protection because it involves duties we owe to God’s divine authority. This is something with no parallel in secular worldviews. No holder of a secular worldview experiences a deeply troubling conflict between what he or she sincerely believes and the commands of civic authorities the way devout religious believers do. As the founders realized, the Christian religion is a fundamental and irreducible good for society which cannot be subsumed into a larger secular category. Religion is special because while the Establishment Clause assures that a religion may not use the coercive arm of the state to promote its agenda, the state and federal governments are under no such interdiction to promote secular values and objectives. Governments are free to promote the values and objectives of any secular activist groups applying enough pressure, such as those of LGBTQ groups. This is why the Free Exercise Clause as the framers meant it is needed now more than ever.

Chapter 4

RELIGIOUS FREEDOM AS FREEDOM OF SPEECH

THE IMPORTANCE OF FREE EXPRESSION

In 1990, religious liberty was dealt a blow in the United States from which is yet to recover. In *Employment Division v. Smith* (1990), the Supreme Court cast aside almost three decades of free exercise jurisprudence decision and all but erased the Free Exercise clause from the First Amendment. Prior to *Smith*, the state could not deny religious exemptions without demonstrating a compelling state interest, which had to be pursued in the least restrictive way. It was this decision that prompted Congress to enact the Religious Freedom Restoration Act discussed in the previous chapter. The issue in *Smith* was whether the state of Oregon erred in denying unemployment benefits to two men belonging to the Native American Church who were fired for the centuries-long practice of using sacramental hallucinogenic peyote in their religious practice. The Court ruled that burdens on religious freedom no longer had to be justified by a compelling state interest if laws are neutral and generally applicable.

This case opened to door to state persecution of Christians under public accommodation laws, because as Richard Duncan notes, "under *Smith* the general rule seems to be that government may prohibit what religion requires or require what religion prohibits" (2001, p. 850). Justice Scalia opined that if religious groups or individuals want an exemption from a generally applicable law, they should seek it through the political process. This would put matters of conscience up for a vote, which is a "solution" the First Amendment exists to prevent; fundamental rights are not subject to legislative whim. America is not a democracy whereby government reflexively carries out the will of the majority. We are a constitutional republic in which government derives its powers from the consent of the governed. It is a form of government that rejects the tyranny of the majority and protects the rights of those who defy the orthodoxies of the day—or at least it is supposed to be. But, as Vincent Bonventre remarks: "Scalia's formulation has effectively removed free exercise of religion from its previously preferred place where it was immunized from abridgement except for the most compelling government reasons" (2018, p. 665). However, Scalia offered an exception for cases involving "hybrid rights;" that is Free Exercise claims conjoined with Free Speech or other First Amendment claims. From *Smith* onwards, the Court has only grudgingly recognized the Free Exercise Clause for no other reason that it is, embarrassingly, in the Constitution.

Because of the *Smith* holding, most religious defendants in LGBTQ rights v. religious freedom cases have relied on the Free Speech Clause, although many simultaneously bring a religious liberty claim. The reasoning behind this is that religious expression is conduct, and the courts have treated conduct as speech when conduct conveys a message. This has not always been the case because traditionally free speech protection applied only to verbal utterances. "However, as other delivery mechanisms were held to fall within the ambit of free speech law, freedom of speech was increasingly understood to involve a broader 'freedom of expression,' and categories such as speech-plus-conduct, expressive conduct, and symbolic expression were developed" (Kersch, 2006, p. 265).

Freedom of expression is a fundamental human right because it reinforces other rights. It enables people to pursue their own paths in life, set their own goals, and to defy social orthodoxies. If a person cannot dissent from the general will, society is not truly free. Free speech is never absolute however. The Supreme Court identifies some categories of speech of "low value" that may constitutionally be restricted by the state such as fighting words, incitement to riot, defamation, fraud, child pornography, obscenity (although modern rap lyrics and movies call this into question), and commercial speech. Absent these exceptions, the Supreme Court has zealously protected free speech. In *Brandenburg v. Ohio* (1969) the Court ruled that the state lacks power to proscribe speech based on either content or viewpoint, noting that "the constitutional guarantees of free speech and free press do not permit a State to forbid or proscribe advocacy of the use of force or of law violation except where such advocacy is directed to inciting or producing imminent lawless action and is likely to incite or produce such action."

Some progressive academics feel that Americans should sacrifice free speech rights in the name of equality. They point to countries in Europe that have "hate-speech" laws and would like us to become more like them. Caroline Corbin tells us that "we tend to overvalue First Amendment rights, and that overvaluing tends to come at the expense of equality" (2015, p. 301). Karl Marx would agree, because the emotional pull of equality can only result in expanding state power. Ronald Krotoszynski (2015) also abhors American free speech "absolutism" and points to Germany and Canada, that have hate-speech laws, as examples fit for emulation. Do we want to live in a country that bans books such as *Mein Kampf*, or criminalizes holocaust deniers? *Mein Kampf* is a racist rant, but if I want to read it to gain insight into Hitler's character, what right has the state to forbid me? Similarly, to deny the holocaust is ignorant considering the overwhelming evidence, but why should I be jailed for stupidity? In Canada, psychologist Phillippe Rushton has been investigated by the Ontario Human Rights Commission for "inciting racial hatred," with the evidence being his peer reviewed scientific work on race differences (Kay, 2006).

The slippery slope problem with regard to hate speech is who gets to define it? If scientific work published in peer reviewed journals can be defined as hate speech, anything can, including speech that defines marriage as between one man and one woman. George Dent counsels the LGBTQ movement against using the hate speech argument against religious doctrine because it may backfire: “The homosexual movement seeks to ostracize traditional religion, and government treatment of religious doctrine as hate speech furthers that goal. However, gay activists should consider that hate speech laws can easily be turned against them. Gay activists often vilify traditional religionists as bigots and hate-mongers” (2007, p. 619). If one group can be denied free speech, then so can all others. Christians who believe in traditional marriage are gagged today; whose turn tomorrow?

An ominous indication of where the nation is headed in terms of free speech is President Biden’s appointment of Richard Stengel to take the team lead position on the US Agency for Global Media. Stengel strongly supports free speech limits, saying that “… the intellectual underpinning of the First Amendment was engineered for a simpler era. The amendment rests on the notion that the truth will win out in what Supreme Court Justice William O. Douglas called “the marketplace of ideas’” (in Favocci, 2020, np). He is another progressive who views our First Amendment as outdated and meant for a “simpler era,” but the First Amendment is now needed more than ever as a bulwark against authoritarian big government, which is why liberal Democrats continue to scorn it. The left does not believe in the American tradition that the cure for erroneous or offensive speech is more speech. Speech from the right is simply labeled “incendiary” and thus must not be allowed a public hearing. As for Stengel, Constitutional scholar Jonathan Turley notes that: “Since it would be difficult to select a more anti-free speech figure to address government media policy, one has to assume that Biden will continue the onslaught against this core freedom as president” (2020, np).

CONDUCT AS SPEECH

State regulation of conduct with an expressive component must be subject to strict scrutiny. The question is: When does conduct qualify as expressive such that the Free Speech Clause, and thus strict scrutiny, is triggered? The classic case in this area is *Spence v. Washington* (1974). In

1970, Harold Spence hung an American flag upside down and festooned it with peace symbols to protest the Vietnam War for which he was arrested, charged, and convicted for desecrating our national symbol. Upon overturning Spence's conviction, the Supreme Court announced a simple test for determining if conduct is expressive and triggers First Amendment protection: (1) Conduct is expressive if a person intended to express a particular message, and (2) that message is understood by the audience. Spence was using the flag to express ideas which all those who viewed would understand. The issue in LGBTQ rights v. religious freedom cases is whether the conduct of religious dissenters meets these criteria to allow them to prevail.

The *Spence* standard was reinforced in *Texas v Johnson* (1989). Gregory Johnson, protesting the Reagan administration's policies during the 1984 Republican National Convention in Dallas, set the American flag on fire. Johnson was charged with violating a Texas state law, which criminalized desecrating the national flag and was convicted. The Texas Court of Criminal Appeals overturned Johnson's conviction, whereupon the state of Texas appealed to the Supreme Court. In a 5-4 decision, the Supreme Court affirmed the Texas Court of Criminal Appeals' decision and concluded that Johnson's action was "sufficiently imbued with elements of communication to implicate the First Amendment." Thus, the Court ruled that flag burning was expressive conduct protected by the First Amendment, and that protecting the flag did not trump the right to engage in political speech. Justice Brennan argued Johnson was convicted for "his expression of dissatisfaction with the policies of this country, expression situated at the core of our First Amendment values." The Court also ruled that offensiveness is not a valid reason to prohibit expressive speech and that actions used to express ideas cannot be regulated by the state.

COMPELLED SPEECH

The Free Speech Clause is interpreted as both the right to speak freely and the right to refrain from speaking at all. Being forced to speak, verbally or symbolically in the form of conduct, is compelled speech according to the Supreme Court. An early compelled speech case is *West Virginia State Board of Education v. Barnette* (1943) in which children in a family of Jehovah's Witnesses refused to salute the flag and were sent home from school. The Court held that schoolchildren could not be required to pledge allegiance to the flag because such a requirement compelled "affirmation of a belief and an attitude of mind," and unconstitutionally violated the "individual freedom of mind." Compelled conduct triggers a free speech claim if someone is compelled to convey a message with which he or she disagrees. Put plainly, having to speak a message with which one disagrees under duress is state tyranny and has no place in the United States—unless the message happens to be that of LGBTQ activists.

Compelled speech is further illustrated in *Wooley v. Maynard* (1977). George Maynard, a Jehovah's Witness, viewed the New Hampshire motto, "Live Free or Die" that he was required to display on his vehicle's license plate as repugnant to his moral, religious, and political beliefs. As an Idahoan compelled to carry around "Famous Potatoes" on his license plate, I would gladly swap it for New Hampshire's macho motto. Maynard, however, did not wish to convey New Hampshire's message, so he cut the words "or Die" off his plate and was convicted of violating state law. He twice refused to pay the fine on religious grounds and was jailed. The Supreme Court overruled his conviction on the grounds that the statute in effect required individuals to "use their private property as a 'mobile billboard' for the State's ideological message." The Court held that the state's interests in requiring the motto did not outweigh free speech principles under the First Amendment, including "the right of individuals to hold a point of view different from the majority and to refuse to foster... an idea they find morally objectionable." It also held that to require him to do so was compelled speech, and that the state may not "'invade the sphere of intellect and spirit which it is the purpose of the First Amendment of our Constitution to reserve from all official control."

Thus, the Court ruled that individuals have a right to hold a point of view different from the majority and to refuse to foster an idea they find morally objectionable. This ruling means that state regulation of conduct with an expressive component must be subject to strict scrutiny. The precedent established by this case is a victory for freedom of expression and freedom to abstain from expression against state coercion. Maynard was free not to affirm a message objectionable to him *created by others*. How much more important is it that he must be free from actually being coerced into *creating* the very message he finds repugnant? This should be doubly important because he would be compelled both to act and to speak affirmatively, not just compelled to silently affirm a message. Maynard was obviously not compelled to create the message to which he objected, but religious small business owners across the country are being compelled by state public accommodation laws to create the very messages that they oppose.

Modern free speech jurisprudence has been kind to secular free speech issues, but rarely to religious free speech issues. A lesson from *Wooley* is that the state's interests should be achieved by the least restrictive method possible. LGBTQ cases involve gay and lesbian couples demanding services that religious business owners will not provide. In no case has the business owner refused to serve these people based on their homosexual status, but rather based on being required to participate in, or facilitate an event, containing a clear message that they did not wish to send. When state compulsion creates a clash between what people believe and what they must communicate, free strict scrutiny should be triggered. Rather than sacrificing a religious person's free expression, the state could direct those wishing services the religious provider considers repugnant to other providers who do not. This achieves state interests by "the least restrictive means" and protects dissenters' free exercise and free speech rights.

Individuals refused services cry that their dignity is offended, but dignity runs both ways. Demanding that private business owners give up sincerely held beliefs in order to participate in the public marketplace offends their dignity also, not to mention their rights of free speech and free expression. Religious exercise may not be verbal speech, but it may be regarded as symbolic speech in that it is intended to be communicative. If a person refuses to photograph a same-sex wedding, to bake a cake containing a celebratory message for a same-sex wedding, or to create floral arrangements for one, that person is communicating disagreement with such a ceremony and exercising his or her right not to be compelled to do so. Compelling them to labor in furtherance of a same-sex marriage is tantamount to compelling them to speak in favor of same-sex marriage. This is different from Maynard's wish to be free of coerced expression because the coerced expression must be created and affirmed by the very people who object to it!

A recent free speech case involving religious objections to complying with a state statute is *National Institute of Family and Life Advocates v. Becerra* (2018). In 2015, California passed its Reproductive FACT Act (RFA), mandating that pro-life pregnancy centers provide information to their patients on how to obtain a state-funded abortion. The National Institute of Family and Life Advocates sought to enjoin the enforcement of the act as forcing staff and volunteers to violate their consciences in violation of their First Amendment rights. In *Becerra*, the United States Supreme Court ruled the RFA unconstitutional, noting that there is no such requirement in California that abortion clinics post pro-life information in their facilities. In effect, the RFA required pro-life pregnancy centers to advocate abortion, the very practice that they oppose, which clearly alters the content of their speech. The Court noted that: "States cannot choose the protection that speech receives under the First Amendment, as that would give them a powerful tool to impose 'invidious discrimination of disfavored subjects.'" Justice Kennedy's concurring opinion provided a stinging rebuke to the California legislature's self-congratulatory statement that the RFA was part of California's "forward thinking:"

> But it is not forward thinking to force individuals to be an instrument for fostering public adherence to an ideological point of view they find unacceptable. It is forward thinking to begin by reading the First Amendment as ratified in 1791; to understand the history of authoritarian government as the Founders then knew it; to confirm that history since then shows how relentless authoritarian regimes are in their attempts to stifle free speech; and to carry those lessons onward as we seek to preserve and teach the necessity of freedom of speech for the generations to come. Governments must not be allowed to force persons to express a message

> contrary to their deepest convictions. Freedom of speech secures freedom of thought and belief. This law imperils those liberties.

There are at least three disturbing aspects of the case. The first is the way the California legislature compelled the speech of those with whom it ideologically disagreed while leaving unburdened the free speech rights of those with whom it agreed, and congratulated themselves by calling it "forward thinking." The second is that defending California's RFA was Xavier Becerra, the person Joe Biden has named as his secretary of Health and Human Services. In his brief before the Court, Becerra argued that forcing pro-lifer centers to prominently display pro-abortion messages was not compelled speech, and, absurdly, that doing so was not contrary to their values. One wonders what damage to free exercise and free speech this man may do if confirmed. The third is that the Supreme Court decision was made purely along ideological lines, with all four liberal judges dissenting from the Court majority. Apparently, even liberals on the highest court in the land want to stifle speech that does not fit the left's anti-Christian ideology. Although *Becerra* is a welcome free speech victory for Christians, it is not one involving LGBTQ issues.

Conjoining Free Exercise and Free Speech Enfeebles the Free Exercise Clause

As useful as it may seem, relying on free speech claims when the real issue is religious objection, further enfeebles the Free Exercise Clause and makes it a mere sub-category of the Free Speech Clause and subordinate to it. In effect, this is saying that religious free exercise can receive the same constitutional protection as secular conduct, but nothing more. This is not what the founders meant free exercise to be. They made the Free Exercise Clause the "first liberty" distinct from others, and certainly not one to be bracketed with the Free Speech Clause. If the founders meant it the way that current jurisprudence sees it, they would not have included the Free Exercise Clause in the First Amendment in the first place. Furthermore, the Office of

Legal Policy makes the point that the framers of the Constitution used language that implies that the Free Exercise Clause has more force than the Free Speech Clause because in the former they used "prohibiting," and in the later they used "abridging." The Office notes that:

> ..."prohibiting" and "abridging" function substantively as part of the description of the categories of laws the government is disabled from enacting. Moreover, "prohibiting" and "abridging" are denotatively and connotatively distinct. "Prohibiting" means to forbid or prevent, while "abridging" means to reduce or limit. Thus, "prohibiting" connotes a finality, certitude, or damning not present in "abridging", which connotes limitations falling short of the finality of prohibition or prevention (1986, p. 17).

Recall that *Smith* precipitated the infamous notion that the Free Exercise Clause is a subsidiary of the Free Exercise Clause. Although Justice O'Connor ruled with the majority in *Smith*, she noted the distinctiveness of the Free Exercise Clause: "The First Amendment's command that religious liberty is an independent liberty, that it occupies a preferred position, and that the Court will not permit encroachments upon this liberty, whether direct or indirect, unless required by clear and compelling governmental interests of the highest order." While O'Connor's words are true to the Constitution, *Smith* has left us with a Free Exercise Clause that is a "subsidiary" of the Free Speech Clause. Daniel Conkle notes that while this is presently so, the Free Exercise Clause can still be the icing on the Free Speech Clause cake: "Free Exercise Clause can be understood to play an important—albeit subsidiary—function by permitting legislative accommodations of religion and by ensuring preferred constitutional protection for religious speech and religious association" (2001, p. 115). However, far from getting preferred constitutional protection on free speech/free expression grounds, most religious expression cases have been given short shrift, as we shall see played out in the Supreme Court's Establishment Clause jurisprudence related to public schools.

Stripping Free Exercise and Free Speech from Public Schools

Abraham Lincoln once wrote: "The philosophy of the school room in one generation will be the philosophy of government in the next". Lincoln's words were intended to support the moral role of Christianity in schools because of his belief that "The only assurance of our nation's safety is to lay our foundation in morality and religion" (Federer, 1994, p. 392). Teaching Christian values in school was so important to the Founding Fathers that they made it a part of the Northwest Ordinance, enacted in 1787 by the last Congress of the Confederation. The document made plain what the purpose of schools was to be: "Religion, morality, and knowledge, being necessary to good government and the happiness of mankind, schools and the means of education shall forever be encouraged" (Brown, 1912, p. 99). Two years after the penning the Ordinance, many of the same men sitting in the first Congress under the new Constitution proposed the religious clauses of the First Amendment.

Early in the history of America, the Bible was used in schools as a text for instilling moral principles. The Bible was eventually replaced by books such as Noah Webster's *Primer,* which was filled with moral Bible verses. Webster wrote in his *Advice to Children* that the purpose of education is to "enlighten the minds of youth in religious and moral principles and restrain some of the common vices of our country" (Sampson, 2005, p. 473). The Bible is banned in schools today (teachers have been reprimanded and fired for having one on their desks), and Webster's *Primer* would likewise be laughed at and shunned by progressives for its moral content.

The first case setting in motion the banishing of Christianity from public schools was *Engel v. Vitale* (1962). The case involved Board of Regents of New York State writing a non-sectarian prayer for recitation at the start of each school day. The Board viewed moral and spiritual training as part of a school's mandate and a tool for the development of moral character and good citizenship. The prayer was entirely voluntary, and any student objecting did not have to participate. The prayer was to be recited following the pledge of allegiance, and reads as follows: “Almighty God, we acknowledge our dependence upon Thee, and beg Thy blessings upon us, our teachers, and our country. Amen.” Opposition from ten parents in the New Hyde Park school district resulted in a suit to stop the recitation. The motion failed in district court which ruled that the prayer was constitutionally permissible because it was voluntary. This ruling was upheld by the New York Court of Appeals, but the parents, joined by the ACLU, appealed to the Supreme Court. The Court ruled the prayer in violation of the Establishment Clause, thus conflating children praying with Congress establishing a state religion.

Given this logic, the *Star-Spangled Banner* is also an unconstitutional establishment of a state religion since it proclaims: “Praise the Power that hath made and preserved us a nation! Then conquer we must, when our cause it is just, and this be our motto: ‘In God is our trust’”. Justice Potter Stewart’s dissent included these commonsense comments on the Court’s majority ruling that school prayer amounted to the State of New York establishing an official religion:

> The Court does not hold, nor could it, that New York has interfered with the free exercise of anybody’s religion…But the Court says that, in permitting school children to say this simple prayer, the New York authorities have established “an official religion.” I cannot see how an “official religion” is established by letting those who want to say a prayer say it. On the contrary, I think that to deny the wish of these school children to join in reciting this prayer is to deny them the opportunity of sharing in the spiritual heritage of our Nation.

Not content with barring children from asking God to bless themselves, the school, and their teachers, atheists went after the Bible in *Abington v. Schempp* (1963). Pennsylvania and Maryland had Bible reading in their curricula, arguing the truth that it serves the promotion of moral values and the perpetuation of American institutions. The Schempp family filed a suit because, although students could be excused from Bible readings if parents objected, this did not satisfy them. The Supreme Court ruled that both prayer or Bible reading in schools to be unconstitutional. Justice Clark noted that most parents desire Christian moral precepts to be taught in public schools, but their wishes must be sacrificed to atheism. Justice Stewart argued in his dissent that the Court is biased against Christianity, and noted that, "a refusal to permit religious exercises thus is seen not as the realization of state neutrality, but rather as the establishment of a religion of secularism, or, at the least, as government support of the beliefs of those who think that religious exercises should be conducted only in private".

The Supreme Court then went after the Ten Commandment in *Stone v. Graham* (1980). Sydell Stone's parents challenged a Kentucky state law that required the posting of a copy of the Ten Commandments in public schools. Although the Ten Commandments are the basis of Western legal tradition, the Court ruled that displaying them could give students the impression that the state was promoting the beliefs they represent. Apparently, the state has no business promoting non-violence, truth, or coveting what is not yours! The Court's dicta in the case is disconcerting: "If the posted copies of the Ten Commandments are to have any effect at all, it will be to induce the schoolchildren to read, meditate upon, perhaps to venerate and obey, the Commandments". Is moral guidance no longer a "legitimate state interest"? Heaven forbid that schoolchildren might read, meditate upon, venerate, and obey the Ten Commandments! Let our schoolchildren meditate on obscene rap lyrics, pornography, lust, greed, and envy instead.

In *Wallace v. Jaffree* (1985), the Supreme Court ruled that children could not even meditate on God. The case involved a 1981Alabama statute authorizing one-minute silence in schools "for meditation or voluntary prayer", and a 1982 statute authorizing teachers to lead willing students in a prayer to "Almighty God…the Creator and Supreme Judge of the World". A federal judge declared the statutes constitutional because they promote the view that religious observances should be accommodated in a non-coercive way, and certainly do not establish a Church of the United States. The Supreme Court disagreed and ruled the statutes violated the Establishment Clause. In Justice Warren Burger's dissent, he wrote: "The notion that the Alabama statute is a step toward creating an established church borders on, if it does not trespass into, the ridiculous. The statute… affirmatively furthers the values of religious freedom and tolerance that the Establishment

Clause was designed to protect". Burger went on to point out the Court's hostility to religion: "To suggest that a moment-of-silence statute that includes the word 'prayer' unconstitutionally endorses religion.... manifests not neutrality but hostility toward religion". The Free Exercise Clause says that Congress is forbidden to prohibit "free exercise", period. It does not say Congress must not prohibit free exercise "except in the public square".

In Justice William Rehnquist's biting dissent, he pointed out how alien the Court's ruling would have been to previous generations of Americans, especially the generation that wrote the Declaration of Independence, the Constitution, and the Bill of Rights:

> It would come as much of a shock to those who drafted the Bill of Rights as it will to a large number of thoughtful Americans today to learn that the Constitution, as construed by the majority, prohibits the Alabama Legislature from "endorsing" prayer. George Washington himself, at the request of the very Congress which passed the Bill of Rights, proclaimed a day of "public thanksgiving and prayer, to be observed by acknowledging with grateful hearts the many and signal favors of Almighty God." History must judge whether it was the Father of his Country in 1789, or a majority of the Court today, which has strayed from the meaning of the Establishment Clause.

If the state of Alabama was behaving in unconstitutionally, so were George Washington and all his contemporaries who wrote the document. Indeed, as far as the majority of the anointed ones on the Supreme Court are concerned, all individuals and institutions in America prior to the Court's mysterious finding of "tension" between the religious clauses were in violation of the Constitution. This is how far the Courts have taken us toward making this nation not just a non-Christian nation, but an anti-Christian nation.

The Supreme Court delivered another blow to religious liberty in *Lee v. Weisman* (1992). In this case, the Court interpreted the Establishment Clause so broadly that its boundaries could not be seen, but somewhere in that vast expanse the Free Exercise clause was buried. The problem ensued when a Providence, Rhode Island, school invited a rabbi to deliver a non-sectarian prayer at its graduation ceremony in 1989. The parents of Deborah Weisman objected and requested an injunction barring the prayer. A district judge denied the Weismans' motion, but the Weismans' continued their objections and won a victory in a federal appeals court. The school district then appealed to the Supreme Court, arguing that the prayer was nonsectarian and that if Deborah objected, she was free to remain seated during the prayer and free not to attend the ceremony. However, using Justice Kennedy's coercion test in a way opposite of way it was intended, the Court ruled, however, that Deborah was "psychologically coerced" into bearing the "burden" of having to listen to the prayer, and if she absented herself, she would forfeit the intangible benefit of the graduation ceremony. Thus, millions of high school graduates across the nation cannot engage in what could be a moving spiritual experience because one student was offended.

Apparently forgetting that he authored the infamous decision in *Smith* that all but erased the Free Exercise Clause, Justice Scalia made some scathing remarks in this case that seems to suggest that he regrets *Smith*. Scalia wrote mockingly that that the Court has gone beyond what it knows it's doing and that "interior decorating is a rock-hard science compared to psychology practiced by amateurs". He further added that: "In holding that the Establishment Clause prohibits invocations and benedictions at public school graduation ceremonies, the Court... lays waste a tradition that is as old as public school graduation ceremonies themselves, and that is a component of an even more longstanding American tradition of nonsectarian prayer to God at public celebrations generally".

The next important case in the relentless march against Christianity in our schools was *Santa Fe Independent School District v. Doe* (2000). In this case the Court held that even the practice of opening high school football games with a prayer, *initiated by students,* is unconstitutional. The complainant in this case could not argue that coercion to participate was involved as in *Weisman,* since attendance at a football game is entirely voluntary, yet Justice Stevens found coercion. He noted that students are faced with the "choice between whether to attend these games or to risk facing a personally offensive religious ritual…The Constitution, moreover, demands that the school may not force this difficult choice upon these students". In Stevens' view, a community-affirming prayer is an "offensive religious ritual" that students should not have to bear as an expense for attending a football game. Students voluntarily praying were surely surprised to find that the Court considered them agents of state efforts to establish a religion, or that they were forcing a "difficult choice" on others. What about the difficult choice "forced" on students by having to hear what a Justice cast in the mold of Stevens may call an "offensive patriotic ritual" in the playing of the national anthem, which contains references to God? We may hear of such a case in the near future as atheism gain ever more traction in American political discourse. The Court's ruling in this case violates the free speech, as well as free exercise rights, of Christian students and tells them that their beliefs and desires are subordinate to the beliefs and desires of others. Chief Justice Rehnquist's dissent noted the hostility of some Justices toward Christianity:

> But even more disturbing than its holding is the tone of the Court's opinion; it bristles with hostility to all things religious in public life. Neither the holding nor the tone of the opinion is faithful to the meaning of the Establishment Clause, when it is recalled that George Washington himself, at the request of the very Congress which passed the Bill of Rights, proclaimed a day of "public thanksgiving and prayer, to be observed by acknowledging with grateful hearts the many and signal favors of Almighty God".

How far hostility toward religion has gone was starkly in evidence in a May, 1995, decree, issued by U.S. District judge Samuel Kent in a school prayer case that would eventually end up in the United States Supreme Court in 2000 as *Santa Fe Independent School District v. Doe* discussed above, Kent announcing that any student uttering the word "Jesus" at a school graduation would be arrested and locked up. He further added:

> And make no mistake the court is going to have a United States marshal in attendance at the graduation. If any student offends this court, that student will be summarily arrested and will face up to six months incarceration in the Galveston County Jail for contempt of court… Anyone who violates

> these orders, no kidding, is going to wish that he or she had died as a child when this court gets through with it (McDowell & Hostetler, 1998, p 53).

This obnoxious bully who denied students their freedom of religion and free speech was himself jailed for 33 months in 2009 on five counts of sexual assault on female employees and obstruction of justice (Powel, 2009).

Judicial hostility to religion reaches into higher education. In *Christian Legal Society v. Martinez* (2011), the Court ruled against a challenge by the Hastings chapter of the Christian Legal Society (CLS) to the policy of the University of California Hastings College governing official recognition of student groups. Members of CLS were required to sign a "Statement of Faith" and to live in accordance with Christian beliefs and values and disqualified from membership anyone who engaged in "acts of sexual conduct outside of God's design for marriage between one man and one woman". Because of this rule, the CLS was denied registered student organization (RSO) status. The CLS complained that it was the only group denied the right to participate in the life of the law school community on equal terms with other groups because of its faith-based nature, and that: "To require a religious group like CLS to admit nonbelievers is a severe burden on its freedom of association". CLS is the only group ever to be denied RSO status at Hastings.

Justice Alito wrote in his dissenting opinion that the bylaws of other RSOs at Hastings had provisions allowing the denial of membership to students disagreeing with the views and objectives of the organization as an essential part of any group's identity and message. The CLS was thus uniquely burdened due to its Christian views. Justice Alito also noted that the Court's ruling turned a blind eye to three Constitutional rights of the CLS denied them by Hastings: (1) Freedom of religious expression (its bylaws were deemed unacceptable to Hastings, so it would not allow them to express them); (2) freedom of speech (CLS was denied access to campus bulletin boards, facilities, and the school newspaper), and (3) freedom of association (unlike other RSOs, CLS was not permitted the freedom to choose with whom it wants to associate). It is important to note that the CLS did not deny membership based on sexual orientation but rather on sexual conduct. It is as unlikely that a practicing homosexual would want to join the CLS as an African American is to want to join the KKK or a Jew the Nazi Party. Thus, Hastings' policy in no way protected homosexuals; it is nothing less than an attack on Christian expression of First Amendment rights.

The *Martinez* Court disregarded its own precedence established in *Widmar v. Vincent* (1981). In *Widmar*, the Court ruled that the refusal of the University of Missouri to accommodate the religious meetings of a campus religious group as unconstitutionally abridging its freedoms of speech, association, and free exercise of religion, the very same rights that the Court denied CLS in *Martinez.* Of course, what has happened to change the Court's jurisprudence over the 40-year span between the two cases is the advent of LGBTQ rights and the concurrent diminution of religious rights.

In a series of cases, the Supreme Court has slowly laid waste to a rich constitutional history of religious freedom and practice in the hearts of the young people of America. This has led: "to a society that lacks a unifying or common narrative. When religion is exorcised from the public schools, we raise generation after generation of citizens with no clear sense concerning the foundations of moral values, ethical behavior, or interpersonal conduct. As a result, many Americans struggle with issues of worth and identity, lacking a clear sense of either self or community" (Shrader, 2005, p. 5). A culture that commands us to be silent about our Christian convictions is heading toward moral anarchy and spiritual degradation. This is the tragedy wrought by an unaccountable legal priesthood sitting on the highest court in the land that believes it knows the Constitution better than its authors.

Chapter 5

Religious Liberty and the Legalization of Same-Sex Marriage

America's Culture War and Cultural Marxism

There is cultural war going on for America's soul. On the far left of the war is a coherent intellectual program containing an assemblage of Marxist/Freudian ideas known as Cultural Marxism. The roots of this program may be traced back to Antonio Gramsci (1891–1937) and to a Marxist think tank known as the Frankfurt School in Germany in the early 1930s, which called its system of thought *Kulturbolshewismus* ("Cultural Bolshevism"). The central idea of Cultural Marxism is that Marxism failed to gain traction in the West because the values of capitalism and Christianity are too deeply embedded in Western society, and that if it is to take told, it must concentrate its efforts on cultural rather than economic issues. Because Christianity is Marxism's most potent enemy, Gramsci believed that war against Christianity must be waged relentlessly: "Marxists must change the residually Christian mind... to alter the mind—to turn it to its opposite—so that it would become *not merely a non-Christian mind but an anti-Christian mind*" (in Malachi, 2008, p. 250; emphasis added). The ideas of Cultural

Marxism are propagated vigorously today in our universities under the guise of "critical theory."

The goal of Cultural Marxism is "the conquest of the system", which is to be accomplished by "The long march through the established institutions" (Buden, 2018, p. 129). The goal of capturing and reshaping the institutions of Western culture, such as higher education, the media and entertainment industries, the courts, and political parties, is socialism. Once you control the movie and music industries you have an open pipeline to pump endless sleaze into the minds of impressionable young people, while at the same time mocking Christian morality. Gain access to the press, schools, and universities, and you have opportunities through more cerebral pipelines to distort American history, to vilify Christianity, the traditional family, capitalism, and those nasty white males who made the unparalleled success of the West possible. Finally, capture a political party that rewards sloth and penalizes success, and embraces identity politics to turn the races, sexes, and sexual orientations against one another, and you have the perfect recipe for turning this nation into a second-rate bloated socialist state.

This has been a slow, but a sure and steady process. As Norman Thomas, a six-time Socialist Party candidate for U.S. president, said in a 1944 speech: "The American people will never knowingly adopt socialism. But, under the name of 'liberalism,' they will adopt every fragment of the socialist program, until one day America will be a socialist nation, without knowing how it happened. I no longer need to run as a Presidential Candidate for the Socialist Party. The Democratic Party has adopted our platform" (in Miller, 2010, p.264). Thomas knew whereof he spoke. The 2016 Democratic National Convention in Philadelphia opened with a prayer by Christian minister. Almost immediately the crowd booed and jeered her and began chanting "Bernie, Bernie;" leaving no doubt that socialism is now mainstream in the Democratic Party. What is surprising about this is that a Christian minister was invited to offer a prayer at a Democratic Party event in the first place, since during the 2012 Democratic Convention the crowd even booed God. Fast forward to the 2020 Democrat Convention where we saw the words "Under God" twice removed from the Pledge of Allegiance, and no one dared to declare a "God bless you" message at the end of their speech. On the other hand, during the Republican Convention, almost all speakers did.

When the Nazis shut down the Frankfurt School in the 1930s, it moved to Columbia University in New York. Notable Frankfurters were appointed to positions in other elite universities, where they immediately began to repay America's hospitality by applying "critical thinking" to every institution ordinary Americans hold dear. Critical thinking conveys a positive message of openness to all points of view, but in reality, it is the unrelenting pursuit of the negative in order to vilify and obliterate any system of thought that runs counter to the left's anti-Americanism. The most influential member of the Frankfurt School was Herbert Marcuse, who believed that tolerance is only for left-wing ideas and practices: "Liberating tolerance, then, would mean intolerance against movements from the Right and toleration of movements from the Left" (1969, p. 109). Marcuse wanted a utopian socialist society which "is to be ruled *despotically* by an enlightened group whose chief title to do so is that its members will have realized in themselves the unity of Logos and Eros, and thrown off the vexatious authority of logic, mathematics, and the empirical sciences" (in Kosalowski, 1981, 416). Marcuse's ideas have formed the intellectual foundation for the academic left and its intolerant political correctness. In many university social science and humanities departments in the Western world he has achieved his goal of converting "illusion into reality and fiction into truth" (Marcuse, 2002, p. 252).

Marcuse channeled Marx and Freud in his best-selling *Eros and Civilization.* This work became the Bible of Cultural Marxism because it sold the fatal attraction of sexual freedom to its readers. Sex sells everything from aftershave to sports cars, so why not socialism? Marcuse described individual freedom as a life free of the constraints of morality; man "is free only where he is free from constraint, external and internal, physical and moral—when he is constrained neither by law nor by need" (1966, p. 187). He wanted to remove all constraints on sexual behavior, including behaviors most people consider perverse: "the perversions uphold sexuality as an end in itself" (1966, p. 50). The ultimate goal of this unbridled sexuality was the destruction of the family, the other enemy of Marxism: "This change in the value of and scope of libidinal relations would lead to a disintegration of the institutions in which the private interpersonal relations have been organized, particularly the monogamic and patriarchal family" (1966, p. 201).

Roger Kiska and Paul Coleman (2012) list a number of cases from abroad in which sexual freedom has strengthened the state to intrude on religious freedom, and thus to all freedoms. These cases include a Swedish pastor sentenced to one month in prison (later overturned) for delivering a sermon on sexual immorality, redemption and grace which referenced "sexual orientation;" an elderly Croatian Catholic school teacher who was sued for "hate speech" for teaching the Catholic position on homosexual behavior from a state approved textbook; a criminal investigation launched against a Roman Catholic bishop in Ireland under hate speech laws for delivering a homily on "the arrows of a secular and godless culture" which allegedly insulted a humanist, and efforts in Spain to criminally prosecute a bishop for delivering a homily during a Good Friday mass, in which he celebrated the virtues of the sinless life and warned against the "particular sins of the age"—a thinly veiled reference to homosexual behavior.

Cases such as these make it easy to agree with political scientist Stephen Baskerville that: "The greatest threat to religious freedom – and therefore to freedom generally – in the Western world today is the sexual agenda" (2011, p. 91). The loss of freedom is, of course, is the stated goal of Cultural Marxism, for how can we be ruled "despotically" by the self-anointed elite until we have been divested of all freedoms? Note how Baskerville alludes to the slow and stealthy way that this has progressed consistent with Cultural Marxist strategy: "The erosion of religious freedom in the West is gradual, like the proverbial frog in the kettle. Without a decided response, Christians will not only be 'marginalized,' as many already complain; they will lose their most basic freedoms, as will others" (p. 93). Sexual liberation provides government with power to intrude into areas of our lives we used to consider private. If you applaud this, go ahead, but as Baskerville says, be prepared to eventually mourn your own loss of freedom.

Although the founders of Cultural Marxism gave it its name ("*Kulturbolshewismus*") and coined its most famous phrases, and although their many books and articles are easily found, there are a number of left-wing blogs on the Internet calling the existence of Cultural Marxism a wacky right-wing anti-Semitic conspiracy theory. It is considered anti-Semitic because most members of the original Frankfurt School were Jews; which is as absurd as saying that abhorring Nazism is anti-German because most Nazis were Germans. It is considered wacky and lumped together with really wacky conspiracy theories to imply guilt by association. These alleged conspiracies include Obama was born in Kenya, climate change is a hoax, JFK was assassinated by the CIA, big pharma is suppressing a cancer cure, Princess Diana was murdered; the list is endless. Yet real conspiracies do occur. A dictionary definition of a conspiracy is: "The act of two or more persons, called conspirators, working secretly to obtain some goal". Among successful conspiracies, are the American, French, and Russian revolutions, while Guy Fawkes' plot to blow up Parliament, and the various conspiracies against Hitler's life, are examples of unsuccessful conspiracies.

True, Cultural Marxism is not a conspiracy in the traditional sense of the term wherein there is a cabal of secret conspirators directing the attack from the center. Unlike notable historical conspiracies, it is not a hub-and-spokes affair in which one or more principal conspirators at the hub have entered into agreements with others at the spokes to take action to achieve their goal. Cultural Marxism is akin to the evolutionary socialism of the British Fabian Society. The Fabians initially adopted a wolf in sheep's clothing as its logo, later replaced by a tortoise, representing its goal of a slow, imperceptible transition from Christianity and capitalism to atheism and socialism. One of Fabianism's most famous members, George Bernard Shaw, described the Fabian strategy as "methods of stealth, intrigue, subversion, and the deception of never calling socialism by its right name" (Stormer, 1964, p.26).

Cultural Marxism does not have a logo, but if it is a wacky conspiracy theory, then the voluminous literature written by its adherents revealing their destructive views on religion and the family is just an empty intellectual exercise lacking any policy recommendations. The people in the music, movie, and journalism industries, the people teaching "critical thinking" classes, or the judges in their courtrooms, may have never heard of the Frankfurt School or of any of its long dead members, but they are knowingly or unknowingly carrying out its agenda. Cultural Marxism served as the primary inspiration for New Left student movement in the 1960s (their placards read: “Marx, Mao, Marcuse”) and it continues to exercise significant influence in many spheres of life today. Like a cancer, Cultural Marxism—an unseen and undetected rot—has spread silently and unknowingly over decades to invade almost every cell in American life. As with cancer, in its early stages the damage to America’s soul was difficult to diagnose, but would have been easy to treat; in its later stages, it is easy to diagnose but difficult to treat.

THE REPERCUSSIONS OF OBERGEFELL V. HODGES

Obergefell v. Hodges (2015) is the landmark decision of the Supreme Court legalizing same-sex marriage that represents the high-water mark in the culture wars that have been waged ever since the sexual revolution of the 1960s. Since that time American culture has been, in Judge Robert Bork’s telling phrase, “slouching toward Gomorrah.” This period saw the ascent of liberal progressivism and its politics of blanket equality, political correctness, entitlement, envy, and the rejection of traditional American values. What was previously limited to a few exotic beatniks spilled over to a flood of hippies and leftist intellectuals who lauded the hedonism of the hippy lifestyle as signaling America’s liberation from “bourgeois” Christianity, capitalism, and morality. Following that, what used to be safely confined to the professoriate in the social sciences and humanities, oozed out of the ivory tower to infect the rest of society, and a significant proportion of the goals of Marcuse’s *Eros and Civilization* has been realized.

Having said that, I have no quarrel with the *Obergefell* decision legalizing same-sex marriage; my concern is that it opened the floodgates to attacks on Christians who exercise their beliefs in the public square. The newly discovered right pronounced in *Obergefell* emboldened LGBTQ activists to embark on a crusade against religious rights. Many people have come to believe that if same-sex marriage is a constitutional right and a moral norm of equality, why should there be any public space for accommodating, or even tolerating, opposing views? As Maggie Gallagher points out: "Gay marriage advocates have crafted a public argument that presumes there is no possible good reason to oppose gay marriage. According to some gay marriage advocates, only animus and hatred explains why, after an appropriate time to get used to the idea, any American would seriously object to gay marriage" (2010, p. 263).

Such attitudes have led LGBTQ activists to refuse to recognize the difference between serving them with goods and services for any occasions and actively facilitating a same-sex marriage. They insist that businesses owned by devout Christians must either violate their religious identities and do this or face crippling legal penalties and be driven out of business. Conform or withdraw from society was the counsel of Colorado Democratic Senator Pat Steadman when he said of people whose religion forbids them to participate in same-sex weddings: "Get thee to a nunnery and live there then. Go live a monastic life away from modern society" (in Laycock, 2014, p. 871). This is the kind of bigoted message that was once aimed at homosexuals— "Live your scandalous life if you must, but live it in the closet outside of mainstream society." Steadman evidently does not see the intolerance in his insistence that religious business people must check their moral principles at the shop entrance or be squeezed out of civic life. For such religious people, their businesses are an extension of their Christian ministry; religion is not something practiced only by ordained ministers. These people do not compartmentalize their religious and professional lives, even if the state insists that they must.

In *United States v. Winsor* (2013), the Supreme Court invalidated a key section of the Defense of Marriage Act that restricted the terms "marriage" and "spouse" to opposite-sex couples. *Winsor* elevated the level of scrutiny in gay rights cases. Although sexual orientation has not achieved strict scrutiny status, homosexuals have been transformed into a quasi-protected class and afforded heightened scrutiny. It was only two years later when the Supreme Court ruled in a 5-4 decision in *Obergefell v. Hodges* that same-sex marriages are legal in every state. There were two issues before the Supreme Court in *Obergefell*: (1) Does the Fourteenth Amendment require a state to license a marriage between two people of the same sex? (2) Does the Fourteenth Amendment require a state to recognize a same-sex marriage when the marriage was lawfully licensed and performed in another state? Writing for the majority in *Obergefell,* Justice Kennedy concluded: "The Court, in this decision, holds same-sex couples may exercise the fundamental right to marry in all States". Justice Kennedy also wrote: "The nature of marriage is that, through its enduring bond, two persons together can find other freedoms, such as expression, intimacy, and spirituality. This is true for all persons, whatever their sexual orientation. There is dignity in the bond between two men or two women who seek to marry and in their autonomy to make such profound choices".

The four dissenting Justices were scathing in their written dissents. Justice Scalia called the decision "a naked claim to legislative—indeed, super-legislative—power; a claim fundamentally at odds with our system of government", and Chief Justice Roberts invited anyone who wishes to celebrate the Court's decision to legalize same-sex marriage to do so: "But do not celebrate the Constitution. It had nothing to do with it". Justice Scalia wrote: "The five Justices who compose today's majority are entirely comfortable concluding that every State violated the Constitution for all of the 135 years between the Fourteenth Amendment's ratification and Massachusetts' permitting of same-sex marriages in 2003". Scalia also took the ruling as an opportunity to attack the Court's usurpation of the legislative process and dangers such a usurpation may lead to:

> Today's decree says that my Ruler, and the Ruler of 320 million Americans coast-to-coast, is a majority of the nine lawyers on the Supreme Court. The opinion in these cases is the furthest extension in fact—and the furthest extension one can even imagine—of the Court's claimed power to create "liberties" that the Constitution and its Amendments neglect to mention. This practice of constitutional revision by an unelected committee of nine, always accompanied (as it is today) by extravagant praise of liberty, robs the People of the most important liberty they asserted in the Declaration of Independence and won in the Revolution of 1776: the freedom to govern themselves.

The primary concern of the four dissenting justices raised by this decision was, however, the affect it will have on religious liberty. In Justice Thomas' dissent he wrote:

> In our society, marriage is not simply a governmental institution; it is a religious institution as well. Today's decision might change the former, but it cannot change the latter. It appears all but inevitable that the two will come into conflict, particularly as individuals and churches are confronted with demands to participate in and endorse civil marriages between same-sex couples... [and this has] potentially ruinous consequences for religious liberty.

Justice Alito's comments are the most worrisome. He chides the Court majority for their discovery of a new right unimaginable just a few decades ago, and then forcing all Americans to accept it. He notes the chilling effect the decision will have on the freedom of speech, religion, and association, and the bullying bigotry it will justify.

> Today's decision usurps the constitutional right of the people to decide whether to keep or alter the traditional understanding of marriage. The decision will also have other important consequences. It will be used to vilify Americans who are unwilling to assent to the new orthodoxy. In the course of its opinion, the majority compares traditional marriage laws to laws that denied equal treatment for African-Americans and women. The implications of this analogy will be exploited by those who are determined to stamp out every vestige of dissent... I assume that those who cling to old beliefs will be able to whisper their thoughts in the recesses of their homes, but if they repeat those views in public, they will risk being labeled as bigots and treated as such by governments, employers, and schools... If a bare majority of Justices can invent a new right and impose that right on the rest of the country, the only real limit on what future majorities will be able to do is their own sense of what those with political power and cultural influence are willing to tolerate.

The fears expressed by the dissenters in *Obergefell* were already a reality years before, but they have increased and strengthened since the decision was handed down. Religious believers have increasingly become the new pariahs targeted for state intrusion designed to deny them leeway to define their moral convictions the way homosexuals can now define theirs. Homosexuals can now claim the right to marry their partners, and I applaud that right, but that right should not entail the right to use state power to compel others to support, participate in, or endorse it. Religious dissenters know that same-sex marriage is now the law of the land, and they simply want to be left alone to live their lives in accordance with their beliefs.

The Flawed Analogy with Interracial Marriage

Justice Alito notes in the above passage that the moral claims evoked by the ban on interracial marriage in years past was cited in the Court's majority opinion and jumped on to claim that the religious objection to same-sex marriage is animated by the same bigotry: "The implications of this analogy will be exploited by those who are determined to stamp out every vestige of dissent". The analogy with opposition to interracial marriage has the most rhetorical punch of all morality-based arguments for same-sex marriage and for claiming bigotry for those who have issues with it. This argument has been widely used by LGBTQ activists for decades, and is their version of the "race card". Justice Thomas rightly held in his dissent in *Obergefell* that it is a spurious analogy:

> "Laws defining marriage as between one man and one woman do not share this sordid history. The traditional definition of marriage has prevailed in every society that has recognized marriage throughout history".

The interracial marriage issue was settled in *Loving v. Virginia* (1967). The issue before the Court in *Loving* was the marriage of Richard Loving, a white man, and Mildred Jeter, a black woman. Due to Virginia's anti-miscegenation law, the couple had to leave Virginia to get married. Upon their return they were arrested and sentenced to one-year imprisonment, which was suspended on the condition that they leave Virginia. A series of court battles eventually arrived at the Supreme Court. The Court struck down the Virginia statute on Fourteenth Amendment grounds: “There can be no doubt that restricting the freedom to marry solely because of racial classifications violates the central meaning of the Equal Protection Clause”.

Chief Justice Earl Warren quoted the Loving’s trial judge’s rationale for the Virginia law and Loving’s conviction: “Almighty God created the races white, black, yellow, Malay and red, and he placed them on separate continents. And, but for the interference with his arrangement, there would be no cause for such marriage. The fact that he separated the races shows that he did not intend for the races to mix”. On its face, this is an argument made on religious grounds, but it is one man’s claim that he can read the Almighty’s mind as to why the different races are found on different continents, but it is not something found in the *Bible*. The judge’s reference to “separate continents” is based on Acts 17:26: “And he made from one man every nation of mankind to live on all the face of the earth, having determined allotted periods and the boundaries of their dwelling place.” Deuteronomy 7:3 was also used to justify anti-miscegenation laws: “Do not intermarry with them. Do not give your daughters to their sons or take their daughters for your sons”. But Deuteronomy 7:4 is clear that it was not race to which it refers, but to marriage to people who worshiped other gods: “for they will turn your children away from following me to serve other gods, and the LORD’s anger will burn against you and will quickly destroy you”. This is supported by Corinthians 6:14-15: “Do not be bound together with unbelievers; for what partnership have righteousness and lawlessness, or what fellowship has light with darkness?”

While a biblical rationale for opposing interracial marriage requires eccentric interpretation, the rationale for opposing same-sex marriage is unambiguous and accepted by all three monotheistic religions. It is beyond question that all biblical references to marriage, beginning with Genesis, see it as a lifetime commitment between a man and a woman. All references to homosexuality in the bible condemn it (see for instance, Leviticus 20:13, Romans 1:26-27 and First Corinthians 6:9). Unlike the beliefs of those who were opposed to interracial marriage, those who refuse to recognize same-sex marriages make their stand on solid religious ground. However, I am of the opinion, shared by many theologians, that much of the harshness of the Old Covenant's Mosaic laws have been abrogated, and that Christians now live under the New Covenant of Christ's love for all, including homosexuals.

Unlike the same-sex marriage issue, religion played a supporting role in the fight against anti-miscegenation laws. In *Perez v. Sharpe* (1948) challenging California's law against interracial marriage, the California Supreme Court became the first court to strike down an interracial marriage ban, and did so in light of *religious* arguments. As Fay Botham (2009, p. 310) notes:

> [The argument] hinged upon several key points of Catholic doctrine: first, that Jesus Christ is the "founder of the Roman Catholic Church"; second, that marriage is a sacrament "instituted by Jesus Christ"; third, that the Catholic Church has no law forbidding "the intermarriage of a nonwhite person and a white person"; and fourth, that the Church "respects the requirements of the State for the marriage of its citizens as long as they are in keeping with the dignity and Divine purpose of marriage.

Arguments were also made by a number of religious groups in *Loving* that bans on interracial marriage, and the religion-based justifications for them, distorted the understanding of both Christianity and marriage. These groups became involved, according to Susan Gold, "because of their commitment 'to end racial discrimination and prejudice' and because of the 'serious issues of personal liberty' raised by the Loving's ordeal" (2009, p.72). Both the Court majority in *Obergefell* and LGBTQ activists are seriously in error in conflating real religious objections to same-sex marriage with concocted religious objections to interracial marriage.

The analogy between interracial and same-sex marriage is fundamentally different in at least two ways as they apply to their legal repercussions. First, following the legalization of interracial marriage, no dissenters were forced to participate in an interracial marriage on pain of ruinous financial penalties and possibly jail, but religious dissenters who operate wedding-related businesses are forced to affirm same-sex marriage or face such penalties. Second, unlike the distortions and idiosyncratic interpretations of Biblical passages used to oppose interracial marriage, Old Testament opposition to homosexuality is seen by many as unambiguous. The question is begged, however, is this an accurate assessment; can it be subjected to alternative interpretation? Christians can maintain the authority of the *Bible* and also affirm sexual diversity because a loving God does not deny anyone the opportunity to be what they are by nature.

While I am no theologian, I cannot agree with teachings that cast homosexuality as an insult to God, since God created homosexuals the way they are. I am convinced that homosexuality is just as biologically based as heterosexuality, but my opinion is irrelevant. The relevance lies in the beliefs of those being persecuted by the state because they adhere to them. Because these people adhere to Old Testament views, it does not mean that they hate homosexuals, or they are bigots who wish to harm them anymore than they hate heterosexual adulterers and Lotharios. It is what they regard as sinful behavior they abhor regardless of the sexual orientation of the sinner. With Douglas Laycock, I know of: "no American religious group that teaches discrimination against gays as such.... The religious liberty issue with respect to gays and lesbians is about directly facilitating the marriage, as with wedding services and marital counseling" (2014, p. 8).

The Flawed Analogy with Jim Crow Laws

LGBTQ activists and their media supporters also often make the analogy between refusing to facilitate a same–sex wedding with refusing to serve blacks in the old South. Jacquelyn Cooper makes such an analogy and calls it "modern day segregation." She reveals that she does not understand the religious objections at all when she writes: "If a liberal chef serves a conservative patron, the chef is not professing 'I support conservative views,'" and that "A florist may detest lilies, but if a customer wants lilies, the florist will provide them" (2013, p. 427). Cooper seems oblivious to the fact that there are no religious objections to conservatives or to lilies. A devout Christian chef will gladly cook a meal for a gay couple because there is no moral objection to doing so, and a Christian florist who "hates lilies" will sell them to a gay customer because there is no morality attached to liking lilies. Anyone of minimal common sense knows that doing so is not analogous to endorsing gay marriage. Her argument is a monumental non sequitur since there is a difference of several orders of magnitude between violating one's religious conscience by facilitating a same-sex wedding versus serving patrons with different political views or floral preferences.

Cooper also states that: "Asking a baker to bake a cake or a florist to make an arrangement does not involve force at all" (2013, p. 427). She is absolutely right at the time that someone merely asks. But when the asker is refused and runs of to state to have it compel the Christian to surrender to the request, then force is most certainly involved. She also invokes Jesus by pointing out that He fed, healed, and ministered to people whose lifestyle he found distasteful, but she neglects to point out that He told them to "go and sin no more." Jesus did not put His stamp of approval on their behavior, or facilitate it in any way, by ministering to them.

Cooper consistently ignores the fact that under Jim Crow laws it was the state that was discriminating. It was not religious conscience that motivated Jim Crow practices; it was state sponsored racism, which makes a world of difference. Under Jim Crow, white businesses were forbidden to serve blacks under penalty of law. White businesses were not in a position to say that they would not lend their talents to facilitate a black wedding but are willing to serve blacks in all other ways. They could not serve them, period. Religious believers, however, are more than willing to serve gays and lesbians for all occasions except for same-sex weddings or comparable occasions. These faith-based exceptions do not remotely compare with refusing service of any kind to a group of people because of the color of their skin. There are principled LGBTQ people who defend the right to refuse to cater to same-sex weddings on either religious or libertarian grounds, but no black person would defend state sanctioned Jim Crow practices on any grounds. The issue is not about discrimination against persons for what they are, but rather about discriminating against an activity that many religious believers consider an act that violates a commandment of God. I have difficulty seeing how anyone cannot grasp the difference.

Another legal scholar, Caroline Corbin, agrees that compelled expressive conduct should only trigger free speech scrutiny when someone is forced by their actions to conveying a viewpoint with which they disagree. There is no argument with this, but she then deals herself the race card from the bottom of the deck: "For example, a restaurant may not decline to serve a black family or a mixed race couple as discrimination on the basis of race is illegal. In the course of serving customers, a waiter must talk to them and write down their orders. Strictly speaking, the law compels speech, both oral and written. But few, I think, would argue that the anti-discrimination law should trigger heightened free speech scrutiny" (Corbin, 2015, p. 287). She is obviously right, but the analogy is wildly fallacious. A waiter has no reason to refuse service in such a case, but talking to the black family or to the interracial couple and taking their order does not involve an issue of religious conscience, nor does it constitute an endorsement of their meal choice. It is an entirely specious analogy, and one that would earn Corbin a solid F grade in logic 101.

Another scholar who conflates refusal to serve gays and lesbians in certain circumstances with the black experience under Jim Crow laws is Taylor Flynn. Flynn finds herself "unnerved by proponents' failure to recognize the dignitary harm at the heart of public *refusals to serve* historically marginalized groups". She sees the issue as analogous to posting a "No gays served here!" sign and sees "Such sign-posting is an embodiment of second-class citizenship" (2010, p. 236). It would be, but the issue is more correctly stated as a refusal to *actively* participate in an event that contravenes a person's religious identity, not one of refusing to serve gays and lesbians. A photographer must attend a wedding and participate in it by recording it on film; a baker must decorate the wedding cake with words and images, and a florist must do much the same, and in some cases arrange flowers at the location of the ceremony. This is facilitating or participating in an event that contravenes deeply held beliefs. It has never been an issue of whether a same-sex couple can get married, have flowers, have their photos taken, or obtain a wedding cake. These goods and services are available in abundance from people anxious to provide them. Nevertheless, there is an infuriating refusal to acknowledge the difference between passively providing a generic service posing no burden on religious conscience on the one hand, and actively facilitating or participating in an activity that does, on the other. They are too smart not to see the obvious difference, but they are not about winning philosophical debates, they are about financially destroying their opponents or destroying their faith.

Courts of law in this country are charged with finding solutions to moral conflicts without privileging or unduly burdening either side. The solution may not be optimal for the staunchest believers of their cause in either camp, but as long as there is a rational justification for the solution it should be acceptable to reasonable people. In the deeply divisive conflict between LGBTQ rights and religious freedom, the positions have hardened and the divisions have deepened, and the courts seem unable to diffuse the situation with balanced and just solutions. Just solutions can surely be found without resorting to coercive tactics that have profound negative effects on religious liberty. To be accepted, the policies promulgated must be widely regarded as just, necessary, and not destructive of fundamental values. Compromises have to be made in situations when not all the need demands of either side can be met, for it is profoundly unjust to disregard the demands of one side entirely to satisfy the demands of the other fully.

Yet, this is exactly what various state civil rights commissions have done. Public accommodation laws mandate that one side must satisfy the demands of the other while completely denying of the other, despite Justice Kennedy's assurance in *Obergefell* that this would not be the case:

> Finally, it must be emphasized that religions, and those who adhere to religious doctrines, may continue to advocate with utmost, sincere conviction that, by divine precepts, same-sex marriage should not be condoned. The First Amendment ensures that religious organizations and persons are given proper protection as they seek to teach the principles that are so fulfilling and so central to their lives and faiths, and to their own deep aspirations to continue the family structure they have long revered. The same is true of those who oppose same-sex marriage for other reasons.

Thomas Berg believes that the same arguments made for recognizing same-sex marriage can be applied to protecting the rights of religious individuals who refuse to recognize it. He argues that "both same-sex couples and religious believers claim that their conduct stems from commitments central to their identity: love and fidelity to a life partner, faithfulness to the moral norms of God—and that they should be able to live these commitments in a public way, touching all aspects of their lives" (2010, p. 207). In other words, gays and lesbians claim a right to have their love and commitment publicly recognized in marriage, and religious people wish to live by the tenets of their faith in their public lives, not just in their homes and churches. Same-sex marriage is protected by law, so why not religious liberty? Of course, religious liberty *is* protected by the First Amendment, but this appears to have been overlooked by the courts. It is a pity that Justice Kennedy did not provide a legal formula by which his promissory words could be put into practice.

Chapter 6

Religious Liberty in the Age of LGBTQ Rights

The Conflict of Views

The sacred right of religious freedom has been taken as a given in the United States since its inception. However, as we have seen, this right, treasured in American history as our "first right," has been slowly eroded with walling off religion from the public square in a series of Supreme Court decisions. This erosion has gathered speed in the first two decades of the twenty-first century as religious liberty has been pitted against LGBTQ rights. As God's creatures, LGBTQ individuals deserve the same rights as everyone else to live their identities free of state interference, but so do Christians. When these two rights butt heads in administrative and civil courts, however, the principled rights of homosexuals have almost always prevailed against the principled rights of Christians. The idea of gay rights trumping religious liberty would have been anathema to the founders in an age when homosexuality was reviled as "The love that dare not speak its name," and religious liberty was seen as America's "first freedom".

Things are very different today as LGBTQ people claim a right beyond their private behavior; that is, the right to have their love and commitment publicly recognized in marriage. Likewise, religious people wish to live by the tenets of their faith in their public lives, not just in their private behavior or in their places of worship. Some scholars see the battle between religious liberty and LGBTQ rights as a zero-sum battle: "Once the nation realizes that there will be a winner and a loser, then the only question is whether religious liberties and free speech rights should be repressed to promote legal recognition of same-sex relationships" (Lindevaldsen, 2010, p. 461). Gay or straight, everyone's answer to this should be a resounding NO! No fair-minded person wants to suppress homosexual rights, but religious liberty and free speech rights are far too precious to be sacrificed for the sake of any cause—any cause at all. Gay rights can be respected without sacrificing the rights of others. Not since slavery has one group had to sacrifice their natural rights to satisfy the demands of another group as are modern Christians.

Throughout history, homosexuals have been faced with the cruel choice of either denying their sexual identities or facing ostracism, prejudice, discrimination, and harsh legal penalties. Up to and including the 1940s, many states used draconian methods designed to "cure" homosexuals, including electric shock treatment, aversion therapy, and castration. In some rare instances, lobotomies were performed on gays and hysterectomies were performed on lesbians. (Painter, 2005) Most people today would surely consider such things as egregious affronts to human rights and dignity. Just over three decades ago the Supreme Court upheld Georgia's anti-sodomy statute in *Bowers v. Hardwick* (1986) on the grounds that it served a legitimate state interest related to "notions of morality". Justice Byron White noted that the Constitution does not confer "a fundamental right to engage in homosexual sodomy". Of course, he is right, but the Constitution does guarantee the right of all citizens to be free to engage in private behavior that does not harm others without government interference.

Seventeen years after *Bowers,* in *Lawrence v. Texas* (2003) the Supreme Court reversed itself, holding that anti-sodomy laws did not serve a state interest and were simply expressions of animus aimed at gays, since opposite-sex sodomy was not criminalized. *Lawrence* freed homosexuals from state intrusion and allowed them leeway to define how they will lead their own lives. The downside to this victory for gays and lesbians is that

Christian business owners are becoming the new pariahs targeted for state intrusion designed to deny them leeway to define *their* lives. The intolerance, intimidation, hate, and legal threats once aimed at gays and lesbians are now aimed at people with a strong religious belief that marriage is only to be between man and woman, and who act on that belief. These people have been the targets of threats, hate mail, and various other forms of intimidation, and courts are penalizing them for refusing to violate their moral conscience.

The moral conscience of Christian believers is often dismissed by gay activists as hatred and bigotry. Andrew Koppleman writes: "A standard–but unfair–rhetorical move within the gay rights movement is to treat all its adversaries as mindless bigots. ...it is a move that is increasingly successful" (2015, p. 939). For instance, Steve Endean of the National Gay Rights Lobby writes that: "Religion-based bigotry is not synonymous with bigotry. It is a uniquely vile form of bigotry as the prejudice, hostility and discrimination behind the words are given a moral stamp of approval" (Laycock, 2014, p. 870). For Endean, religious beliefs and values are nothing but hatred clothed in a veneer of morality. A similar contempt for religious liberty and free speech by gay activists was reported by David Benkof in the *Seattle Post-Intelligencer* (2008, np): "Openly gay Washington state Sen. Ed Murray, D-Seattle, and a representative of the largest Michigan gay-rights group, the Triangle Foundation, have both told me that people who continue to act as if marriage is a union between a man and a woman should face being fined, fired, and even jailed until they relent." Such is the verbiage of the Gestapo, the KGB, or the Stasi—"think and behave the way we say you must or we will come for you".

Despite such attacks, Christians are enjoined to love their neighbors as themselves, which is a tall order we must strive to obey. We cannot claim to love homosexuals but hate their sin, as in the cliché "Love the sinner, but hate the sin". When we label people sinners it is difficult to justify the claim that we love them. We should, however, respect their humanity, dignity, and rights, and wish them no harm. If we define love liberally as a concern for the well-being of others, then we can say that Christians love homosexuals, for they are as much children of God as the rest of us. There are many homosexual Christians who, like heterosexual Christians, have had non-marital sex at some time in their lives. This is the sin we are supposed to abhor, but who among us feel entitled to cast the first stone? "Homosexuals have a right to be a part of the family. They're children of God and have a right to a family". These are the words of Pope Francis, who supports same-sex civil unions, but not same-sex marriage (Arias, 2020, np).

What Christians have no love for is the anti-Christian tactics of radical LBGTQ activists who see the fight against Christianity as total war in which nothing less than unconditional surrender is acceptable. As Rod Dreher notes: "Christians and other religious conservatives, who now understand that the left's culture warriors, having won the gay-rights conflict decisively, are determined to shoot the prisoners" (Dreher, 2015, p. 32). Why do we see such extremism? In his 1921 book *Crome Yellow*, Aldous Huxley noted the nature of the "delicious moral treat" the gay left must feel each time it succeeds in rallying the courts to destroy a Christian small business owner: "The surest way to work up a crusade in favor of some good cause is to promise people they will have a chance of maltreating someone. To be able to destroy with good conscience, to be able to behave badly and call your bad behavior 'righteous indignation' — this is the height of psychological luxury, the most delicious of moral treats" (in Kalder, 2018, p. 174). What joy LGBTQ activists must feel when they contemplate the mental torment and financial ruin suffered by small business owners who have defied the demand to disobey their religious norms.

Sexual Orientation Is not a Choice

Is homosexuality a choice or a biologically assigned status to be respected just as we respect gender and race? Many people see it as a choice, but it is not. The American Psychiatric Association (APA) used to define homosexuality as a mental illness containing aspects of psychopathy, paranoia, and schizophrenia, and mental illness as a condition in which individuals manifest regular subjective distress associated with a generalized impairment in social functioning. Because homosexuality was defined as a mental illness, up to and including the 1940s many states had draconian strategies designed to "cure" people of their homosexuality. There are cases in which gay males were subjected to electric shock treatment, aversion therapy, castration, and in rare instances, lobotomies were performed on gays and hysterectomies were performed on lesbians (Painter, 2005). However, homosexuality per se clearly does not meet the APA requirements for mental illness because most homosexuals are satisfied with their sexual orientation and do not demonstrate any generalized impairment of social functioning. To the extent that they may manifest subjective distress more than heterosexuals, it may be attributable to their stigmatized social status.

Recognizing this, the APA removed homosexuality from its list of mental illnesses in 1973 and relabeled it a "sexual preference." The term "preference" implies choice among equally available others. Choice suggests alternatives are possible, which enabled family members and religious counselors to bombard homosexuals with moral exhortations and offers of therapy to help them to see that their "choice" was sinful. The choice claim also assumes that we toss a coin or enter into deep deliberation to choose the sex to which we will direct our desires. Who amongst us, gay or straight, did this? What rational person would choose a sexual orientation that used to be reviled and even criminalized? Most homosexuals say that they have known from an early age that they were sexually attracted to members of the same sex. (Ryan, Huebner, Diaz, & Sanchez, 2009). Their sexual orientation thus conforms with the way their brains, genes, and hormones bias them, despite strong social and legal pressures urging the contrary.

It is a widely accepted "fact" that homosexuals constitute 10% of the human population. The 10% statistic is a propaganda weapon for a radical movement known as the US National Gay Task Force whose campaign slogan is "We are everywhere." The statistic is based on studies by Alfred Kinsey, who used bogus sampling methods that ensured the overrepresentation of homosexuals in an effort to "normalize" his own lifestyle. Kinsey had a clear agenda in elevating the prevalence of homosexuality. Kinsey lived in an open marriage with his wife, engaged in many deviant acts, tried to sanitize child sex abuse, and claimed that 95% of men engage in deviant sexual behavior such as incest and homosexual sodomy. According to Judith Reisman and Edward Eichel: "No man in modern times has shaped public attitudes to, and perceptions of, human sexuality more than the late Alfred C. Kinsey. He advocated that all sexual behaviors considered deviant were normal, while polemicizing that exclusive heterosexuality was abnormal and a product of cultural inhibitions and societal conditioning" (1990, p. 2).

The actual prevalence of homosexuality is an open question, but there are a number of large studies using correct sampling methods that provide evidence that a small but stable percentage of people regard themselves as unequivocally homosexual. An American study estimated the prevalence to be 2.1% of men and 1.5% of women (Gilman et al., 2001). A British survey found the prevalence of males who were gay to be 2.8% (Mercer et al., 2004), and a Dutch study found 2.8% of men and 1.4% of women were homosexual (Sandfort et al., 2001). A Canadian study of 289,767 students found that only 1.5% of males identified as either bisexual or completely homosexual, although 3.5% said they have had sex with a male in the previous year (Saewyc, et al., 2007). A 2012 Gallup poll of more than 120,000 U.S. adults found that that 3.4% percent identified as lesbian, gay, bisexual, or transgender (Gate & Newport, 2012). These figures are a far cry from Kinsey's 10%.

In recognition of the growing scientific consensus that the roots of a homosexual identity are biological (albeit with environmental input), the phrase "sexual orientation" has replaced sexual preference. The growing awareness of this led to the decriminalization of homosexual behavior in 2003. Unfortunately, the debate about the origins of homosexuality is frequently couched in either/or terms; either 100% biological or a choice influenced by developmental experiences and situational factors. Like many other things, the truth is never simple. While there is no such thing as a "gay gene," after reviewing the genetic, epigenetic, neurobiological, and hormonal evidence, two prominent researchers concluded that: "The preponderance of evidence from sexual orientation research strongly suggests that human sexual orientation has biological underpinnings and that it is tightly regulated at the molecular level" (Nygun & Vilain, 2014, p. 178).

Thus, someone with an abiding unambiguous, and singular attraction to their own sex is probably closer to the "100% biological" end, while homosexual behavior sometimes engaged in by people claiming heterosexual identity is probably attributable to situational factors with a small biological input, such as strong sexual urges fueled by elevated testosterone levels.

If a homosexual identity is "tightly regulated at the molecular level," it is not likely that it can be changed. The best evidence that a gay identity cannot be changed are gays who have tried to change of their own volition but could not. Exodus International, an "ex-gay" Christian ministry founded in 1976, claimed that homosexuality could be cured by prayer and counseling, but after almost four decades of fruitless effort, Exodus International was dissolved in 2013. Alan Chambers, the president of Exodus International, noted that: "The majority of people that I have met, and I would say the majority meaning 99.9% of them have not experienced a change in their orientation or have gotten to a place where they could say that they could never be tempted or are not tempted in some way or experience some level of same-sex attraction" (in Throckmorton, 2012, np). Exodus International's four-decade crusade reveals that there are a number of gays who, for whatever reason, would like to change but who can no more do so than a straight person can change theirs. We should accept the fact that God made some people homosexual and others heterosexual, just as He made some people white and some people black.

STATUTORY V. CONSTITUTIONAL RIGHTS

Some see the clash between LGBTQ rights and religious liberty as a clash between two equally protected rights. For instance, Carl Stychin writes that: "Liberal democracies are faced with what appears to be an irreconcilable clash of two conflicting rights" (2009, p. 729). This is wrong. What we have is a clash between inalienable rights enumerated in the Constitution and alienable *statutory* rights, which historically have always been reconciled in favor of a constitutional right. Alexander Hamilton noted in *Federalist Paper No. 78*: "Whenever a particular statute contravenes the

Constitution, it will be the duty of the judicial tribunals to adhere to the latter and disregard the former" (1788, np). Justice Kennedy expressed the identical position in the 1989 Texas flag burning case—*Texas v. Johnson*: "For we are presented with a clear and simple statute [the Texas "breach of the peace" statute] to be judged against a pure command of the Constitution [freedom of speech]". Hamilton and Kennedy were simply stating that the United States Constitution sits above and governs all statutory law beneath it, and if a statute conflicts with it, the "pure commands" of the Constitution prevail.

A constitutional right and a statutory right are thus two very different things. Statutes are written by a legislative body laying out commands or prohibitions on citizens under its jurisdiction. They are legal rules enacted in response to issues of the moment usually considered to be pressing. A statute may be amended or repealed as an issue resolves itself, if it conflicts with the national or state constitution, or if there is significant public opposition to it. Such an amendment or repeal requires only the vote of the majority of legislators of the jurisdiction that enacted it. Acts of the legislature are not lawful per se. In other words, just because a legislature enacts a statute, it does not mean that it is necessarily a lawful exercise of its authority. Laws enacted by the states are, however, presumptively lawful unless successfully challenged in the courts.

If a law is contested, it is up to the judiciary to determine if the law passes constitutional muster. When a statute falls foul of a state constitution or the United States Constitution it is void, regardless of the good faith will of its legislators. If the case is deemed to be of constitutional importance, it may eventually find itself in the United States Supreme Court, which alone may decide if the legislature has acted beyond the scope of its authority. The Court has the final say as to the constitutionality of statutes passed by either state or federal legislatures, and has done so on numerous occasions. The *Justia US Law* (2017) website lists 968 state statutes, beginning with *United States v. Peters* in 1809, to *Pavan v. Smith* in 2017, which the Supreme Court has ruled unconstitutional. In other words, *all* cases in the past in which statutes have conflicted with the enumerated rights contained in the United States Constitution have been struck down. This is still the case with all statutes that offend the Constitution, except statutes relating to LGBTQ issues, then the Constitution seems to have gotten lost.

In *Wisconsin v. Yoder* (1972), Chief Justice Warren Burger was emphatic about the standard to be applied whenever government statutes interfere with religious liberty: "The essence of all that has been said and written on the subject is that *only those interests of the highest order* and those *not otherwise served* can overbalance legitimate claims to the free exercise of religion" [my emphasis]. It is thus black letter law that state or federal legislation may not limit the rights of individuals contained in the United States Constitution unless the governmental interest is of the "highest order", and cannot be "otherwise served". States can grant their citizens more rights than exist in the Constitution, but it cannot take rights away. While it is commendable to provide rights not included in the Constitution, newly minted rights should never be granted preference at the expense of the ancient and natural rights enumerated in the Constitution.

Statutory rights are granted by law, and unlike the guarantees of the First Amendment, they are not stated as disabilities on Congress. First Amendment rights prevent Congress from making any laws prohibiting or abridging the free exercise of religion, speech, press, assembly, or petition for redress of grievances. Subsequent amendments in the Bill of Rights prohibit certain kinds of government actions (prohibiting unreasonable searches, excessive bail, etc.), but they do not specifically prohibit the passage of certain kinds of laws with respect to these amendments. The uniqueness of the First Amendment lies in the founder's realization the rights contained therein are special—inalienable—and not mere civil privileges granted by the state. Statutory laws that have the effect, even if not the intention, of preventing the free exercise of religion, are violating this First Amendment disability. This does not mean that the statute is unconstitutional per se, it means only that it trespasses into that territory when it does not provide provisions to accommodate exceptions to the law on First Amendment grounds.

The statutory rights clashing with the enumerated rights contained in the United States Constitution of concern here are LGBTQ rights contained in public accommodation laws. The relevant enumerated rights are the free exercise of religion, free speech, freedom of association, and the Thirteenth Amendment right to be free from involuntary servitude. These natural rights guaranteed by the Constitution are being stripped away under the guise of LGBTQ rights. The courts routinely rule in favor of newly minted statutorily granted anti-discrimination rights over ancient enumerated Constitutionally protected rights. This affront to the Constitution and our Christian heritage is deplored by law professor Douglas Laycock, who writes: "If the Court feels free to enforce the *unenumerated* rights it likes, and to strip all independent meaning from the *enumerated* rights it does not like, it's hard to see how the existence of a written Constitution affects its decisions... To refuse to enforce rights that are expressly in the Constitution is as mistaken as enforcing rights that are not in the Constitution" (1990, p. 112; emphasis added). As a constitutionally guaranteed right, the free exercise of religion is an affirmative substantive right that should always stand above state statutes that have the *effect*, even if not the *intent*, of penalizing the free exercise of one's faith. Like the man who aims at A but hits and kills B, the issue is not whether a state statute specifically targets religious conscience but whether it hits it.

Religious Liberty and Compelling State Interest

The framers clearly noted the possibility of conflict between religious liberty and the state, for without this possibility there would be no need of the Free Exercise Clause. The Free Exercise Clause does not bar all state prohibitions on religious liberty, but religiously motivated actions that do not present a clear danger to the state are (supposed to be) constitutionally protected. No state or federal law exists that intentionally discriminates against practicing Christians, but sometimes government passes a neutral law that incidentally impinges on certain religious beliefs or practices. If an individual or group contests the law claiming that their beliefs or practices should be accommodated, the courts may use one of three standards of review to assess the merits of the case: strict scrutiny, heightened scrutiny, or rational basis.

If a court finds that there is a fundamental freedom essential to ordered liberty involved it will use the strict scrutiny test. A fundamental right includes all rights contained in the First Amendment, and others such as the right to privacy, to vote, to travel, and so on. Strict scrutiny is also applied to a suspect classification. Race, religion, and national origin are always treated as suspect classes, although other classifications have sometimes been included. To pass strict scrutiny, the state must prove that a law impinging on a fundamental liberty furthers a "compelling governmental interest" and be "narrowly tailored" so that a right is not abridged any more than necessary to achieve the government's interest. The burden is on the government to prove the constitutionality and necessity of legislation exposed to strict scrutiny. The Constitution carries a presumption of religious freedom, and the state must bear the burden of overcoming it.

The heightened, or intermediate scrutiny, standard is applied to so-called quasi-suspect groups (gender, age, legitimacy of birth, and sexual orientation). Unlike the strict scrutiny standard, the courts do not look as closely at the purpose or effect of the legislation under the intermediary scrutiny standard of review. A law passes constitutional muster under this standard if it is found to be substantially related to an important government interest, but the burden of proof still rests primarily with the government.

The least restrictive standard of review is the rational basis test. If neither a fundamental right or suspect or quasi-suspect classification is implicated, a state may enact any number of laws that are presumptively constitutional as long they are rationally related to a legitimate government purpose, even if the purpose is not necessarily compelling. That is, the courts do not look at whether a statute does in fact further a legitimate government interest. The burden of proof in such a case lies with the party bringing suit to show that the law is entirely irrational.

Prior to the LGBTQ rights movement, the federal government and the various states have always viewed religious liberty as a fundamental right unless the state could prove that an infringement of freedom of religion served a compelling government interest. There is no hard and fast definition of what a "compelling" government interest is, but in James Madison's amendments to the 1776 Virginia Declaration of Rights, which became the basis of the Bill of Rights, he gave a definition of what constitutes something so compelling as to justify government abridging a fundamental right:

> That religion, or the duty which we owe to our Creator, and the manner of discharging it, can be directed only by reason and conviction, not by force or violence; and therefore, that all men are equally entitled to enjoy the free exercise of religion, according to the dictates of conscience, unpunished and unrestrained by the magistrate, unless the *preservation of equal liberty and the existence of the State are manifestly endangered* no man or class of man ought on account of religion to be ... subjected to any penalties or disabilities, unless under color of religion the preservation of equal liberty, and the existence of the state be manifestly endangered (Madison, 1776, np; emphasis added).

Thus, in the opinion of the author of the Constitution, the state could interfere with religious exercise if the "existence of the state be manifestly endangered," but if the state's existence is not so endangered, religion may be exercised "unpunished and unrestrained by the magistrate." This constitutes a high bar for the government. Madison's language did not make it into the wording of the Bill of Rights, but it signaled that religious liberty has limitations when there is a conflict between a person's religious practices and legitimate state interests in its safety and security.

A clear instance of Madison's manifest endangerment trumping sincere religious belief is the 1993 bombing of the World Trade Center in New York that killed six people and injured over a thousand. The mastermind behind the bombing, Sheik Omar Abdel Rahman, tried to justify his actions at his sentencing hearing as his religious duty to wage war on the infidel. No one would deny that the government has a legitimate interest in suppressing a "religious duty" to kill and maim, because religious conscience must submit itself to the government's duty under God to preserve peace and civility in society.

Rahman certainly manifestly endangered the state, but does the practice of polygamy do so? Polygamy was the issue in the first Supreme Court case involving the Free Exercise Clause in *Reynolds v. United States* (1878). George Reynolds was a member of the Church of Jesus Christ of Latter-Day

Saints which at that time believed it was the duty of men to practice polygamy, and if they did not, they faced eternal damnation. The Court recognized the history of religious freedom in the United States, but noted that there are limits to practices that harm society:

> Polygamy has always been odious among the northern and western nations of Europe, and, until the establishment of the Mormon Church, was almost exclusively a feature of the life of Asiatic and of African people. At common law, the second marriage was always void, and from the earliest history of England polygamy has been treated as an offence against society... we think it may safely be said there never has been a time in any State of the Union when polygamy has not been an offence against society… polygamy leads to the patriarchal principle, and which, when applied to large communities, fetters the people in stationary despotism… .

There is no Biblical support for the practice of polygamy that would lend credence to Reynolds' claim. There are characters in the Old Testament such as Solomon and David who were polygamous, but there is a difference between the Bible simply narrating ancient practices and affirming them. The Bible does not endorse all that it records; its truth is in what it *reveals*, not in everything it records. It is illogical to claim that failing to practice polygamy will lead to eternal damnation. After all, there are only so many women to go around, and if elite members of a congregation took a lion's share (Brigham Young, the Mormon leader, had 55 wives), this would knowingly put a lot of other members of the flock in danger of hell fire. Thus, not only is polygamy not given a seal of approval anywhere in the *Bible*, the doctrine is logically self-contradictory, as modern Mormons admit.

The Court further proclaimed that to recognize Reynolds' religious defense against criminal indictment would "permit every citizen to become a law unto himself," and that the state could regulate religious conduct if it had a compelling interest for doing so. The *Reynolds* Court gave examples of human sacrifice and the burning of widows on their husbands' funeral fires as non-Christian religious practices that the state has a compelling interest to prevent. Society cannot and should not allow all practices hiding under the umbrella of religious freedom. It cannot allow acts that jeopardize the health, safely, and lives of others in the name of religion, such as parents refusing a child a life-saving medical procedure such as a blood transfusion or a crucial vaccination. If any and all practices were safe under religion's umbrella, I might be tempted to found a religion forbidding its members to pay income taxes. I would soon have many converts feigning true belief, even though it contravenes Jesus' command to "render onto Caesar." A free exercise claim is not valid if it contradicts a clear command of God. To believe otherwise is to burden the Free Exercise Clause with a weight too great to bear, and it is up to the Supreme Court to separate the religious wheat from the chaff. Sometimes it gets it right, but sometimes its notion of what constitutes manifest endangerment is beyond the pale.

For instance, in *Braunfeld v. Brown* (1961), the Court ruled that legislation designed promote some valid goal that did not directly burden a religious practice was Constitutionally sound. Abraham Braunfeld was an owner of clothing and home furnishing store in Philadelphia and an Orthodox Jew whose religion required him to observe the Sabbath, from sundown on Friday to sundown on Saturday. He compensated for this by opening his store on Sundays, which violated a 1959 statute law prohibiting non-essential forms of commerce on Sundays. The Court ruled that while Braunfeld's free exercise of religion would have been violated if the state had required him to open on Saturday, but requiring him to follow the state's "Blue Law" to close on Sunday did not. Although the requirement certainly burdened his finances, in the Court's eyes it did not burden his religion. Where is the manifest endangerment to the state in a Jew opening his store on Sundays? Surely his religious beliefs were burdened by requiring him to close his store on Sundays, thus forcing him to silently affirm a Sabbath that was not his own.

In *Sherbert v Vener* (1963), Justice William Brennan wrote that previous Free Exercise claims had been rejected by the Court because the regulated conduct "invariably posed some substantial threat to public safety, peace or order". It stretches the meaning of such words to the limit to assert that Braunfeld posed such a dire threat. However, the Supreme Court adopted the strict scrutiny standard in *Sherbert.* Adele Sherbert, a Seventh-day Adventist, was fired for refusing to work on Saturday, the Seventh-day Adventist Sabbath. She was unable to find other employment not requiring her to work on Saturday, so she filed for unemployment benefits. The state of South Carolina refused her claim because she failed to accept available employment when offered. The state's decision was upheld by the South Carolina Supreme Court, but the United States Supreme Court overturned it and held that Sherbert's conscientious objection to working on Saturday is a fundamental right, and was not "conduct within the reach of state legislation."

The United States Supreme Court has shown a willingness to grant broad religious exceptions to laws of general applicability in cases not involving LGBTQ rights. One such case is *Gonzales v. O Centro Espírita Beneficente União do Vegetal* (2006). This case involved a small Brazilian religious group called *Centro Espírita Beneficente União do Vegetal* (UDV) whose members receive communion in the form of a tea called *hoasca* brewed from plants containing a schedule I hallucinogenic substance. The U.S. Customs seized a shipment of the substance sent to the UDV and threatened it with prosecution. The Government acknowledged that its actions constituted a substantial burden on the sincere exercise of the UDV religion, but argued that this burden was overridden by a compelling state interest, and that applying the Controlled Substances Act was the least restrictive means of advancing it. The compelling interest involved protecting the health and safety of UDV members and preventing the acquisition of the substance from non-church members. The question before the Court was "Does the Religious Freedom Restoration Act of 1993 require the government to permit the importation, distribution, possession and use of an otherwise illegal drug by a religious organization?" Applying the strict scrutiny standard of review, the Supreme Court found for the UDV, ruling that the government was unable to show that its claim of compelling interest outweighed the burden imposed on the UDV's free exercise of religion.

Another such case is *Holt v. Hobbs* (2015), which involved an Arkansas prison inmate who claimed his right to grow a half-inch beard he believed is required by his Muslim faith. Not all Muslims are required to wear a beard, but the Court held that under the guarantee of the Free Exercise Clause the protection is "not limited to beliefs which are shared by all members of a religious sect." Prison officials had denied Holt that right, citing as a compelling interest the possibility that contraband could be hidden in a beard. In a unanimous decision, the Supreme Court ruled that Holt's rights to live according to his religious conscience outweighs the burden placed on the prison's security risk since it can find less restrictive ways of maintaining safety and security.

Given these diverse cases, one wonders who decides if a religious practice so manifestly endangers the state that it warrants state interference. The simple answer is that it can be any government entity testing the limits of its power, or any religious practice that the state entity feels necessary to suppress. Take for example the city of Houston's efforts to subpoena the sermons of five pastors in 2014. What danger to the existence of Houston was contained in those sermons that made Houston's petty officials want to seize them? The sermons were nothing more dangerous than to urge congregants to exercise their free speech rights to speak out against a city ordinance allowing transgendered individuals to choose to use either a male or female bathroom. Texas Attorney General Greg Abbott sent a letter to Houston saying that: "Whether you intend it to be so or not, your action is a direct assault on the religious liberty guaranteed by the First Amendment. The people of Houston and their religious leaders must be absolutely secure in their knowledge that their religious affairs are beyond the reach of the government" (in Sanburn, 2014, np). No crazier issue has ever occupied legal beavers than this, but the real tragedy is that religious liberty has been so degraded that it has been placed below an insane issue like who gets to do their business where. After all, if a person really is transgender, no one in the bathroom would know that "she' was born a "he", or vice-versa. But if a male looking like Grizzly Adams simply declaring that he was a female went into a woman's bathroom strutting his stuff, would you like your wife or daughter to be a witness to it?

Ultimately, what constitutes a compelling state interest is what the United States Supreme Court says it is. Apparently, the integrity of state unemployment claims, preventing the importation and use of psychedelic drugs, or maintaining prison security, does not rise to the level of a compelling state interest because the government must find less restrictive ways of achieving its ends. Until the Supreme Court says otherwise, a compelling state interest is whatever state statutes or civil rights ordinance say that it is. A compelling state interest according to these laws is that gays and lesbians must obtain whatever services they require, from whomever they require them, and the devil take the hindmost to religious liberty. State bureaucrats do not seek less restrictive ways to achieve this "crucial" interest, such as simply directing gays and lesbians to alternative vendors eager for the business. They would rather flex their muscles and show these religious "bigots" who is boss and set about destroying them.

Chapter 7

FREEDOM, EQUALITY, DISCRIMINATION, AND INVOLUNTARY SERVITUDE

EQUALITY VERSUS FREEDOM

I have a libertarian live-and-let-live philosophy of life, and strongly oppose any government interference with any personal, family, or business decisions that do not involve tangible harm to others. People should be free to live their lives and pursue their interests as they see fit if they do not physically or financially harm others in the process. This includes the rights of people and businesses to discriminate if they are willing to bear the cost of ostracism and boycotts that such discrimination may generate. Affixing the label "discrimination" to anything immediately casts that action as unreasonable, bad, and intolerable. The term has become a trigger word conjuring up pictures of Bull Conner, lynch mobs, and "Whites Only" signs in the old South. Most Americans see the word denoting unjust or prejudicial treatment of certain categories of people based on arbitrary and unreasonable grounds, but never on reasonable moral grounds. Stripped of all its negative connotations, discrimination simply means "to make a distinction and act accordingly". Leftists cannot even imagine any moral grounds for discrimination since, above all things, they value equality more than freedom. Equality is the banner under which demands for non-discriminatory treatment are made by LGBTQ activist groups seeking to avail themselves of services others are unwilling to provide based on sincere religious grounds.

There has always been a tension between those who favor equality over freedom and those who place freedom over equality, with conservatives and libertarians placing freedom above equality, and liberals placing equality over freedom. Of course, civic and political equality is considered a positive given for both political wings, but if equality demands exceed these boundaries there is always a trade-off, since both principles cannot be maximized at the same time. Because we have freedom of choice, and because people have different levels of conscientiousness and cognitive ability, a certain level of socioeconomic inequality is inevitable, which many liberals do not seem to understand. No government on earth can guarantee equality of outcome, but it can guarantee equality of opportunity. Both sides of the political aisle should agree to this. It has been convincingly shown by many studies that the most equal societies in the world are the freest societies in the world (e.g., Giebler, & Merkel, 2016), which implies that such societies have achieved the best balance between equality and freedom. This applies only to civic and political equality. These equalities assure that all able bodied and able minded people can become what their talents and ambitions will allow.

In the present context, the trouble is that the principle of equality is inflationary, continually making greater claims against other interests and cannibalizing other human rights in the process, including the right to be free of being a servant to the demands of others. The freedom to exercise fundamental rights should never be sacrificed in the name of equality. The refusal to cater to a same-sex couple's wishes to their marriages is without doubt discrimination, but the refusal of such services is freedom to act according to the dictates of conscience. It is the freedom to refuse to endorse practices that violate centuries-old beliefs and practices. State public accommodation laws have taken away service providers' precious freedom to refuse what is repugnant to them. The consequences of such laws are well put by law professor Richard Duncan: "When a legislature acts to protect homosexual behavior under antidiscrimination laws, it elevates homosexual practices to the status of protected activities while at the same time branding many mainstream religious institutions and individuals as outlaws engaged in antisocial and immoral behavior" (1994, pp. 397-398). I have no quarrel with homosexuals who wish to publicly affirm their love in marriage; I only quarrel with those who seek to force Christian business owners to likewise affirm it under threat of legal sanction.

The Constitutional basis for filing discrimination suits is the equal protection clause of the Fourteenth Amendment stipulating that no state may deny any person in its jurisdiction "the equal protection of the law". The courts have heretofore interpreted the antidiscrimination intent of this clause as being limited only to intentional discrimination that is arbitrary or unreasonable, but not to discrimination that aimed at avoiding the endorsement of a cause repugnant to the discriminator(s) even though there is discrimination "in fact". Examining the intersection of religious freedom and nondiscrimination, a constitutional scholar explains: "When we say that 'discrimination' is wrong, what we actually mean is that wrongful discrimination is wrong, and when we affirm that governments should oppose it we mean that governments should oppose it when it makes sense, all things considered, and when it is within their constitutionally and morally limited powers, to do so" (Colby, 2013, p. 2 citing Richard W. Garnett).

According to Deborah Dewart, a stalwart defender of freedom in several Supreme Court cases: "What the Equal Protection Clause clearly forbids is irrational, arbitrary or unreasonable discrimination. Discrimination is not 'arbitrary' where its purpose is to avoid endorsing a cause" (2012, p. 8). Dewart's reasoning is that because some Christians consider homosexual behavior a sin and not a civil right, discrimination against same-sex couples who wish to be availed of their services to facilitate their marriage is entirely reasonable because *not* to discriminate would be to endorse what they consider sinful. It must be strongly emphasized again that in none of the cases we will explore have individuals or businesses discriminated against homosexuals based on their sexual orientation; that would indeed be unreasonable and arbitrary. In all cases, the discrimination involved either the facilitation of a same-sex marriage or endorsing some other message that the party or parties involved found abhorrent to their moral sensibilities.

The United States Supreme Court distinguished between reasonable and unreasonable discrimination in *Hurley v. Irish American Gay, Lesbian, and Bisexual Group of Boston* (1995). The Court unanimously ruled that private organizations were permitted to exclude a group if it represented a cause contrary to the values or message the organization wants to convey. The case involved the South Boston Allied War Veterans Council, organizers of the annual St. Patrick's Day Parade, refusing the Irish American Gay, Lesbian, and Bisexual Group of Boston a place in the parade. In the unanimous opinion, Justice Souter wrote that to require private citizens to include a group advancing a message that the organizers do not wish to convey in order to make private speech conform with the public accommodation requirements of Massachusetts "violate[s] the fundamental First Amendment rule that a speaker has the autonomy to choose the content of his own message and, conversely, to decide what not to say". This ruling means that the government lacks the constitutional power to mandate the speech of individuals, groups, or organization when they do not agree with the message that other groups want to express, even if it violates a state's public accommodation law.

Although *Hurley* was decided on free speech grounds, it could have also been decided on the First Amendment's Free Association clause, as was *Boy Scouts of America* et al. *v. Dale* (2000). This case involved the Boy Scouts revoking James Dale's membership after he announced that he was gay. The Court held that New Jersey's public accommodation law that demanded that Dale be readmitted to the boy scouts was in violation of the Boy Scouts of America's First Amendment right of Freedom of Association. In a 5-4 decision, Chief Justice Rehnquist, delivering the opinion of the Court, noted that the Boy Scouts is devoted to instilling its system of moral values in young people that are inconsistent with homosexual conduct. He added:

> It also asserted that the right to engage in free association activities is protected by the First Amendment. This right is crucial in preventing the majority from imposing its views on groups that would rather express

> other, perhaps unpopular, ideas. Forcing a group to accept certain members may impair the ability of the group to express those views, and only those views, that it intends to express…freedom of association ... plainly presupposes a freedom not to associate.

Despite these rulings, under public accommodation laws the courts are increasingly telling individuals, organizations, and businesses that they must labor for, associate with, and endorse messages they find repugnant in the name of non-discrimination, regardless of their religious beliefs. Being told that you cannot say "No!" to promoting, participating in, or laboring for something that one finds morally objectionable makes one a slave without choices. According to the Office of Legal Policy, this is partly because the courts have reversed the way they have approached constitutional rights to view them as positive rather than negative: "The so-called 'Affirmative Age' of government has transformed the way in which we approach constitutional rights by emphasizing entitlements over responsibilities, equality over liberty, and positive over natural law" (1986, p. iii). David Bernstein makes some incisive remarks about the tension between equality and liberty, discrimination, the thin-skinned, and how seeking legal remedies for hurt feelings enhances state power over our lives:

> If Americans are going to preserve their civil liberties... they will need to develop thicker skin. One price of living in a free society is toleration of those who intentionally or unintentionally offend others. The current trend, however, is to give offended parties a legal remedy, as long as the offense can be construed as "discrimination." A society that undercuts civil liberties in pursuit of the "equality" offered by a statutory right to be free from all slights will ultimately end up with neither equality nor civil liberties…The violation of civil liberties required to achieve this kind of equality will diminish constitutional restraints on the government, and the additional power garnered by the government, introduced for noble purposes, will end up in the hands of people who use it to promote their own interests (2003, pp. 14-15).

Many believe that crushing the precious the rights of religious dissenters is justified because it advances LGBTQ rights, and thus the rights of a minority. Such people should heed the words of Ayn Rand: "The smallest minority on earth is the individual. Those who deny individual rights cannot claim to be defenders of minorities" (in Miniter, 2011, p. 278). If government intrudes into one Individual's life on behalf of another, it provides it with a leeway to further intrude on everyone's life, and to censor speech and demand conformity of beliefs, attitudes and behavior. This should alarm you whatever your politics or sexual orientation because, while the intrusion may favor you today, it may not tomorrow. The equal rights of all must be protected, but not at the expense of more fundamental rights hard-won by previous generations who considered them inalienable. The statutory rights of LGBTQ individuals can be protected without stomping on the constitutional rights of Christians. Same-sex couples are fully entitled to goods and services provided to others, but they are not entitled to force individuals and institutions that object to their message to endorse it, at least according to the Constitution as written. Faith-based businesses should be accommodated by opt-out provisions in the libertarian spirit of live and let live if we want to preserve liberty. Empowering state officials to punish people for their religious convictions necessarily invests them with enormous discretionary power, which will inevitably be wielded in other spheres of life over which they have been granted power.

Chillingly, there are people in America that support such an expansive role for government that would allow it to intrude even into one's private conscience. Harvard law professor Adrian Vermeule is one such person. Vermeule does not identify as a Cultural Marxist, but in his *Atlantic* article (2020) he channels Herbert Marcuse faithfully. He wants big government to promote his notion of equality and well-being, even "against subjects' own perception of what is best for them". Vermeule is a professor in an elite university, so naturally he knows better than you or the founding fathers how to live your life, what you should value, and what you should believe in. His vision of the relationship between individuals and their government rises dangerously close to totalitarianism with his Orwellian assertion that his all-powerful government bureaucracy "will be seen not as an enemy, but as the strong hand of legitimate rule... Subjects will come to thank the ruler whose legal strictures, possibly experienced at first as coercive, encourage subjects to form more authentic desires for the individual and common goods, better habits and beliefs that better track and promote communal well-being" (2020, np). Notice that he calls you and me "subjects." Did not Americans cease being subjects in 1776?

Vermeule calls his system "common-good constitutionalism", and wants judges to read into the Constitution principles and meanings that would turn it into a mere cosmetic document. His vision for America is chillingly reminiscent of the totalitarianism of Plato's *Republic* (the rule of elite philosopher Kings undergirded by the "noble lie"), Rousseau's general will (the will of the majority is absolute and binding on all), and Marx's dictatorship of the proletariat (elimination of private property rights and the redistribution of wealth). This is exactly what the American Constitution was designed to avoid. Our constitutional government does not exist to manipulate our beliefs, desires, or habits to produce an oppressive conformity; this is something Orwellian dictatorships strive for. Vereule says that he wants to promote "the common good", but he would do well to ponder C. S. Lewis's warning that: "Of all tyrannies, a tyranny exercised for the good of its victims may be the most oppressive" (1970, p. 292).

INVOLUNTARY SERVITUDE

Not only are the various civil rights commissions violating the First Amendment rights of Christian vendors who refuse to violate their religious consciences, they are violating their Thirteenth Amendment right to be free of involuntary servitude. Being told you cannot say "No!" when ordered to work against one's will for the benefit of another is involuntary servitude. As Deborah Dewart put it in a writ of certiorari before the Supreme Court: "A requirement to actively perform personal services imposes a direct and crushing burden—a critical component in some cases. Courts decline to specifically enforce personal service contracts because enforcement might constitute involuntary servitude. …Thirteenth Amendment concerns lurk just beneath the surface" (2012, pp.130-131).

The Thirteenth Amendment ended slavery and involuntary servitude in the United States in 1865, but the latter is making a comeback with the advent of same-sex marriage. The relevant part of the Thirteenth Amendment reads: "Neither slavery nor involuntary servitude, except as punishment for a crime, whereof the party shall have been duly convicted, shall exist in the United States, or any place subject to its jurisdiction". What does the law have to say about involuntary servitude today? Courts have the authority to require a person to perform affirmative acts a person has a legal duty to perform, but this only applies to civic duties such as serving on juries, paying income tax, and selective service registration. It is pointed out that: "It has generally been held that this power does not extend to *compelling the performance of labor or personal services*, even in cases where the obligated party has been paid in advance" (Free Legal Dictionary, nd, np; emphasis added). Apparently, this prohibition against compelling performance of labor or personal services does not apply to devout Christian business owners when confronted by LGBTQ demands.

The United States Congress has defined involuntary servitude quite plainly in U.S. Code § 7102, with section B being particularly relevant to Christian businesses. That is, "the use or threatened use of a law or legal process" to make any person labor involuntarily to meet the demands of others.

> The term "involuntary servitude" includes a condition of servitude induced by means of—(A) any scheme, plan, or pattern intended to cause a person to believe that, if the person did not enter into or continue in such condition, that person or another person would suffer serious harm or physical restraint; or (B) the abuse or threatened abuse of the legal process. The term abuse or threatened abuse of the legal process means the use or threatened use of a law or legal process, whether administrative, civil, or criminal, in any manner or for any purpose for which the law was not designed, in order to exert pressure on another person to cause that person to take some action or refrain from taking some action.

United States Supreme Court rulings have been consistent with U.S. Code § 7102. In *Bailey v. State of Alabama* (1911), Justice Holmes noted that involuntary servitude has a broader meaning than slavery: "The plain intention was to abolish slavery of whatever name and form and all its badges and incidents; to render impossible any state of bondage; to make labor free, by prohibiting that control by which the personal service of one man is disposed of or coerced for another's benefit which is the essence of involuntary servitude". Justice Holmes' use of the phrase "badges and incidents" is apropos here. An "incident" is something that occurs as a casual result of something else, and the clearest incident of involuntary servitude is the compulsory service of one person on behalf of another. A badge of slavery harkens back to some locations in the Old South where slaves sometimes wore copper badges to identify them as being available to be hired by others on behalf of their masters. Being identified as a devout Christian vendor is arguably a badge of slavery which could lead to incidents of involuntary servitude, and thus surrendering one's right of religious conscience, or losing one's livelihood and facing crippling fines if one refuses.

In the case of *United States v. Kozminski* (1988), the Supreme Court defined involuntary servitude as a compulsory condition in which someone must perform work on behalf of another or be subject to legal sanctions. According to the Court, it is a condition:

> in which a person lacks liberty especially to determine one's course of action or way of life" ... [it] "necessarily means a condition... in which the victim is forced to work [for the benefit of another] by the use or threat of physical restraint or physical injury, or by the use or threat of *coercion through law or the legal process*...we find that in every case in which this Court has found a condition of involuntary servitude, the victim had no available choice but *to work or be subject to legal sanction.* (emphasis added).

Constitutional law thus explicitly forbids what state civil rights commissions across the country are attempting to do; that is, to force Christian business owners to provide their services to facilitate same-sex weddings and to provide other services they consider sinful. Not only do these petty state officials violate the Free Exercise and Free Speech Clauses and part B of U.S. Code § 7102, they violate the plain intent of the Thirteenth Amendment. Plainly put, the right of anyone's access to the services of another by public accommodation laws must be construed narrowly when it runs up against the unalienable constitutional rights of free exercise of religion, freedom of speech, the ownership and use of private property, liberty of contract, and freedom from involuntary servitude. Using the examples of a photographer and a baker being forced to labor against their wills, Deroy Murdock states that:

> Denying a woman the right to choose whether or not to take pictures at a wedding constitutes art at gunpoint.... If bakers must spend hours and hours creating cakes unwillingly, this is involuntary servitude. Is this picking cotton in the blazing sun while being whipped? No. Is this exerting one's labor against one's wishes? Yes. This insults the free society. Ironically, Christians are losing the Wedding Cake War because they are too Christian. Rather than forgive, they need to fight (2016, np).

James Madison spoke passionately about the unalienable right of exercising religious conviction to the General Assembly of the Commonwealth of Virginia in 1785: "The Religion then of every man must be left to the conviction and conscience of every man; and it is the right of every man to exercise it as these may dictate. This right is in its nature an unalienable right" (Curry and Battistoni, 2000, p. 150). Madison would be outraged as gays and lesbians demand for themselves what they unjustly want to deny to others, gutting the First Amendment that he and the other framers deemed so fundamental to liberty in the process. If someone refuses to provide a service they find repugnant, the whole history of the United States has heretofore supported that person's right to do so. Baking a cake and inscribing it with words conveying a message makes that baker a publisher, and a publisher has the right to refuse to publish anything he or she wants. There used to be a saying in America that, "You can say anything you want, but you can't make someone else say it for you." This seems no longer to be true, at least as it relates to same-sex marriage. Thomas

Jefferson's words on commerce are appropriate here: "The policy [of good governments] is, to leave their citizens free, neither restraining nor aiding them in their pursuits. Though the interposition of government, in matters of invention, has its use, yet it is in practice so inseparable from abuse, that they think it better not to meddle with it" (1903-04. p. 255). Jefferson is saying that the voluntary exchange of goods and services *agreeable to both parties* free of state pressures is the only moral basis of commerce.

The government does not agree. The ink was barely dry on the Civil Rights Act of 1964 that prohibited discrimination on the basis of race, color, religion, sex or national origin when it was challenged on Fifth and Thirteenth Amendment grounds in *Heart of Atlanta Motel v. United States* (1964). Moreton Rolleston, the owner of the Heart of Atlanta Motel, refused to accept black patrons, arguing that that it violated his Fifth Amendment rights by depriving him of his property without due process of law and of his ability to choose his customers and operate his business as he saw fit. Rolleston also claimed that forcing him to rent rooms to blacks violated the Thirteenth Amendment by placing him in a position of involuntary servitude. The Supreme Court ruled against Rolleston, holding that the Fifth Amendment did not forbid the regulation of interstate commerce and thus his due process rights had not been violated. As for his Thirteenth Amendment claim, the Court ruled that the amendment was enacted to end discrimination, and therefore it could not be used as a tool to support discrimination.

LGBTQ activists often point to *Heart of Atlanta Motel* to support their view that business owners such as Rolleston can indeed be forced to provide services against their will. To be clear, as a libertarian I believe that anyone has the right refuse to sell, rent, or lease to anyone for any reason if that person is willing to bear the economic and social consequences. I disagree with Rolleston's actions, but defend his right to take them. In my mind, as in Jefferson's, there should be no legal consequences, since the state has no business involving itself in private exchanges that are not fraudulent. I know, of course, that this viewpoint is socially unpopular and has no purchase in the courts any longer. The point I wish to make is that case is distinguishable from same-sex marriage cases in at least two ways.

First, Rolleston's refusal was based squarely on racist grounds, which has no biblical, constitutional, or moral support, while religious objectors to same-sex marriage may rely on the support of all three. Society has a bona fide reason to eliminate the racism that Rolleston exercised, but certainly no reason at all to eliminate the freedom of religion exercised by those who refuse to facilitate or participate in a same-sex wedding. Rolleston would have abruptly reversed his policy had he been subjected to the disgusting attacks and crushing legal and financial burdens that religious objectors have faced, but these objectors have not because they see their refusals as complying with the commands of God. Rolleston's refusal was unreasonable and arbitrary discrimination, while those of religious objectors are reasonable and consistent with their sincerely held religious beliefs that are supposed to be constitutionally protected.

Second, the Thirteenth Amendment was not enacted to end discrimination, although some may find it implicit in its wording. It was enacted to end slavery and involuntary servitude, period. If discrimination is read into it, it is the distinction between he who must labor unwillingly and he who is the beneficiary of that labor. Rolleston was not subjected to involuntary servitude because he did not have to create anything special for black guests, the rooms were just there awaiting occupancy. Nor did he have to participate in any way in the activities of his guests in their rooms. On the other hand, the religious business owners discussed in this book have happily supplied gays and lesbians with generic goods and services—cakes, cookies, flowers, photographs, and so on, for any occasion—with the sole exception of providing special services for a same-sex celebratory occasion. This refusal is not based on LGBTQ animus in a way that Rolleston's was based on racial animus, but on matters of religious conscience. Religious objectors are singling out weddings, not homosexuals. There can be no doubt that when Christians are forced at the barrel of the government gun to labor on the demand of others that they are subject to involuntary servitude as defined by U.S. Code § 7102, by Supreme Court precedent, and by any commonsense moral understanding of the concept.

Although liberals dismiss involuntary servitude claims as applied to Christian vendors, they are happy to apply such claims in other contexts. For instance, Cynthia Bailey writes of involuntary servitude in the context of the 1996 welfare reform legislation that required welfare recipients to work or be in training to receive benefits. This legislation (Workfare) was designed to instill a work ethic among welfare recipients, get them used to the idea of earning a paycheck, providing them with a sense of self-discipline, and improve their self-esteem. It sought to distinguish between welfare recipients willing to work, abstain from drugs, and otherwise prove their virtue from those who were not. Bailey was incensed by people having to work for their sustenance and wrote: "Absent from any discussion of workfare, however, is the recognition that workfare is coerced labor. Indeed, one of the most important principles of the Thirteenth Amendment of the United States Constitution is that the right to one's labor is inalienable. By forcing welfare recipients to work, their right to self-determination is fundamentally compromised" (1995, p. 287). The right to one's labor is indeed inalienable, but Bailey should remind state civil rights commissions of that because they have made that right an alienable one for Christians.

Workfare is an opportunity, and not an imposition. Recall the Court's words in *Kozminski* stating that involuntary servitude exists when a person has "no available choice but to work or be subject to legal sanction." No such sanctions were threatened against welfare recipients if they refused employment or training. Unlike Christian vendors, they were entirely free to refuse the government's offer. If they did so, no legal sanctions were applied; they were simply denied access to benefits that the rest of us have to work to provide. If you and I work and pay taxes to provide for those who will not, are we not laboring, albeit, voluntarily, for the benefit of others, Professor Bailey? Furthermore, objectors to Workfare cannot claim any kind of high moral duty to refuse work. On the contrary, each has a duty to provide for the physical and spiritual well-being of their family. They have no right to expect others to take care of this responsibility.

What constitutional rights of welfare recipients are violated by telling them that they must work for their supper, just like everyone else? The right to be lazy? The right of free access to your money and mine? If such rights are in the Constitution, I can't find them. Bailey surely has a quite bizarre notion of what constitutes a right and what involuntary servitude is. Should

Bailey decide that the life of leisure is for her, does she really believe that she would still be entitled to her salary? If welfare recipients must labor for their benefits, it is for themselves and for their families, not for you or your family. Involuntary servitude is plainly defined as working against one's will for the benefit of others. No government agency is threatening to take away anything from those required to work for their keep except the bogus "rights" Bailey thinks they are entitled to. Indeed, the welfare reform legislation provided welfare recipients the opportunity to join with the rest of us as productive members of society.

Why do liberals feel that working to receive benefits paid for by others is involuntary servitude while working to provide benefits for another against one's will is not? After all, the taxpayers who fill the government's ATM must work for their daily bread, so why not those who feed from it? The consequences of "involuntary servitude" for welfare recipients and for taxpayers were overwhelmingly positive, both for them and for society. Within a few short years after Workfare was introduced, the welfare caseload was cut in half, and employment rates and earnings among single mothers increased significantly (Rector, 2003). In 2003, about 3 million fewer children lived in poverty than in 1995, and we had the lowest level of black child poverty in the nation's history (Rector, 2003). So, liberals are aghast at "involuntary servitude" that lifted millions out of poverty but fine with genuine involuntary servitude that impoverishes Christian small business owners! During the Obama administration, which evidently believed that the success of welfare is measured by how many people are on it, work requirements were gutted, and many reverted to exercising their "rights" to be lazy and dependent (I recognize that there are many people who simply cannot work for one reason or another and excuse them from that assessment). In 2017, President Donald Trump, who believes that the success of welfare is measured by how many people leave it, reversed the Obama administration policy. No doubt Biden will reverse Trump.

JUST AND UNJUST LAWS

Public accommodation laws that violate constitutional rights granted by the Creator are unjust laws and should not be respected. Law is a wonderful thing without which there would be anarchy, insecurity, fear, and victimization of the weak by the strong. Violating the law of a duly constituted authority should only occur if a law is unjust. We all live our lives under authorities greater than us: parents, teachers, employers, and even briefly, the traffic cop. All the holders of authority are under higher authorities, as are they in turn. In the United States, all authorities are themselves under the authority of constitutional law.

Christians believe that there is a higher law than man-made law: the ultimate authority of God. The apostle Paul notes that although God is the ultimate authority from whom all other authority comes, it is our Christian duty to obey just earthly authority. In Romans 13.1 Paul wrote that God has outlined three earthly authority structures—the family, the church, and the government—because each provides us with direction in our lives: "Let every person be subject to the governing authorities. For there is no authority except from God, and those that exist have been instituted by God". Paul also says in Romans 13.7: "Give to everyone what you owe them: Pay your taxes and government fees to those who collect them, and give respect and honor to those who are in authority", Jesus Himself said: "Then give back to Caesar what is Caesar's, and to God what is God's" (Luke, 20.25).

The state's most fundamental role is to protect citizens from the evil intentions of others, both foreign and domestic: "The one in authority is God's servant, an agent of wrath to bring punishment on the wrongdoer" (Romans. 13:3, 4). If the state is to follow God's word as His agents, it must allow citizens to follow God unhindered. The state is designed to preserve social order so that its people may live, in Paul's words, "peaceful and quiet lives" in a sinful world. This is a vision of the state designed to protect negative rights, and not one designed to provide positive rights, which may only be achieved by trampling on the negative rights of others. Jesus and Paul call for us to be in submission to governing authorities, but they do not say that we must obey them in all cases. We should submit to those in authority and obey all just laws, but we should not submit to laws that are contrary to the will of God.

How do we distinguish between a just and unjust law? Mathew Lippman notes that an unjust law is one "used to repress individuals and limit their rights. The respect that is accorded to the legal system can mask the dysfunctional role of the law. Dysfunctional means that the law is promoting inequality or serving the interests of a small number of individuals rather than promoting the welfare of society or is impeding the enjoyment of human rights" (2020, p. 23). The various states are unjustly "serving the interests of a small number" of LGBTQ activists while "impeding the enjoyment of human rights" of Christians. True, they are targeting only a small number of Christian vendors (to my knowledge, no business owners of any other faith have been targeted), but a right denied to them is potentially a right denied to anyone in similar circumstances. In his *Letter from a Birmingham jail*, civil rights leader, Dr. Martin Luther King Jr., made a clear distinction between just and unjust laws, and how we are morally obligated to obey the former and morally obligated not to obey the latter:

> One may well ask: "How can you advocate breaking some laws and obeying others?" The answer lies in the fact that there are two types of laws: just and unjust. I would be the first to advocate obeying just laws. One has not only a legal but a moral responsibility to obey just laws. Conversely, one has a moral responsibility to disobey unjust laws. I would agree with St. Augustine that "an unjust law is no law at all." How does one determine whether a law is just or unjust? A just law is a man-made code that squares with the moral law or the law of God. An unjust law is a code that is out of harmony with the moral law. To put it in the terms of St. Thomas Aquinas: An unjust law is a human law that is not rooted in eternal law and natural law. Any law that uplifts human personality is just. Any law that degrades human personality is unjust.

King was of course concerned with the civil rights of blacks in the segregated South, but his words are just as applicable to Christian business owners subject to public accommodation laws that "degrade their human personality". A just state is one that ensures that no man takes from another man what properly belongs to him, especially his moral conscience. Government can only give to someone what it takes from someone else. If it forces Christians to accommodate the desires of others, it takes their dignity and autonomy from them. A state powerful enough to do this is tyrannical, but such a state exists for Christians who want to live their faith in all aspects of their lives, both public and private. All governments are run by flawed individuals who will take as much power as we the people will grant them. It thus pays us to be wary of all earthy governments, especially governments that promise to grant positive rights at the expense of the inalienable negative rights of others. Good laws are laws that satisfy an inner-morality, and bad ones are laws that require contradictory obligations. The 19th century French philosopher and legal scholar, Frederic Bastiat, warned of the consequences of laws that compel law-abiding citizens to submit to laws that require contradictory moral and legal obligations: "When law and morality contradict each other, the citizen has the cruel alternative of either losing his moral sense or losing his respect for the law" (2006, p.10).

Chapter 8

TWO ICONIC RELIGIOUS LIBERTY V. ANTI-DISCRIMINATION CASES

JACK PHILLIPS AND MASTERPIECE CAKESHOP

Who would have thought at the dawn of the 21st century that cakes, flowers, and photographs would provide fodder for American political debate? Even before the nationwide legalization of same-sex marriage, various civil rights commissions targeted Christian wedding vendors who refused to lend their services to same-sex marriage. To be clear, it is not the desire for marriage commitment among homosexuals that is a problem for religious liberty. The problem is the demand of radical activists—typically aided by the ACLU—determined to destroy the lives of anyone who does not endorse their agenda in word and deed. The courts have been very friendly to the LGBTQ cause, and openly hostile to the cause of religious liberty. Two major cases addressed in this chapter illustrate this because the alleged offensive behavior of religious objectors to the LGBTQ message was mirrored by the same alleged offensive behavior of secular objectors to religious messages. The two religious objectors have faced years of court battles and face financial ruin while the secular objectors were excused.

The quintessential case involving free-exercise jurisprudence clashing with anti-discrimination jurisprudence is the case of the devoutly religious Colorado baker, Jack Phillips, owner of Masterpiece Cakeshop. In 2012, Phillips refused to bake a custom cake for the same-sex wedding of Charles Craig and David Mullins and was charged with violating Colorado's anti-discrimination laws. He did not refuse the request based on sexual orientation, because he said he would refuse an order for a custom cake celebrating same-sex marriage to anyone, and did so when Craig's mother attempted to order one. According to the ACLU, which joined with the state and with Craig and Mullins in the civil action against Phillips: "The [Colorado Civil Rights] Commission also ordered Masterpiece Cakeshop to change its company policies, provide 'comprehensive staff training' regarding public accommodations discrimination, and provide quarterly reports for the next two years regarding steps it has taken to come into compliance and whether it has turned away any prospective customers" (ACLU, 2013, np).

In a court case appealing the commission's decision, the court upheld the commission's ruling and Phillips was actually *ordered* to bake same-sex wedding cakes if asked to do so. Under Colorado law he could jailed for contempt of court if he refused. The judge cited Colorado state law prohibiting businesses from refusing service based on race, sex, national origin, or sexual orientation. The plaintiffs did not deny that Phillips told them: "I'll make you birthday cakes, shower cakes, sell you cookies and brownies, I just don't make cakes for same-sex weddings" (in Crossland, 2013, np). The distinction between selling cakes to anyone for secular purposes and participating in a ceremony that Christians believe is repugnant to God is presumably plain to everyone except petty bureaucrats in Colorado and their supporters. Baking a custom cake celebrating same-sex marriage is tantamount to endorsing it, but the court essentially told Phillips that he has no right to follow his faith, must create compelled speech, and must embrace same-sex marriage or face financial ruin and jail.

Phillips' attorney, Nicolle Martin, called the court's ruling Orwellian and "offensive to everything America stands for. They are turning people of faith into religious refugees.... Is this the society that we want to live in –

where people of faith are driven out of business?" (Starns, 2014, np). The requirement of Phillips to submit he and his staff to "sensitivity training" to mold their thoughts in politically correct directions smacks of totalitarianism, and his forced submission of reports to the state is essentially "designed to demonstrate that he doesn't exercise his belief system anymore – that he has divested himself of his beliefs" (Starns, 2014, np).

Phillips appealed the ruling to the Colorado Supreme Court, which refused to hear the case. Ria Tabacco Mar, staff attorney for the ACLU's LGBT Project, applauded the court's decision, saying: "We all have a right to our personal beliefs, but we do not have a right to impose those beliefs on others and harm them" (ACLU, 2013, np). Who is imposing their personal beliefs and harming whom? Phillips was going about his life baking cakes and not imposing anything on anyone. He did not preach on Craig and Mullins' doorstep, let alone demand that they accept his message. It was Craig and Mullins that came to him demanding that he violate his faith by helping them to celebrate their wedding. This is the very definition of imposing. If Phillips does not have the right to impose his beliefs on Craig and Mullins, which he did not, they should not have the right to impose their beliefs on Phillips, which, through state power, they did.

When a state attempts to impose a set of beliefs on anyone that he or she finds repugnant and then orders them to perform an act that affirms those beliefs is the very essence of tyranny. The pretense of state neutrality to religion is laid bare, for the state could hardly be less neutral to religion than when it places one private citizen at the disposal of another, even though it violates the conscience of the laborer and makes him a little more than a vassal. James Madison referred to religious conscience as the "most sacred of property", but religious individuals are being forced to use that property, and the property that constitutes their livelihood, to serve a practice that violates everything their consciences hold dear. This is tyranny of the most egregious sort that few ever expected to see in the USA.

Phillips' case eventually made it to the Supreme Court as *Masterpiece Cakeshop, Ltd. v. Colorado Civil Rights Commission*; the first religious liberty versus LGBTQ case to do so. Before *Masterpiece* was decided by the Court, law professor Eric Segal (2017, np) wrote: "The Supreme Court should rule against Phillips on his free-exercise-of-religion claims because the commission's actions were not directed at his religious beliefs or practices but rather at his refusal to sell his commercial product to customers based, in the commission's view, on the customers' sexual orientation". How can the commission's actions not be directed at his religious beliefs and practices? It is true that on its face the commission is simply directing him to bake a cake, but how can baking a cake with a message abhorrent to his religious beliefs *not* be directed at his religious beliefs? And how was Phillips' refusal based on the customers' sexual orientation when it was acknowledged by Craig and Mullins that he would sell them any baked goods they desired except a commissioned cake to celebrate same-sex marriage. It was the kind of cake, not the kind of customer, that Phillips refused.

In *Masterpiece*, the Colorado Civil Rights Commission's position was that the statute under which Phillips was charged was neutral and generally applicable, and in theory it is. However, it was found to be neither neutral nor generally applicable in practice, as illustrated in the case of William Jack. Mr. Jack entered the Azucar Bakery in Denver and asked Marjorie Silva to create a cake inscribed with "Homosexuality is a detestable sin. Leviticus 18:22". Silva refused to do so, and Jack filed a complaint with the Colorado Civil Rights Commission claiming religious discrimination. In Phillips' case, the Colorado Court of Appeals said that his refusal to endorse the message on the cake would send his undenied "opposition to same-sex marriage", and that this amounted to discrimination against the couple wanting him to send their message. In Silva's case, however, the court said that her objection to the "offensive nature of the requested message" did not discriminate against Jack. The Commission ruled that Silva's willingness to create cakes with other Christian themes for Jack exonerated her, while Phillips' willingness to create other cakes with secular themes for Craig and Mullins was deemed irrelevant. In other words, the court ruled in Silva's case that the cake's message would be hers and not Jack's, so she need not express it. In the Phillips case, the court held that the message would be the gay couple's and not Phillips', and thus he must create it and send it.

In both cases, it was the kind of message on the cake, not the kind of customer that was the determining factor in Phillips' and Silva's refusal. I support fully the right of Phillips and Silva to decide what commissions they will accept and which they won't, because if we don't have the right to discriminate, we only have the illusion of freedom, but we are not really free. Nevertheless, there is a clear double standard here; either it is the baker's message or it is the customer's, it can't be one thing in Phillips' case and another thing in Silva's. Professor Doug Laycock had a number of concerns with the different ways the Phillips and Silva cases were handled and the hostility toward religion of the court:

> The Civil Rights Commission and the Court of Appeals each found William Jack's Leviticus message offensive, and they protected the conscience of the baker who refused to spread that message. They did not find a same-sex couple's wedding cake offensive; they were offended by the idea that anyone might have a religious objection. The Court of Appeals analogized Phillips's religious belief to a belief so "irrational" that it could only be a pretext for discrimination. In free speech terms, this is viewpoint discrimination. In free exercise terms, it is neither neutral nor generally applicable (Laycock, 2018, p. 782).

In their writ of certiorari to the Colorado Court of Appeals, Gates, Shanefelt, and Epstein (2017, p.13) also noted the discriminatory way the state of Colorado operates in matters of religious liberty. They noted that there are a number of sites that serve only same-sex weddings ready and willing to serve people like Craig and Mullins, and state: "Although many of these sites explicitly provide services exclusively for same-sex weddings, the Colorado authorities have not applied CADA [Colorado Antidiscrimination Act] against these sites. Instead, using an explicit double-standard, it is only the tiny minority of religious bakers who face the full fury of the Colorado law".

In *Masterpiece*, the Supreme Court held that the state officials acted with "clear and impermissible hostility toward the sincere religious beliefs that motivated his action". The Court noted that "some of the commissioners at the Commission's formal, public hearings endorsed the view that religious beliefs cannot legitimately be carried into the public sphere or commercial domain, disparaged Phillips' faith as despicable and characterized it as merely rhetorical, and compared his invocation of his sincerely held religious beliefs to defenses of slavery". The Court also noted a Commission statement to the effect that Phillips can believe "what he wants to believe, but he cannot act on his religious beliefs". Evidently, the Commission accepted the Obama administration's position that the Free Exercise Clause should be limited to belief and worship. Justice Kennedy chided the ACLU's argument that opposition to same-sex marriage is discrimination based simply on sexual orientation, writing that: "Your identity thing is just too facile". Kennedy further noted the obvious thing that the ACLU and other religious persecutors simply refuse to see. Suppose, he says: "I have nothing against gay people but I just don't think they should have a marriage because that's contrary to my beliefs. It's not their identity; it's what they're doing". Justice Kennedy appears to be one of the few able to recognize the obvious difference between a person's status and an event he or she wants another person to facilitate.

Although the Court ruled in Phillips' favor, unfortunately it did so on only on overly narrow procedural grounds. It ruled only on the grounds that the Commission did not employ religious neutrality and were disrespectable and hostile to Phillips' rights to free exercise. The Court's narrow ruling did not address the broader issues of free exercise, free speech, and involuntary servitude. It appears as though the Court is most reluctant to dive into the real constitutional meat of religious claims against the tyranny of state civil rights commissions. Hopefully, it will do so in future cases with three new originalist Justices appointed by the Trump administration who are believers in what the Constitution actually says.

Shortly after Phillips prevailed in *Masterpiece*, Colorado sued him again, this time because he declined to design a cake celebrating the gender transition of attorney Autumn Scardina. Scardinia told Phillips that she wanted a: "a three-tiered white cake" with a "large figure of Satan, licking a nine-inch black dildo. I would like the dildo to be an actual working model that can be turned on before we unveil the cake" (in Harsanyi, 2019, np). Scardina claimed that Phillips refused to create the requested obscenity for her simply because she is transgender, not because of the message. It is doubtless true that few bakers would create such a monstrosity, regardless of their religious beliefs or the customer's sexual identity. One of the commissioners hearing the suit called Phillips a "hater", and others actually voiced their support for the comments that the Supreme Court in *Masterpiece* called disrespectful and hostile. After the Alliance Defending Freedom filed a federal lawsuit against the state on Phillips' behalf, the Commission dismissed the case. Instead of appealing the Commission's dismissal, Scardina filed a lawsuit with a district court seeking more than $100,000 in damages, fines, and attorney's fees. On April 29, 2020, the district court refused Phillips' motion to dismiss the case, thus burdening him with more years of ridiculous expensive and emotionally draining litigation.

The reason for the relentless persecution of this devout man was well put in Nicole Russell's (2020, np) op-ed piece in the *Washington Examiner* in which she echoed Justice Kennedy in *Masterpiece*:

> Phillips is not refusing to serve anyone because of their gender identity or sexuality, he is simply standing firm in the idea that he cannot be forced to create or endorse a message that violates his religious beliefs. But the media, ACLU, gay and transgender activists, and other liberals broadcast Phillips as some kind of zealous, religious bigot. In the process, they have proved themselves to be anti-religious bigots who want to force their own beliefs on others. It's why they want to force nuns to provide birth control. It's why they want to force churches to hire whom the government mandates they hire. And it's why they want to force people like Jack Phillips to say and do what they want.

Barronelle Stutzman and Arlene's Flowers

In 2013, Barronelle Stutzman, a then 68-year-old grandmother and owner of Arlene's Flowers, declined to provide flowers for a same-sex marriage for long-term customer and friend, Robert Ingersoll, because her personal involvement in the celebration of a same-sex marriage would amount to a denunciation of her faith. Even though she has employed and served many members of the LGBTQ community, Ingersoll, the state of Washington, and the ACLU has waged years of war against Arlene's Flowers and Stutzman personally. The antidiscrimination lawsuits filed against her threaten the assets of Arlene's Flowers as well as personal assets Stutzman owns beyond the flower shop. During her long legal battle, Stutzman has been boycotted, cursed at, and has even received death threats. Bob Ferguson, Washington's Attorney General, offered to settle the suit for $2,001 if Stutzman would agree to cater same-sex weddings or not to cater to weddings at all. Stutzman replied that Ferguson does not understand or appreciate her religious objections, and wrote:

> Since 2012, same-sex couples all over the state have been free to act on their beliefs about marriage, but because I follow the Bible's teaching that marriage is the union of one man and one woman, I am no longer free to act on my beliefs.... I certainly don't relish the idea of losing my business, my home, and everything else that your lawsuit threatens to take from my family, but my freedom to honor God in doing what I do best is more important. Washington's constitution guarantees us "freedom of conscience in all matters of religious sentiment." I cannot sell that precious freedom. You are asking me to walk in the way of a well-known betrayer, one who sold something of infinite worth for 30 pieces of silver. That is something I will not do. ... You chose to attack my faith and pursue this not simply as a matter of law, but to threaten my very means of working, eating, and having a home (in Backman, 2015, np).

In February 2015, a district court judge ruled that both the state and Ingersoll may collect damages and attorney fees from Stutzman personally and from her business. This ruling means that Stutzman may lose her business, her home, and her savings. The court also ruled that she must either agree to decorate same-sex weddings or stop doing weddings altogether. Stutzman has said that she would gladly sell pre-made floral arrangements for use at a same-sex ceremony but would not design custom arrangements to celebrate one. Custom arrangements involve substantial participation in the wedding, and this participation would prevent her from being true to her faith. Stutzman designs and creates floral art that celebrates weddings and delivers it to the wedding venue; she attends the ceremony and adorns the site and does what she can to make the ceremony a success. This is clearly participation in the wedding. The depth of her involvement in a wedding is expressed by Stutzman:

> I discuss with the bride and groom their wedding plans and get to know their relationship and personalities; I spend weeks creating dozens of custom floral designs that include not just flowers but also fabrics, pictures and other objects; I bring those designs to the ceremony; and I decorate the venue with my centerpieces and the wedding party with my bouquets, boutonnieres and corsages. I am personally involved in celebrating these weddings... Doing this well requires an artist like me to pour my soul into the event — to believe in the celebration. As happy as I am to serve gay customers, I just can't take part in wedding ceremonies — events I view as sacred — that violate my faith (2019, np).

Stutzman appealed her conviction to the Washington Supreme Court relying on the Supreme Court's "expressive speech" jurisprudence with a conjoined free religious expression claim. Stutzman's refusal to pour her soul into a same-sex marriage expresses her belief in God's word and acting on God's word is the fundamental right of free expression. However, the Washington Supreme Court clearly revealed how a large part of the judiciary views the status of the Free Exercise Clause: "the only fundamental right implicated in this case is the right to religious free exercise", but it refused to even consider Stutzman's religious-liberty claim. The use of the adverb "only" is an insult to the Constitution, its framers, to America, and to God. How can a fundamental right, which the court acknowledged it was, be so cavalierly dismissed? The court dismissed the free exercise claim as of "lesser importance" than a free speech claim, even though the framers placed the former in front of the latter. It also stated that a constitutional free exercise claim must be "balanced" with the state statute barring discrimination. In "balancing the claims, the Washington Supreme Court placed its thumb on the scale in favor of a mere public accommodation statute and it left the pan containing the Constitution's "first liberty" swinging impotently in the fog of legal whitewash.

As for Stutzman's free speech claim, the court ruled that her work is not an "inherently expressive" act. In a unanimous decision, the court wrote: "Certainly, she argues that she intends to communicate a message through her floral arrangements. But the major contest is over whether Stutzman's intended communications actually communicated something to the public at large—whether her conduct was 'inherently expressive.' And her actions in creating floral arrangements for wedding ceremonies do not satisfy this standard". This is a strange comment, since all wedding floral arrangements express a message that the public "at large" understands. Floral arrangements play an iconic role in wedding ceremonies, and their design is an artistic process that often requires the collaboration of the couple to be married.

Thus, the Washington Supreme Court holds that the state can force citizens to participate and endorse acts they believe to be immoral. Stutzman's attorney, Kristen Waggoner, commented on the ruling: "The message of these rulings is unmistakable: the government will bring about your personal and professional ruin if you don't help celebrate same-sex marriage. Laws that are supposed to prohibit discrimination might sound good, but the government has begun to use these laws to hurt people – to force them to conform and to silence and punish them if they don't violate their religious beliefs on marriage" (Alliance Defending Freedom, 2015, np).

In June of 2018, the Supreme Court granted Stutzman's petition for a writ of certiorari appealing the Washington court's decision. However, rather than deciding the issue of religious freedom once and for all, the Court merely vacated the judgment of the Washington Supreme Court and remanded the case back to it for further consideration in light of its ruling in *Masterpiece*. In June 2019, the Washington Supreme Court again ruled against Stutzman, stating that there was no evidence of religious hostility on the part of the state in her case.

There may have been no actual hostile words in the state's brief aimed at Stutzman, but the state's anti-Christian/pro LGBTQ stance is revealed by its response to Ben Borgman, the gay owner of the Bedlam Coffee Shop in Seattle. Borgman kicked out a group of Christians when he discovered that they were passing out antiabortion leaflets in the street expressing their religious beliefs. Borgman not only threw them out, he went on a vulgar and blasphemous rant, stating "Will you tolerate my presence if I go get my boyfriend and f*** him in the a** right here?" In Stark contrast to Stutzman's gentle refusal of Ingersoll, Borgman told the Christians to "f*** off and don't come back".

Despite Borgman's violation of Washington's public accommodation law the state did nothing other than send him form letters, to which Borgman did not reply. Neither did the state do anything about his non-response. What is galling is that the state justified its decision not to investigate Borgman on the grounds that he served the Christian group on other occasions. However, when Stutzman points out that she served Ingersoll and his partner for almost 10 years and would gladly do so again, the state dismissed the point as "irrelevant". Identical conduct is thus relevant in one case but irrelevant in another! This is invidious status-based discrimination. In their brief to the Washington Supreme Court, Stutzman's attorneys stated that only religious hostility can explain the disparity between how Stutzman and Borgman were treated:

> As these actions show, the State views Christians like Mrs. Stutzman as foes to be prosecuted, not citizens to be protected. In Washington, those people of faith always lose. If they are creative professionals declining to celebrate same-sex marriage, the State deploys its full arsenal to punish them, even personally. If they are customers enjoying coffee, the State refuses to protect them. But the rules change for others. The State allows gay and lesbian proprietors like the Bedlam Coffee owner to reject Christians while dismissing the religious convictions of Christians exemplifies not just disparate treatment but outright religious hostility (Ahend, Connelly, & Waggoner, 2019, pp. 9-10).

Stutzman has once again requested the U.S. Supreme Court to take her case. If the Court agrees to hear the case, it will require it to rule on Washington's stark and egregious First Amendment violations: denial of free exercise, compelled speech, and freedom of association. Her attorneys may also consider the Thirteenth Amendment prohibition of involuntary servitude. She certainly has a good case in light of *Masterpiece* in which the Justices observed about a wedding cake: "The use of artistic talents to create a well-recognized symbol that celebrates the beginning of a marriage clearly communicates a message…" If a commissioned cake "clearly communicates a message", how much more so is the service Stutzman is being forced to provide? It remains to be seen if the Court will hear the case or let the Washington decision stand and ruin the health and finances of this elderly Christian woman (aged 76 at the time of writing). If the Court does not, religious freedom will be gone, and the more "progressive" states will be free to ruin people of faith and marginalize them in their communities.

The Double Standard in the Application of Public Accommodation Laws

There is a clear double standard in the way both Colorado and Washington apply their public accommodation laws. The cases of Phillips and Silva in Colorado and Stutzman and Borgman in Washington share all legally salient features in that they all refused service to statutorily protected persons (religion or sexual orientation). The gaping difference in these cases is that while Christians are required to service same-sex weddings, their complaints when they are denied services because of their Christian views fall on deaf ears, thus relegating them to second class citizenship. Christians are compelled to speak the LGBTQ message, but supporters of the LGBTQ are not compelled to speak the Christian message. Neither side, of course, should ever be compelled to send a message with which they do not agree. We have seen that the Supreme Court has ruled against compelled speech on many occasions in the past, but what about now in the age of LGBTQ activism? Will the Court finally address *constitutional* issues, as is their mandate, and stop hiding behind narrow procedural issues?

As noted above, the Supreme Court did not rule on Phillips' compelled speech claim in *Masterpiece*, and thereby left open the issue of whether state public accommodation laws may compel speech in this brave new world of state intolerance toward Christianity. We should thus revisit *Hurley v. Irish American Gay, Lesbian, and Bisexual Group of Boston.* In *Hurley*, the Supreme Court rejected any suggestion that a public accommodations law could justify compelling speech. The Court ruled that the Massachusetts statute, on its face, did not target speech or discriminate:

> The state court's application, however, had the effect of declaring the sponsors' speech itself to be the public accommodation. Since every participating parade unit affects the message conveyed by the private organizers, the state courts' peculiar application of the Massachusetts law essentially forced the Council to alter the parade's expressive content and thereby violated the fundamental First Amendment rule that a speaker has the autonomy to choose the content of his own message and, conversely, to decide what not to say.

In other words, public accommodation statutes may not declare another person's speech to be a public accommodation or grant protected individuals the right to participate in that person's speech. The same logic should apply to other state public accommodation laws that are unobjectionable on their face. The language of the First Amendment clearly refers to the free exercise of religion as an important substantive value that the state may not prohibit. The language in no way suggests that it matters whether a state-imposed burden on religious exercise arises from a law aimed specifically at prohibiting religion or from a law that on its face or in its intent is neutral toward religion. A law's impact depends on what it hits as well as what it aims at. The "peculiar application" of public accommodation law in LGBTQ cases crush the free exercise and free speech right of religious objectors, and burdens then with involuntary servitude and the command to embrace the LGBTQ message. When a law does this, it ceases to be an antidiscrimination statute and becomes a regulator of religious conscience, speech, association, and labor. Religious objectors should be afforded same right that the parade organizers in *Hurley* had; that is, the: "autonomy to choose the content of [their] own message and, conversely, to decide what not to say".

The gay couples involved in these cases claim only dignitary harm, and Colorado and Washington have not attempted to show any harm beyond that. Dignitary harm is not enough to justify restriction on Phillips' and Stutzman's constitutional rights, and surely Phillips and Stutzman have significant dignitary harm claims. The Constitution does not impose a duty on citizens to avoid offending the dignity of others regardless of whether the indignity suffered is intentional or unintentional. Dignitary harm is covered in tort law, and "the interests protected by the torts that can be considered 'dignitary'—offensive battery, false imprisonment, defamation, intentional infliction of emotional distress, and invasion of privacy" (Abraham & White, 2018, p. 322). As the Supreme Court noted about dignitary harm in *Masterpiece*, the refusal to participate in a same-sex wedding can "be well understood in our constitutional order as an exercise of religion, an exercise that gay persons could recognize and accept without serious diminishment to their own dignity and worth".

The only person in these cases that could arguably be accused of causing dignitary harm is Ben Borgman for the foul offensive battery and defamation he visited on his Christian customers. His behavior was in stark contrast to both Phillips and Stutzman, who respectfully declined their services. The state does not seem to care, of course, about the dignitary harm caused by the vile abuses Phillips and Stutzman have suffered from LGBTQ activists over many years. We have created statutes to protect the rights of certain members of society that simultaneously disregard the rights of other members, and which have obliterated the distinction between hurt feelings and actionable tort claims.

The only tangible harm suffered by either gay couple was the gasoline and time involved in locating a willing baker or florist. In their writ of certiorari to the Colorado Court of Appeals, Gates, Shanefelt, and Epstein (2017, p.13) present a Google Maps figure showing that the nearest alternative bakery (Elegant Bakery) is only two-tenths of a mile from Masterpiece Bakery. I did a similar Google Maps search and found that the distance from Arlene's Flowers to an alternative flower shop (Simplified

Celebrations) is eight-tenths of a mile. Contrast the miniscule tangible harm done to the gay couples to the immense tangible harm suffered by Phillips and Stutzman. Both have endured huge financial losses, large amounts of time, and the deep emotional stress involved in defending multiple lawsuits. Douglas Laycock notes that "The harm of regulation on the religious side is permanent loss of identity or permanent loss of occupation, and that far outweighs the one-time dignitary harm or insult harm on the couple's side" (2018, p. 65). We should all be appalled that state governments in the "Home of the free" can and do present God-inspired citizens with a deplorable choice—obey your conscience or lose your livelihood. Can we not all agree that in a free society any business agreement assumes willing participants, and that forced participation is tantamount to state sponsored slavery? It behooves all Americans of any sexual orientation to heed Justice Robert Jackson's words in *West Virginia State Board of Education v. Barnette* (1943): "If there is any fixed star in our constitutional constellation, it is that no official, high or petty, can prescribe what shall be orthodox in politics, nationalism, religion, or other matters of opinion or force citizens to confess by word or act their faith therein."

It would also be instructive to heed the words of James Madison in the 1785 *Memorial and Remonstrance.* He was vehemently opposed to any interference whatsoever by the state on religious matters, as these words attest:

> We maintain therefore that in matters of Religion, no man's right is abridged by the institution of Civil Society and that Religion is wholly exempt from its cognizance. Because if Religion be exempt from the authority of the Society at large, still less can it be subject to that of the Legislative Body. The latter are but the creatures and vicegerents of the former. Their jurisdiction is both derivative and limited… It degrades from the equal rank of Citizens all those whose opinions in Religion do not bend to those of the Legislative authority (1785, np).

Phillips and Stutzman did not bend to legislative authority in the matter of same-sex marriage and were thus became degraded "from the equal rank of Citizens". The courts and legislative bodies have gravitated to the point where people with "hurt feelings" have been elevated almost to the rank of a constitutionally protected category. Worse yet, the only "hurt feelings" that seem to matter are those of LGBTQ people who can find numerous businesses willing and eager to provide their marriage needs but chose to go to those which will not, and then destroy them with their "take no prisoners" tactics. Religious dissenters have no legal recourse to soothe their hurt feelings. Leftists who cheer when anti-discrimination laws are hijacked and weaponized against our First Amendment freedoms should pause to consider what the weakening of these constitutional rights really means. While it is Christians who are having their rights eroded today, it will not end there. Ours is not an America that our freedom loving founders would recognize.

Chapter 9

PHOTOGRAPHS, CAKES, AND PIZZAS

ELAINE HUGUENIN AND ELANE PHOTOGRAPHY

Although the Masterpiece Cakeshop and Arlene's Flowers are the best known of the religious liberty cases, there are a blizzard of other such cases. An early case of state rejection of religious freedom is a 2006 New Mexico case in which Elaine Huguenin, co-owner of Elane Photography, refused on religious grounds to photograph the same-sex "commitment ceremony" (not a wedding per se since New Mexico did not recognize same-sex weddings at the time) of Vanessa Willock and Misti Collinsworth. The lesbian couple promptly hired another photographer, but Willock filed a complaint with the New Mexico Human Rights Commission (NMHRC) against Elane Photography. The NMHRC found against Elane Photography and awarded Willock attorney fees. Ms. Huguenin appealed the NMHRC decision to the New Mexico Court of Appeals, arguing that that "Photographers, writers, singers, actors, painters and others who create First Amendment-protected speech must have the right to decide which commissions to take and which to reject" (Liptak, 2013, np). The issue was similar to the compelled speech issues in *Spence, Johnson,* and *Maynard*; to wit: whether the state can require a photographer to create expressive images and picture books conveying messages that conflict with her religious beliefs and violate the

First Amendment's ban on the rights of free speech. Ignoring Supreme Court free speech precedence, the New Mexico Court of Appeals ruled that the state can, and affirmed the NMHRC and a district court's rulings.

Elane Photography then appealed to the New Mexico Supreme Court, which upheld the decision of the Court of Appeals. Justice Richard Bosson concurred with the majority opinion, but he did not seem to be quite comfortable with it. In his written opinion Bosson stated: "The Huguenins are not trying to prohibit anyone from marrying. They only want to be left alone to conduct their photography business in a manner consistent with their moral convictions.... they are compelled by law to compromise the very religious beliefs that inspire their lives. Though the rule of law requires it the result is sobering". Indeed, it is. He also wrote that while religious convictions deserved respect, believers should "compromise, if only a little, to accommodate the contrasting values of others". How does one compromise with what the Huguenins take as a command of God, and why should it be the Huguenins who had to compromise, "if only a little", and not the lesbian couple? The compromise for Willock and Collinsworth had to make was to find another photographer, which they easily did. The compromise for the Huguenins would have been to labor involuntarily for many hours to produce a message they find abhorrent to their consciences. The actual "compromise" forced on the Huguenins by the state was an order to pay court costs and $6,637.94 in attorneys' fees to Willock and Collinsworth. Such costs constitute a heavy burden on a small photography business.

After viewing the concept of compromise through rainbow tinted glasses, in the final paragraph of the Court's decision, Bosson did the same with the concepts of tolerance and respect:

> In the smaller, more focused world of the marketplace, of commerce, of public accommodation, the Huguenins have to channel their conduct, not their beliefs, so as to leave space for other Americans who believe something different. That compromise is part of the glue that holds us together as a nation, the tolerance that lubricates the varied moving parts of us as a people. That sense of respect we owe others, whether or not we believe as they do, illuminates this country, setting it apart from the discord

> that afflicts much of the rest of the world. In short, I would say to the Huguenins, with the utmost respect: it is the price of citizenship.

Where is the tolerance and respect for the Huguenins? Bosson thinks that the Huguenins can "channel their conduct" while disregarding their beliefs but fails to understand that their beliefs channel their conduct. Substitute Willock and Collinsworth for the Huguenins in Bosson's statement and ask why it was the Huguenins and not them that have to "leave space for other Americans who believe something different." After all, it was Willock and Collinsworth that imposed the burden on the Huguenins who were minding their own business until the lesbian couple approached them. Bosson also says that this burden "is the price of citizenship." So, the price of being American is to labor against one's deeply held faith on behalf of another and forfeit religious liberty. Apparently, this is true if you are a Christian business owner and the other party is gay, lesbian, or anything in between.

Recall that the federal RFRA states that: "Government shall not substantially burden a person's exercise of religion even if the burden results from a rule of general applicability." So, why was the court able to rule against Elane Photography? It was able to do so because the Supreme Court ruled the federal RFRA does not apply to the states in *City of Boerne v. Flores* (1997). The *Boerne* decision enabled the Commission to rule that because the state provides businesses a license to sell goods and services to the general public, they may not reject customers based on race, religion, or sexual orientation. This is perfectly agreeable, but Elane Photography did not reject Willock and Collinsworth because of their *status* as lesbians, but because of an *event* the couple wanted to celebrate and capture with pictures taken on site and later arranged by Elaine Huguenin into a celebratory album.

If the federal RFRA does not apply to the states, how about New Mexico's own RFRA? This act reads in part: "Nothing in the New Mexico Religious Freedom Restoration Act authorizes a government agency to burden a person's free exercise of religion". Despite these bold words, it did not protect Elane Photography because the New Mexico Supreme Court held that the New Mexico RFRA applied only to government agencies that interfere with religious exercise and not to disputes between private litigants. The New Mexico RFRA notes that an exception to the protection of religious liberty is lawful if "the application of the restriction to the person is essential to further a compelling governmental interest and is the least restrictive means of furthering that compelling governmental interest". What is so "compelling" that it justifies stripping a constitutional right from one person to satisfy a statutory right of another? And what was the "least restrictive means" the state could have employed to satisfy that statutory right without infringing on the constitutional rights of another? Surely, the simple answer would have been to provide the lesbian couple with a list of photographers who would be delighted with their business.

In its petition for certiorari to the United States Supreme Court, Elaine Huguenin's legal counsel argued a compelled speech claim, leaving aside a free exerciser claim as apparently being fruitless given current Supreme Court jurisprudence. They noted that: "Ms. Huguenin's artistic expression pervades her work. During the picture-taking process, Ms. Huguenin uses her artistic eye to frame and capture images that convey the story she wants to tell. She also choreographs many of the scenes depicted in her photographs" (Lorence, et al., 2013, p. 5). They then go into great detail as to how Huguenin spends time poring over and selecting the pictures that suit her artistic tastes and expressive goals. She then creates a photo album by arranging the images to tell her desired message about the event. This labor is certainly participating in the event. Huguenin's legal counsel then proceeded to clearly show that it was her speech that was being compelled: "Ms. Huguenin, and not her customer, is the speaker communicating through her photographs and books. Her actions in choreographing, capturing, selecting, editing, producing, and arranging the final photographs and storybooks all affect, and ultimately determine, the messages conveyed through her images and books" (p.5). They go on to note that Huguenin automatically obtains federal copyright protection over all her work, and that this confirms conclusively that she is the communicating speaker.

Elaine Huguenin was not just prohibited from expressing a religious belief with which the state of New Mexico disagreed; she was also compelled to affirm the state's position as her own. We saw in *Wooley v. Maynard* that the Court held that George Maynard did not have to affirm New Hampshire's message by displaying it on his license plate. New Mexico went a step further than New Hampshire by compelling Elain Huguenin not merely to display an expressive message created by others, but to create the very message offensive to her religious conscience. Surely the compelled *creation* of speech infringes on the First Amendment to a far greater degree than does the compelled display of speech created by others.

Under the logic of the NMHRC, if asked to do so, writers or artists who take public commissions could be ordered to write an article or paint a picture celebrating same-sex themes that conflict with their religious beliefs. Yet the Supreme Court unanimously held in *Hurley* that the First Amendment right against compelled speech is "enjoyed by business corporations generally." What is Elane Photography if not a business? Nevertheless, in 2014, the United States Supreme Court denied Elane Photography's petition for certiorari, thus letting the New Mexico Supreme Court's ruling stand, and by doing so put its seal of approval, not only on the abridgement of religious freedom and involuntary servitude, but also on the abridgement of freedom of speech which it stoutly defends in non-religious cases.

Such a non-religious compelled speech case came before the Supreme Court just one year after denying certiorari to Elane Photography and illustrates how it is applied one way in non-religious cases, and quite another in religious cases. The question before the court in *Agency for International Development v. Alliance for Open Society International, Inc.* (AOSI) (2013), was whether non-governmental organizations should be required to have an explicit anti-prostitution policy in order to receive federal funding. In the majority opinion, Chief Justice Roberts wrote that they are not, because: "It requires them [AOSI] to pledge allegiance to the Government's policy of eradicating prostitution." Were not the proprietors of Elane Photography required to pledge allegiance to the state sponsored LGBTQ agenda, thus sacrificing their First and Thirteenth Amendment rights on the altar of statutory anti-discrimination laws? Apparently, Americans can hold, or refuse to hold, any position on any imaginable issue without government interference—with the exception of same-sex marriage and other LGBTQ issues.

Betty and Richard Odgaard and Görtz Haus Gallery

Illustrative of the way some couples purposely seeking services from religious people who they know will refuse them is the case of Betty and Richard Odgaard. In 2013, Lee Stafford and Jared Elders approached the Odgaards, a devout Mennonite couple, to host their wedding. The Odgaards were owners of the Görtz Haus Gallery; an art gallery, lunch bistro, flower, and gift shop, but their primary source of income was to plan, facilitate, and host wedding ceremonies. Although the Odgaards have willingly hired and served gays and lesbians throughout the Gallery's history, their religious beliefs do not allow them to facilitate same-sex weddings. To do so would send a message to other Mennonites that their belief that marriage is a religious covenant ordained by God between a man and a woman is untrue.

When the Odgaards related this to Stafford and Elders, they filed suit with the Iowa Civil Rights Commission (ICRC). Betty Odgaard replied to the complaint by noting that: "We hire and serve gays and lesbians… and we respect that good people disagree with our religious conviction against hosting a ceremony that violates our faith. We simply ask that the government not force us to abandon our faith or punish us for it" (in Anderson & Ford, 2014, p. 10). When word got out about their refusal, the Odgaards received e-mails containing death threats and hateful messages saying such things as they were "finished" and "doomed." and referring to them as "mother f***** racist sons of bitches from hell," and saying "F**k you, f**k your God, f**k your religion." These are the kind of hateful bigots the state puts before decent Christians who just want to live their lives in accordance with their faith and to be left alone.

The ICRC tried to force the Odgaards into performing the wedding despite Stafford and Elders admitting, contrary to their previously sworn statements, that they had been married months before they asked the Odgaards to host another. This is a clear indication of targeting to destroy, and should have resulted in a case against Stafford and Elders for defrauding the ICRC for giving false information. How can a couple in possession of something claim any sort of harm by being denied that which they already possess? Given their fraudulent claim, Stafford and Elders lacked standing to bring the case because standing requires that a plaintiff show 'injury-in-fact'. Yet the ICRC insisted that the Odgaards must plan, facilitate, and host what they consider an insult to a religiously significant expressive event, thus forcing them to promote a public message with which they disagree. The ICRC also insisted that the Odgaard's exhaust all administrative avenues before seeking relief in the courts. The ICRC's administrative procedure subjected the Odgaards to 38 intimidating, intrusive, insulting, and arguably irrelevant questions. According to their legal counsel in a writ of certiorari to the Iowa Supreme Court to dismiss the case:

> Among other things, these questions asked the Odgaards to reveal to the Commission their religious beliefs, their sexual orientation, and the sexual orientation of their employees and customers. The Commission warned that the Odgaards were "REQUIRED" [ICRC's emphasis] to submit documentation in support of this intimate, private information, and placed a legal duty on them to preserve all documents and evidence that could conceivably relate to the complaint filed against them (Harty, et al., pp. 26-27).

Despite the fraud perpetrated by the gay couple, the Iowa Supreme Court refused to dismiss the case. Faced with state bullying, and obnoxious attacks by LGBTQ activists, the Odgaards settled the suit by paying $5,000 to Stafford and Elders and agreed to stop hosting all weddings. Without the income generated by hosting wedding, the Odgaards were forced to close their life's work rather than violate their faith. Stafford and Elders pocketed their fraudulently gained lucre, and, with state collusion, destroyed the livelihood of an elderly Christian couple. A *Sioux Center News* Article commented: "While heartbroken to see their life's work end this way, the Odgaards' faith is stronger than ever and they're certain they did the right thing in staying true to their beliefs. A local church later purchased the gallery as a house of worship, which would mean it can continue to express the Odgaards' Christian faith — and this time, even the state of Iowa has to respect it" (2018, np)

But hold on a second, perhaps the state of Iowa does not agree that it must respect a house of worship. The tyrannical ICRC has declared that prohibitions against discrimination on the basis of sexual orientation and gender identity, and against practices limiting access to bathroom and locker to biological males and females, "sometimes" apply to churches. In a brochure titled *Sexual Orientation and Gender Identity*, the ICRC pronounced that:

> Iowa law provides that these protections do not apply to religious institutions with respect to any religion-based qualifications when such qualifications are related to a bona fide religious purpose. Where qualifications are not related to a bona fide religious purpose, churches are still subject to the law's provisions. (e.g., a child care facility operated at a church or a church service open to the public)" (Iowa Civil Rights Commission, nd, np).

Of course, a child care facility and church services open to the public encompass most of any church's mission. A church's activities must be consistent with its understanding of God's truth, and it should not be made to present a message that contradicts it. The ICRC wants to make it illegal to preach views that would "directly or indirectly" make "persons of any particular gender identity" feel "unwelcome" in conjunction "with church services, events, and other religious activities." Amazingly, it also stated that a "church service open to the public" does not constitute a "bona fide religious purpose" because if it was so considered it would limit application of the law. In other words, Iowa's anti-discrimination law is a de facto ban on free exercise and free speech because it seeks to prevent pastors from preaching their religion's view of sexual morality.

Legal Counsel for Alliance Defending Freedom, Christiana Holcomb, noted that: "Churches have always been protected from government intrusion, and they still are. They have a firmly established freedom to teach their beliefs and set internal policies that reflect their biblical teachings about marriage and human sexuality. One can hardly imagine a more obvious unconstitutional invasion of the state into the internal affairs of the church" (2016, np). Thankfully, federal district judge Stephanie Rose ruled that churches are not subject to state regulation, and that the ICRC has no business mandating which church activities are religious and which ones are not. She wrote that: "government may neither compel affirmation of a repugnant belief nor penalize or discriminate against individuals or groups because they hold religious views abhorrent to the authorities." Sometimes the Constitution wins, and sometimes we find a judge who knows just who is being discriminated against.

Aaron and Melissa Klein and Sweet Cakes by Melissa

In 2013, Aaron and Melissa Klein, former owners of Sweet Cakes by Melissa, a Gresham, Oregon, bakery, refused to bake a wedding cake for the lesbian wedding of Rachel Cryer and Laurel Bowman, stating that it would violate their religious consciences. The Kleins, parents of five young children, believed their decision was protected by their right to practice their religion as they see fit. The Oregon Bureau of Labor and Industries (BOLI) saw it differently and prosecuted them for violating Oregon's anti-discrimination laws. The Kleins received many hate-filled e-mails and phone calls that they have shared with TV interviewers, one reading: "You stupid bible thumping, hypocritical bitch. I hope your kids get really, really, sick and you go out of business." Wedding vendors became so harassed by gay rights groups that they were forced to stop doing business with Sweet Cakes by Melissa, which had to close its doors. Aaron took a job as a garbage collector making half his previous income.

In July, 2015, BOLI commissioner Brad Avakian, ordered the Kleins to pay damages to the lesbian couple (whom they had served previously with generic baked goods) of $135,000 for "emotional, mental and physical suffering." Avakian had previously made many public statements endorsing gay pride and same-sex marriage, so bias was evident even before the case presented itself. The Kleins initially refused to pay, but the state came after them with a vengeance, garnishing what assets they could, thus completely ignoring the "emotional, mental and physical suffering" of the Kleins and their five young children. The Kleins appealed to the Oregon Court of Appeals, which upheld the BOLI decision. Tyler Smith, the Klein's lawyer, complained about the government's abuse of power: "And that being completely ignored by the state agency, when they're prosecuting based on a statutory classification that this is now a protected status under a statute, when the Kleins have clearly protected constitutional rights that should supersede that and be more protected than a statutory right" (in Hallowell, 2015, np). As previously noted, constitutional law is firmly in Smith's corner: The United States Constitution sits above and governs all statutory law.

After losing in the Court of Appeals, the Kleins appealed to the Oregon Supreme Court, which declined to hear their case. They then appealed to the United States Supreme Court, which vacated the Oregon Court's decision, and remanded this case for further consideration in light of the *Masterpiece* decision. In a brief to the Oregon Court of Appeals on behalf of the Kleins, their attorneys wrote:

> Abandoning the constitutional requirements of neutrality, tolerance, and respect, BOLI's Commissioner, Brad Avakian, spoke dismissively of the Kleins' religious objections before their case even came before him. In the administrative proceedings, BOLI's administrative prosecutor disparaged those objections as a mere "excuse" for discrimination. At the end of those proceedings, the Commissioner not only held the Kleins liable for violating [the Oregon statute], but awarded damages based on Klein's quotation of his sacred text, the Bible. To justify a disproportionately high damages award of $135,000, the Commissioner compared the Kleins' case to completely dissimilar cases of physical violence, prolonged sexual harassment, and religious coercion. Finally, the Commissioner enjoined the Kleins from speaking about their religious beliefs, despite the lack of any basis for such a gag order (Grey, et al., 2019, p. 6).

The case has still to be decided at the time or writing, but because the Oregon Court of Appeals' original ruling already covered the ground the Supreme Court asked it to review, do not expect the Oregon Supreme Court to reverse the appeals court's decision since all seven judges on the court were appointed by a Democratic governor, and we know how liberal Democrats respect the Constitution.

MEMORIES PIZZA

The Case of Memories Pizza shows the extent to which QGBTQ activists will go to destroy a business even if its owner simply expresses opposition to same-sex marriage. Sixty-one-year-old Kevin O'Connor, a co-owner with his daughter own Memories Pizza in Walkerton, Indiana, was interviewed in 2015 by TV reporter Alyssa Marino, who came to their shop in search of a story following the passage of Indiana's new Religious Freedom Restoration Act. Marino asked the O'Conners a hypothetical question about what *would* they do if a same-sex couple asked them to cater a wedding. The O'Conners said that he would not cater such a wedding on religious grounds and added that they would not be denied any other service. Instead of conveying what was actually said, the television station reported that Memories Pizza was the "first business to publicly deny same-sex service." This piece of irresponsible journalism touched off a national media firestorm, and forced the O'Conner family into hiding and to temporarily shut down the store. They received vulgar and threatening telephone calls and had their Facebook pages smeared with gay pornography (Moyer, 2015). All this disgusting behavior for merely *saying* that they would not cater to a same-sex marriage if asked.

Although Connor Friedersdorf supports same-sex marriage, he doesn't like the hateful tactics employed by LGBTQ activists. Writing in the left-leaning *Atlantic* magazine he stated … "that the position I'll gladly serve any gay customers but I feel my faith compels me to refrain from catering a gay wedding is less hateful or intolerant than let's go burn that family's business to the ground". He goes on to write:

> And I believe that the subset of the gay-rights movement intent on destroying their [the O'Connor's] business and livelihood has done more harm than good here... The pizzeria discriminated against nobody…they merely said that it would choose not to serve a gay weeding if asked. Which it never, ever would be, because who asks a small-town pizzeria to cater a heterosexual wedding, let alone a gay one? They were punished for expressing a disfavored opinion to a reporter (2015, np).

Memories Pizza closed permanently in 2018 after the O'Connors were demonized, stigmatized, and marginalized for voicing their Christian views by LGBTQ activists who have been encouraged by the courts and a highly partisan media to dictate the direction of the culture and values of our country. They have employed a very deliberate strategy to turn principled, faith-based opposition to same-sex marriage into bigotry, hatred, intolerance and ignorance. We seem to be on the cusp of Gramsci's goal of turning us into an anti-Christian nation, and Marcuse's toleration only for views from the left, although I doubt if either would have dreamt that LBGTQ individuals would be leading the charge. Christians must fight back, even if they are swimming against the tide if they want to preserve the America that they know for posterity.

There are principled LBGTQ activists who are ashamed of their compatriots' vile and vicious tactics, and who wish to preserve our Christian heritage. Among them is Peter Tatchell, who states that: "Much as I wish to defend the gay community, I also want to defend freedom of conscience, expression and religion" (2016, np). Tatchell, and many other Christian gays and lesbians, do not want to see the Constitution and the Bible trashed in by those who want to force others to deny their faith or lose their business. There must be a deeper issue involved when a same-sex couple requests services from someone who has religious objections to providing them. Although same-sex couples can acquire wedding related services freely elsewhere, many purposely target those who they know will not provide them. If I am gay and want to marry my partner, there are numerous businesses eager to provide services to facilitate the wedding, so why would I to try to force the unwilling to do so? I would want someone that supports me and will gladly do their best job, and I would not leave any aspect of my wedding to someone that does not agree with my lifestyle. Plainly, the issue has nothing to do with obtaining services; it is about malevolently destroying anyone who has the audacity not to approve of same-sex marriage or the LGBTQ agenda in general.

The difference between service versus participation continually appears in these wedding vendor cases. It is one that many people purposely ignore. A recent Supreme Court case that clarifies the clear distinction between serving and participating is *R.G. & G.R. Harris Funeral Homes Inc. v. Equal Employment Opportunity Commission* (2020). Thomas Rost, majority owner of R.G. & G.R. Harris Funeral Homes and a devout Christian, fired funeral director Aimee Stephens after she announced she was transitioning from male to female and intended to dress as a woman at work. In *Harris*, the Court distinguished between active facilitation of a practice that conflicts with religious belief and simple tolerance of such a practice, and that only the former constitutes a substantial burden on religious conscience. In the Court's majority opinion, Justice Gorsuch wrote that while the Court is "deeply concerned with preserving the promise of the free exercise of religion enshrined in our Constitution; that guarantee lies at the heart of our pluralistic society." However, the Court ruled that employing a transgender person does not burden religious practice because doing so is merely tolerating and not actively participating in acts considered sinful. The Court thus characterized passive compliance with antidiscrimination laws as an act of tolerance, and not an impairment on Rost's ability to comply with the dictates of his faith.

The Court's ruling is a commonsense ruling. Rost's only burden was to tolerate Stephens' decision to transition and dress accordingly. The wedding vendors discussed here have tolerated, served, and even employed homosexuals, so why not Rost? Rost was not required in any way to facilitate or participate in Stephens' transition, so a more Christian attitude would have been to respect her gender identity in a loving manner in the same way that a person's racial, national, or sexual identity should be respected. It remains to be seen, however, if the Court will continue to be "deeply concerned with preserving the promise of the free exercise of religion enshrined in our Constitution" in future cases in which the refusal to actively participate in a same-sex marriage is the issue. If the Court's precedence holds that active facilitation constitutes a substantial burden on religious conscience, then we may expect some relief for religious wedding vendors when a same-sex couple comes knocking.

THE COERCION TEST: CHRISTIANS NEED NOT APPLY

In the cases we have discussed that do not involve LGBTQ issues, we have seen that the Supreme Court has ruled that the state must not force individuals or groups to endorse a message or participate in an event repugnant to them. Recall that in *Lee v. Weisman* (the case banning prayers at high school graduations), Justice Kennedy formulated the coercion test for deciding if someone is being forced against their conscience to participate in an event they do not wish to participate in. Writing about the "burden" Deborah Weisman suffered by being exposed to a non-sectarian prayer, Kennedy proclaimed that she had been forced against her conscience:

> a reasonable perception that she is being forced by the State to pray in a manner her conscience will not allow... It is of little comfort to a dissenter, then, to be told that for her the act of standing or remaining in silence signifies mere respect, rather than participation. What matters is that, given our social conventions, a reasonable dissenter in this milieu could believe that the group exercise signified her own participation or approval of it.

We run into another glaring double standard here because, according to civil rights commissions and courts across the nation, providing flowers, baking a cake, or taking pictures for a same-sex wedding does not signify the florist's, baker's, or photographer's participation or approval of that wedding. Yet, the Supreme Court ruled that Deborah's "standing or remaining silent" would signify her participation in, or approval of, the prayer recited at her graduation, and this would mean that the state was forcing her to pray "in a manner her conscience will not allow". If Deborah was forced to participate, and if that participation signaled her approval, by the Court's logic, then, the coercion to participate in a same-sex wedding experienced by the Christian business owners *required* to participate is magnified exponentially. Can it be any clearer that there is one set of legal standards for Christians who run afoul of the LGBTQ agenda and another set for everyone else?

There are significant differences between Deborah's case and the cases of the various wedding vendors. No one approached Deborah and told her that she must attend graduation or face prosecution, or that she could not walk away with impunity when the prayer was about to be recited. In saying that the state was "forcing" Deborah to listen to the prayer, Justice Kennedy surely was employing hyperbole, but the Christian business owners we have discussed were approached, could not walk away, and were quite literally "forced by the State" (or more accurately, the state attempted to force them) to act in a manner their consciences will not allow. Although the coercion test remains part of Supreme Court jurisprudence, apparently Christians need not apply.

Remaining silent is negative non-participation. Deborah did not need to do anything but remain seated to signal her disapproval, and the only cross she had to bear was a few moments of supposed discomfort. She did remain seated, but no civil rights commission hounded her with demands that she must stand and respect the tradition of giving thanks to God at graduation. Not one of her constitutional rights were in danger of being violated as she listened to others exercising their free speech and free exercise rights that her case took from them. On the other hand, if the wedding vendor complied with state demands under penalty of law to take pictures, bake a cake, or arrange flowers celebrating a same-sex wedding, that is unequivocally being forced. It would also be positive participation if the vendors acquiesced to state demands because the person actually has to do something tangible, and attempting to force people to perform those services is a state violation of their fundamental rights. These vendors have been subjected to crushing levels of coercion to put their stamp of approval on an event their Christian consciences will not allow. Deborah's momentary irritation was recognized by the highest court in the land as participation, while the obvious labor demanded of Christian wedding vendors somehow is not. The double standard is again obvious.

In most other circumstances people can refuse to provide their services if doing so would offend their sensibilities without facing state prosecution. In 2016, Bruce Springsteen cancelled a concert in North Carolina because he believed that doing so would signal agreement with the state's bathroom law denying transgendered individuals to use the bathrooms of their choice. Springsteen, or any other provider of services, such as the fashion designers who rushed to be the first to deny their services to Ivanka Trump, should have the absolute right not to do business with entities or individuals promoting issues with which they disagree. But if Springsteen can deny services on principled grounds, why can't Christian business owners? The easy answer is because Christian businesses that refuse run afoul of administrative law and Springsteen did not. Potential attendees denied the pleasure of his concert cannot claim that he violated their rights to his services because they have no such rights. If this musical darling of the left had refused to perform a concert with an overtly homosexual theme to celebrate the *Obergefell* decision, however, the courts may have been persuaded that they did have such rights.

Chapter 10

FEDERAL GOVERNMENT ANIMUS TOWARD RELIGION

THE OBAMA ADMINISTRATION'S ATTACKS ON RELIGIOUS FREEDOM

The eight-year long administration of President Barack Obama waged an unprecedented effort to dethrone religious freedom as the centerpiece of American civil life. Obama often treated the Constitution as if its principles were matters of convenience to be ignored when they got in the way. He infamously framed religious liberty as merely "the freedom to worship as we choose", which infuriated Jonathan Imbody of the *Washington Times*:

> If the president had not been restricting and attacking religious freedom so egregiously, he might merit a pass for using 'freedom to worship' as poor shorthand for religious liberty... The constitutionally guaranteed free exercise of religion in America extends well beyond the freedom to worship. It includes the freedom to live out our conscientiously held beliefs" (2013, np). This hostility is further noted by Walker and Wester, who wrote that while Obama paid obligatory lip service to religious liberty expected from a president, his administration was:

> "immensely hostile to religious liberty … the protections traditionally afforded by religious freedom were severely weakened under the president's stewardship. … history will support the conclusion that his administration worked to delegitimize the beliefs of millions of Americans of diverse faiths and remove them from within the bounds of acceptable discourse (2017, np).

This is not too surprising since Obama virtually marinated in communism, and as president he appointed a number of controversial "czars" with extreme left-wing views. The *Judicial Watch* (2011) lists a litany of leftist policies advanced by these men and women. For instance, diversity czar Mark Lloyd wanted to replace all white people in positions of power in the media with minorities, and praised the "incredible revolution" of Venezuelan socialist president Hugo Chavez. Science czar John Holdren wanted to stem population growth by forced abortions and sterilizations, and Safe and Drug-Free Schools czar Kevin Jennings promoted seminars in schools to expose children to "unorthodox" sexual practices. Green Jobs czar Van Jones, a self-proclaimed anarchist, communist, and anti-white racist, strongly supported Mumia Abu-Jamal, convicted of murdering a white police officer. Communications director, Anita Dunn, gushed over the sadistic dictator, Mao Zedong, her "favorite philosopher," and Energy and Environmental czar Carol Browner was a prominent member of the Socialist International. We can hardly expect such people to value, or even tolerate, religious liberty.

These folks did their best to help Obama keep his promise to "fundamentally transform" America, but thanks to our separation of powers, we have a country we can still recognize, if only dimly. We still have many government officials who treasure our liberties and who fight those who would destroy them. In the House of Representative's 2012 hearing on the Obama administration's many abuses of power, Lori Windham, Senior Counsel for The Becket Fund for Religious Liberty, excoriated it for its many attacks on religious liberty:

> I am very disturbed that the Administration thinks that when an institution steps out and starts to serve the public and opens its arms to

> others, as many religions teach, that somehow they are forfeiting their constitutional rights. And so it is a very disturbing trend that people might believe when you start to serve the public and you start to do good in your country you are then giving up some of your constitutional rights and your freedoms… The Administration has paid lip service to the importance of religious freedom, while at the same time launching an unprecedented government encroachment on the fundamental right of religious freedom. ... If these abuses are permitted to continue, they will create grave injustice and set a terrible precedent for even more serious restrictions on liberty in the future. Every American should be concerned, regardless of political or religious beliefs (2012, np).

THE HEALTH AND HUMAN SERVICES MANDATE IN OBAMACARE

Characterizing Obama as "America's most biblically-hostile U.S. president," David Barton (2016) lists 93 well documented hostile acts against people and institutions of Judeo/Christian faith by the Obama administration ranging from relatively mild insults about white Americans "clinging to their religion and their guns", to major policy decisions that rock the foundations of our free society. Among the most offensive of these acts was the Health and Human Services (HHS) mandates under the Affordable Care Act (ACA). The ACA mandated that all employers, including religious employers, with 50 or more employees must extend health coverage to include sterilization, contraception, abortion, and abortifacients to all employees. Obama boasted before a cheering pro-choice crowd in St. Louis that his mandate forces religious employers to supply them, and added the exclamation: "Darn tootin!" Obama's former HHS Secretary, Kathleen Sebelius, made similar remarks at a pro-choice fundraiser, where she admitted that "we are in a war" with religious dissenters (in Olson, 2012, np). A United States government "at war" with religious liberty! At least, Sebelius was honest about it.

Cardinal Francis George lists four equally unpalatable choices service providers would have to make had the Obama administration been able to fully implement its HHS regulations. They would have to: (1) Break their connection to the church and her moral and teachings. (2) Pay ruinous fines for refusing to provide insurance covering drugs and practices abhorrent to the Church. (3) Sell the institution. (4) Close down. Cardinal George further remarked that: "The Church would love to have the separation between church and state we thought we enjoyed just a few months ago, when we were free to run Catholic institutions in conformity with the demands of the Catholic faith, when the government couldn't tell us which of our ministries are Catholic and which not, when the law protected rather than crushed conscience" (2012, np).

The HHS mandate provided an exemption for religious employers who object to practices contrary to their moral teachings, but it was drawn so narrowly that it did not cover the vast majority of faith-based service organizations. Religious employers were exempt only if their sole purpose is to teach and instill their religious doctrine, hire and serve only people of their own faith, and if they qualified as a religious order or church as defined by the tax code. It has been pointed out that, "Most religious institutions providing health, educational or charitable services to others have no protection. Rev. Larry Snyder notes that even Jesus and His disciples would not qualify for the exemption in that case, because they were committed to serve those of other faiths" (in Dolan, 2012, np). This so-called "accommodation" was impotent since it still forced religious institutions to provide employees with insurance covering services that violate their religious convictions. What happened to the "least restrictive means" mandate of the RFRA? Surely a woman who believes she might have gotten pregnant as a result of last night's fling could sacrifice a latte or two to buy an abortifacient rather than appeal to the state to make the Catholic Church violate its faith. This would be the moral thing to do, but many progressives are not only hostile to the religious foundations of morality, are hostile to the very notion of morality itself, boasting that morality is "the other of liberalism" (Brown, 1992, p. 72).

Apparently, Obama believes that providing contraceptives constitutes a compelling state interest such that the state would be "manifestly endangered" were they not provided by their employers. As noted above, in theory the HHS regulations provide some limited protections, but were written in unclear language and open to "interpretation". A health care worker who suffered a violation of conscience could not file a suit in a court of law because the HHS claimed the exclusive right to hear such complaints, and complaints forwarded to the HHS fell on hostile ears (Goodrich, 2011). The United States Conference of Catholic Bishops complained of this, writing that the HHS: "despite repeated questions and objections from Congress—has allowed valid complaints to languish, sometimes for years, without resolution" (2016, np).

Not too long ago, the idea that the government could demand that the Church violate its principles would have been considered outrageous. Throughout the history of the United States, churches have been left alone to conduct their affairs as they see fit. When the United States acquired the Catholic Louisiana Territory, the Ursuline Sisters wrote to President Jefferson for assurance that the Protestant United States would allow them to continue their charitable work in accordance with their faith. Jefferson replied: "The principles of the constitution and government of the United States are a guarantee to you that it will be preserved to you, sacred and inviolate, and that your institution will be permitted to govern itself according to its own voluntary rules, without interference from the civil authority" (1804, np).

Contrast Jefferson's guarantee to the Ursuline Sisters with that of the Obama administration's strong-arming of the Little Sisters of the Poor. The Little Sisters was founded in 1839, and their spiritual calling is defined by their mission statement contained on their website: "Our MISSION is to offer the neediest elderly of every race and religion a home where they will be welcomed as Christ, cared for as family and accompanied with dignity until God calls them to himself." The Little Sisters provide health care insurance coverage to their employees through the Christian Brothers Employee Benefit Trust, a self-insured church plan. The Little Sisters have always excluded coverage of sterilization, contraception, abortion, and abortifacients from their health care plan, because providing them would be tantamount to condoning them and would violate their public witness to the sanctity of human life, which they believe begins at conception.

After years of futile appeals to the HHS, the Little Sisters appealed to the courts, claiming that complying with the mandate would burden their free exercise of religion. In *Little Sisters of the Poor v. Burwell* (2015), the Tenth Court of Appeals ruled that complying with the mandate did not impose a substantial burden on religious exercise with these dismissive words: "Because we determine Plaintiffs have failed to demonstrate a substantial burden on their religious exercise, *we need not address* whether the Departments have shown a compelling state interest and adopted the least restrictive means of advancing that interest". Dissenting judges noted the lack of understanding of religious duty displayed by the majority, writing that: "All the plaintiffs in this case sincerely believe that they will be violating God's law if they execute the documents required by the government. And the penalty for refusal to execute the documents may be in the millions of dollars. How can it be any clearer that the law substantially burdens the plaintiffs' free exercise of religion?" Indeed, how can it be that the court's majority did not see that daily fines of $100 for each of their 2,719 employees spread over 31 locations nationwide was an extreme burden? Simple math shows that a financial burden amounting to $271, 900 per day would have effectively shut down the Little Sisters' valuable Christian mission.

The case eventually arrived at the Supreme Court. What had happened in the interim was the election of President Donald Trump. Under the Trump administration, HHS's Office for Civil Rights (OCR) launched a new Conscience and Religious Freedom Division dedicated to ensuring compliance with and enforcement of laws that protect religious conscience and free exercise. HHS director Roger Severino explained the new division was needed because for "too long, governments big and small have treated conscience claims with hostility instead of protection, but change is coming and it begins here and now" (Morse, 2018, np). The Trump administration exempted all religious and moral objectors from complying with the HHS mandate under the ACA. These new exemptions precipitated its own legal challenge as *Little Sisters of the Poor Saints Peter and Paul Home v. Pennsylvania* (2020), in which the states of New Jersey and Pennsylvania balked at having to shoulder the financial burden of providing women working for exempted employers with contraceptives. The Court upheld the Trump administration's regulations. Delivering the opinion of the Court, Justice Thomas wrote that:

> For over 150 years, the Little Sisters have engaged in faithful service and sacrifice, motivated by a religious calling to surrender all for the sake of their brother. ... But for the past seven years, they—like many other religious objectors who have participated in the litigation and rulemakings leading up to today's decision—have had to fight for the ability to continue in their noble work without violating their sincerely held religious beliefs.

In a concurring opinion, Justice Alito alluded to *Sherbert* v. *Verner* in which the Court said that "only the gravest abuses, endangering paramount interest" could 'give occasion for [a] permissible limitation' on the free exercise of religion". He added: "Thus, in order to establish that it has a 'compelling interest' in providing free contraceptives to all women, the Government would have to show that it would commit one of "the gravest abuses" of its responsibilities if it did not furnish contraceptives". The two most liberal Justices, Ginsburg and Sotomayor, dissented because the Court's ruling imposes burdens on female employees' access to "seamless health benefits". In their view, the government has a duty to force Catholic nuns to violate their faith to assure their lay female employees had access to contraceptives. Justice Alito noted the faulty logic in the dissenting opinion, and denied that the ruling imposes such burden:

> A woman who does not have the benefit of contraceptive coverage under her employer's plan is not the victim of a burden imposed by the rule or her employer. She is simply not the beneficiary of something that federal law does not provide. She is in the same position as a woman who does not work outside the home or a woman whose health insurance is provided by a grandfathered plan that does not pay for contraceptives or a woman who works for a small business that may not provide any health insurance at all.

There are people who did not appear to like this ruling. Among them are lawyers Tanner Bean and Robin Wilson, who apparently found comfort in the fact that: "Despite its reception, Little Sisters of the Poor is not a solid win for religious liberty. What victory the Little Sisters now enjoy is likely to last only as long as the Trump administration" (2020, p. 256). They went on to tell us that Joe Biden promised that he would restore the Obama-Biden policy that existed previously. Now that Biden is president, the Little Sisters will surely be revisited by the Court. It seems like religious liberty, so long guarded from the heavy footprints of government, will be whiplashed back and forth according to the ideological composition of the Supreme Court and the political party of the president who appoints its Justices.

The demographics of those who voted for Biden in the 2020 election indicate that he has a solid base of popular support for continuing the Obama-Biden administration's anti-religious liberty policies. The AP VoteCast Survey (2020) of more than 110,000 people across the United States showed that voters who declared no religion voted overwhelmingly (72%) for Biden while voters among Christian groups (Protestant, Catholic, "other") the majority voted for Trump. Sixty-one percent of those who attended church once a week or more voted for Trump, while 63% of those who never attended church voted for Biden. Voters who were not working full time voted for Biden over Trump 57% to 42%, and voters who were working full time voted for Trump over Biden 51% to 47%. People who were not currently married voted 58% in favor of Biden, while Trump won Trump won 53% of married voters. In the gender category, 70% who claimed to be "other" than male or female (whatever that is) voted for Biden. Thus, it was mostly the "traditional American"—those who are church-goers, working, married, and who know what sex they are—who voted for the candidate who championed religious freedom.

ILLEGAL RELIGION

The distain for religiously motivated actions is vividly showcased in the 2016 U.S. Commission on Civil Rights report titled, *Peaceful Coexistence:*

Reconciling Nondiscrimination Principles with Civil Liberties. The report was commissioned to consider conflicts between religious freedom and nondiscrimination laws. The title suggests that religious liberty is a civil liberty; it is not. It is a fundamental, inalienable right enshrined by the framers of the Constitution as our first liberty. Despite its title, the report comes out forcefully against the liberty of those who oppose efforts to force them to bend to the demands of radical LGBTQ activists. The report would have been more honestly titled: *The Commission Report on the Abolition of Religious Liberty*. We will get "peace and reconciliation" only if we all conform to the LBGTQ agenda. Douglas Laycock's reading of the report leads him to the same conclusion: "...the text shows no interest whatever in peaceful coexistence; it calls for unconditional surrender by those claiming a right to religious liberty. The majority adopted every argument it ever encountered against protecting the actual exercise of religion and in favor of protecting only the right to believe" (2018, p. 51).

Obama appointee and Committee Chairman, Martin Castro, set the tone of the Commission's attack on religion with a quote which he erroneously attributed to President John Adams: "The government of the United States is not, in any sense, founded on the Christian religion." The quoted statement was written by diplomat John Barlow in the 1797 Treaty of Tripoli with the Barbary States—Tripoli, Tunis, and Algeria—to appease their Muslim leaders. The treaty was designed to protect American ships from the Barbary pirates at a time when the United States was weak, but the "non-Christian" sentence was dropped when the treaty was renegotiated in 1815 after the United States was victorious in the Second Barbary War (Lambert, 2005).

The Commission made the determination that same-sex marriage equality always supersedes religious liberty, but ignores the fact that no Christian business owner has ever used a religious liberty claim to deny any gay or lesbian the right to marry—how could they? They only deny the right of the state to force them into endorsing such a marriage. The report employs the left's tactic of shackling discrimination and hate to religion, and justice and progress to liberalism. Castro's personal disdain for religious liberty is clearly in evidence when he wrote:

> The phrases "religious liberty" and "religious freedom" will stand for nothing except hypocrisy so long as they remain code words for discrimination, intolerance, racism, sexism, homophobia, Islamophobia, Christian supremacy or any form of intolerance. Religious liberty was never intended to give one dominion over other religions, or a veto power over the civil rights and liberties of others (2016, p. 29).

Such bigoted language in a government report is unconscionable. Putting "religious liberty" and "religious freedom" in scare quotes is a way of saying "so-called" religious liberty. Castro employs the usual left-wing strategy of accusing those who disagree with them of moral venality and hypocrisy, and of using religious liberty as a ploy to cover hateful practices. Leftists have honed their skills in demonizing people who disagree with them to a sharp point and have turned them into pitiful objects of scorn. Leftists are winning the cultural war because their computer commandoes control the language in the national debate and get their ideas disseminated. These are clever masters of Orwellian Newspeak who, like Herbert Marcuse, can turn fiction into truth and truth into fiction, but we do not expect to see such magic in an official government report.

Castro accuses Christians who just want to be left alone to live their lives in accordance with their faith of exercising "dominion" and "veto power" over other religions. He says this without proof and without acknowledging that all religions are equally shielded under the First Amendment. However, the effectiveness of this shield has not been tested with people of any faith other than Christianity. Castro fails to recognize that it is the government's embrace of the LGBTQ agenda that is exercising dominion and veto power over people of faith. Nowhere in this 306-page document do the commissioners make the distinction between serving gays and lesbians, and putting their personal stamp of approval on same-sex marriage by facilitating one. The majority of the commissioners may fail to see the difference between serving and participating, but there is a world of difference for men and women of faith.

Castro went on to remark that "In our nation's past religion has been used to justify slavery" (p.123). Yes, it was, but he ignores the fact that it was a world-wide phenomenon, and that Christians in the United States and

Britain fought costly wars to end it in the West. Castro should note that there were no abolitionist movements anywhere in the world that were not founded on Christian principles—not one (Drescher & Engerman, 1998). It also ignores the fact that slavery in Jesus' homeland did not carry the same connotations that we associate with it today. It usually meant debt slavery, or indentured servitude, whereby the unfortunate servant was freed after working off (a maximum of six years) the value of his or her debt. American slaveholders who justified slavery with the *Bible* were either ignorant of the cultural context or simply ignored it.

Another statement signed off on by three Democratic commissioners, made it plain that any attempt to place religious liberty above nondiscrimination laws must be assiduously avoided because civil rights protections ensuring nondiscrimination are of "preeminent importance". According to these bureaucrats, LGBTQ people have every right to demand that Christian business people be placed in involuntary servitude to them because their right is "preeminent". I thought that the Constitution of the United States was preeminent. If a religious objector violates an antidiscrimination statute on grounds of religious conscience and is punished, then the law violates the Constitution. The vexing thing about the First Amendment for the commissioners is that it is indeed the First.

Republican commissioner Peter Kirsanow dissented from the Democratic majority remarking that the recommendations and findings in the report "should serve as an alarm to liberty-loving Americans" (2016, p.108). Kirsanow sees the government juggernaut expanding into all areas of public and private life, which inevitably leads to conflicts between the dictates of God and the dictates of the state among believers. Kirsanow quotes constitutional scholar Ilya Shapiro on the matter:

> The cultural flashpoint surrounding wedding vendors' pleas for toleration is evidence of a more insidious process whereby the government foments social conflict as it expands its control into areas of life that we used to consider public yet not governmental. Indeed, it's government's relationship to public life that's changing - in the places that are beyond the intimacies of the home but still far removed from the state, like churches, charities, social clubs, small businesses, and even "public"

> corporations that are nevertheless part of the private sector. Under the influence of the Obama administration, the Left is weaving government through these private institutions, using them to shape American life according to its vision (2016, pp, 107-108).

The government monster now commands that we discard Constitutional guarantees of religious freedom and free speech rights to suit the radical LGBTQ agenda, but its success in tyrannizing believers should make us wonder who is next. In a *Wall Street Journal* article on the report, William McGurn relates that: "Mr. Castro's is the prevailing view among progressives. Barack Obama alluded to it when he derided small-town Americans bitterly clinging to guns or religion. Ditto for Mrs. Clinton, who in a remark about reproductive rights declared that 'deep-seated cultural codes, religious beliefs and structural biases have to be changed'". McGurn goes on to say that the commission "confirms that the progressive argument is mostly about insulting Americans with differing views" (2016, np).

THE ATTACK ON CATHOLIC CHARITIES

The Catholic Church is especially burdened by state mandates regarding adoption, contraception, and abortion. The Church has many hospitals, schools and universities sitting under its umbrella, and it employs thousands of people, and because Catholic institutions perform the same functions as secular institutions, they are subject to the same laws. The Church has been fine with this since colonial times, but since abortion and homosexual behavior have become legal, it has been told that it must violate its religious principles. The Church has a long and noble history of benevolence to people in need as an expression of its faith, but hard leftists want to drive it out of the charity business if it does not genuflect to their agenda.

The abortion issue has been a thorn in the side of the Catholic Church since it was legalized in 1973, as has been the issue of same-sex couples wishing to adopt children since Massachusetts became the first state to legalize same-sex marriage in 2003. These changes in the law have pitted

Catholic Charities USA (CCUSA) against the wishes of gays and lesbians to adopt children, and against those seeking an abortion or contraceptive devices. CCUSA is the largest private provider of welfare services of all types (food, housing, medical attention, counseling, disaster relief, and many other services) in the nation. Local branches of CCUSA serve millions of people nationwide each year regardless of their religious, social, or economic background. CCUSA also gladly serves homosexuals in matters that do not conflict with religious doctrine.

Both the rights of homosexuals to adopt, and women to have an abortion, were hardly contemplated when the Ursuline Sisters and the Jesuits established the first hospitals, alms houses, orphanages, and other forms of first social welfare in North America in the 1600s (Degeneffe, 2003). Despite centuries of charitable work among the needy, CCUSA is vilified by homosexuals and feminists as hateful and bigoted because it will not provide the services they demand. But it is not really about services they can obtain elsewhere; it is about poking their fingers in the Church's eye by enlisting the law to force a choice on it; serve us or serve no one. But the Catholic Church's position is non-negotiable because its faith and its service to others are unbreakably coupled. A *Catholic Charities Review* article states: "A Catholic specialized service agency is not just a social agency. It is an official charitable agency of the Church. Our social services, therefore, are not just a label auspices. They are an expression of an article of faith" (Degeneffe, 2003, p. 378). If the law demands that a Catholic charity provide a service at odds with its faith, it is demanding that it violate its faith—which it will not do.

Same-Sex Adoption and the Catholic Church

The Catholic Church views marriage as a sacred union between a man and a woman for the purpose of procreation. It believes that it is to the advantage of the child to have both a father and a mother because opposite sexes bring different but complementary socialization skills to the marriage. The Catholic Church does not consider homosexual orientation sinful per se, but it does consider it unsuitable to the raising of children. Thus, it does not approve of placing children with same-sex couples. Catholic Charities is the largest and oldest private organization ministering to abandoned or orphaned children, a position that runs afoul of the Massachusetts Civil Rights Commission. In 2006 the Catholic Church of Boston had to make a choice when faced the conflicting demands of its faith and of the state over the issue of same-sex adoption. It made its choice by announcing that would cease offering adoption services altogether rather than violate its faith. The Bishop of the Archdiocese of Boston wrote: "Sadly, we have come to a moment when Catholic Charities in the Archdiocese of Boston must withdraw from the work of adoptions, in order to exercise the religious freedom that was the prompting for having begun adoptions many years ago" (in Rutledge, 2008, p. 297).

Other Catholic Charities across the nation have also either stopped providing adoption services or have scaled back their services in the face of the loss of public funds. What Massachusetts did, in effect, was to sabotage its own social welfare interests by demolishing its most effective partner in placing its most difficult cases. Catholic Charities placed far more Boston area children in families—many of them difficult to place, such as children with physical or mental health problems, older or unruly children, or mixed-race children—than any other adoption agency in Massachusetts (Rutledge, 2008). The burden here has been placed on children who may no longer be adopted by anyone, although children have been transferred to (now overburdened) secular state agencies. Unlike current politicians, Thomas Jefferson realized the value to society of the work of the Catholic Church in his letter to the Ursuline Sisters in which he even offered them patronage: "It's [the Ursuline services] furtherance of the wholesome purposes of society, by training up it's [sic] younger members in the way they should go, cannot fail to ensure it the patronage of the government it is under" (1804, np).

The antidiscrimination argument is that when religious organizations work for the welfare of children and provide other services to the needy and accept taxpayer money to do so, there attaches an obligation to treat all comers equally. This argument discounts considerations of the freedom of the Church to conduct its operations in accordance with its faith, thus resulting in the loss of a valuable social service not easily replaced. Because the Church refused to bend its knee to the affirmation of the rights of same-sex couples as the state says it must, its decision to cease adoption services altogether has received scathing responses from LGBTQ activists. For example, Jamie McGonnigal writes:

> "Over and over again, the Catholic dioceses have made the conscious decision to abandon orphans and foster children rather than place them in loving, forever homes, based on nothing in their actual belief system.... It is indeed heartbreaking to see those who claim 'Christian' beliefs act so hatefully by leaving thousands of children with nothing to fall back on" (2011, np).

McGonnigal employs the left's tactic of labeling any position other than its own as hate. He ignores the fact that for religions that do not accept the legitimacy of same-sex marriage to comply with state demands that they do means that they must violate religious doctrine, or as McGonnigal dismissively put it, "their actual belief system." The Church has fulfilled its faith-based practice of caring with love as an integral part of their religious mission; what, if anything, has the LGBTQ community done for children? It is the hatred of homosexual activists for Christianity that forced the Church to close shop. LGBTQ individuals chose to approach the Church for same-sex adoption knowing full well that it could not acquiesce, and by doing so advancing their cause of vilifying it. The Church "abandoned" these children with great reluctance, and only because the state says it must, and in doing so abandon its faith.

Catholic objections to same-sex marriage are principled and fundamental. Marriage in the Catholic Church is more than a ceremony; it is a sacrament binding man and woman together. Canon 1055 §1 of the *Catechism of the Catholic Church* on matrimony states: "The matrimonial covenant, by which a man and a woman establish between themselves a partnership of the whole of life and which is ordered by its nature to the good of the spouses and the procreation and education of offspring, has been raised by Christ the Lord to the dignity of a sacrament between the baptized" (nd, np). The Church cannot countenance same-sex marriage without violating the very core of its doctrine. The Church does not condemn homosexual feelings since a person cannot help what he or she feels; it condemns acting on those feelings. Of course, if one's feelings are for one's own sex, not acting on them leaves a person with a life of celibacy shorn of intimacy. While I do not agree with the Churches position on this, it is the Church's position that matters, not mine or anyone else's.

Cardinal Raymond Burke spoke out against the increasing hostility to Christianity on the part of President Obama and his administration in an interview with Izabella Parowicz. He writes about how unimaginable the current war on Christianity would have been just a few short years ago and how "we the people" have let this happen in the context of a culture sufficiently debased that so very many have lost all respect for America's founding principles:

> [T]he President of the United States of America has become progressively more hostile toward Christian civilization…Now he wants to restrict the exercise of the freedom of religion to freedom of worship, that is, he holds that one is free to act according to his conscience within the confines of his place of worship but that, once the person leaves the place of worship, the government can constrain him to act against his rightly-formed conscience, even in the most serious of moral questions. Such policies would have been unimaginable in the United States even 40 years ago... Sadly... a large part of the population is not fully aware of what is taking place. In a democracy, such a lack of awareness is deadly... It is my hope that when they realize what is happening, will insist on electing leaders who respect the truth of the moral law as it is respected in the founding principles of our nation (Burke, 2014, np).

It is a pity that the men and women of the Obama administration did not value freedom as Justice Robert Jackson did in the 1943 case, *West Virginia State Board of Education v. Barnette.* Jackson wrote: "Those who begin coercive elimination of dissent soon find themselves exterminating dissenters. Compulsory unification of opinion achieves only the unanimity of the graveyard". Religious organizations, motivated by religious principles, do so much good in society for the needy, but they require leeway to do so in accordance with those same religious principles. To require them to violate these principles puts a burden on those whom they serve to the benefit of no one, and is manifestly a danger to everyone. The battle over contending rights, values, and identities, while resulting in a symbolic victory for LGBTQ rights, has led to a consequence for needy children that neither side should find palatable. Radical LGBTQ activists who celebrate victories against faith-based institutions are the heartless ones, for they are well aware that such institutions simply cannot violate their faith. They went ahead to test the waters until they made their point, and at the expense of poor children.

Chapter 11

SOME IMPORTANT VICTORIES FOR RELIGIOUS LIBERTY

RESPECTING THE FIRST AMENDMENT: HOBBY LOBBY

There are still courts in America that respect the Constitution—even when the liberty rights contained therein conflict with LGBTQ issues. There are also judges that can still tell the difference between discrimination against individuals and discrimination against events, and between service and participation. We have seen how courts have persistently conflated these things. Although there have been more defeats for religious liberty, there have been some significant victories. Among the most significant is *Burwell v. Hobby Lobby Stores, Inc.* (2014), with which a similar claim brought by *Conestoga Wood Specialties Corp was consolidated.*

Although this was not a case involving an LGBTQ issue (gays have complained that the ruling may prevent them accessing AIDS treatment, but it will not), in it the Supreme Court affirmed the federal RFRA's injunction against burdening the free exercise of religion absent a compelling state interest. The Court also ruled and even if there were a compelling state interest, the government must employ the least restrictive means to advance its interest. While the federal RFRA does not apply to the states, the Supreme

Court's reasoning trickles down to lower courts. If attempting to coerce business people to facilitate or participate in an event they find repugnant is a compelling state interest, the least restrictive means is not draconian legal penalties that would destroy them, but rather to direct those desiring the event to the nearest business willing to entertain them. This is the plain message in the *Hobby Lobby* ruling.

Hobby Lobby Stores is a national arts and crafts chain owned by Daniel and Barbara Green who organized their business around the principles of the Christian faith, including the belief that the use of certain kinds of contraception is immoral. Hobby Lobby operates under the Affordable Care Act (ACA) mandating that employer-provided health care plans must provide contraceptives included abortifacients that *end* pregnancies rather than *prevent* them. The Greens view this as murder because they believe that life begins at conception. Thus, the plaintiffs argued that the requirement that they provide a contraceptive that is effectively the equivalent of an abortion would make them complicit in what their religion considers murder, and that violated the Free Exercise Clause and the federal RFRA.

The Greens filed a motion for a preliminary injunction in district court to prevent the enforcement of penalties. A district court denied them the injunction, and a two-judge panel of the U.S. Court of Appeals for the Tenth Circuit affirmed. The plaintiffs then filed for a hearing before the full Court of Appeals (*en banc).* The full Appeals Court reversed the ruling of its two-judge panel and held that corporations were "persons" for the purposes of RFRA and that persons had protected rights under the Free Exercise Clause. Health and Human Services (HHS) appealed to the United States Supreme Court, arguing that Hobby Lobby is a for-profit company and not a religious organization. It further argued that that the RFRA applied only to persons, and that a corporation is not a person.

The question before the Court was whether closely held corporations were legally persons under the law. Closely held corporations are businesses in which more than 50% of the value of its stock is directly or indirectly owned by five or fewer individuals. In the 5-4 decision, in which all liberal Justices dissented, the Court ruled in favor of the Green's liberty interests. It held that Congress intended for the RFRA to apply to corporations because corporations are composed of and run by individuals for their desired ends. As Justice Alito wrote in the decision: “The plain terms of RFRA make it perfectly clear that Congress did not discriminate in this way against men and women who wish to run their businesses as for-profit corporations in the manner required by their religious beliefs”. The Court further ruled that because the contraception mandate forces religious corporations to fund what they consider abortion against their religious principles it creates a substantial burden on their free exercise. As Justice Alito wrote, if the Greens do not comply, “they will pay a very heavy price—as much as $1.3 million per day, or about $475 million per year, in the case of one of the companies. If these consequences do not amount to a substantial burden, it is hard to see what would”.

The majority opinion noted it was argued, in briefs supporting HHS, that Hobby Lobby could avoid these penalties by dropping employee insurance coverage altogether, although this would also entail substantial economic consequences. The company could face penalties of $2,000 per employee each year, which would amount to roughly $26 million for Hobby Lobby. This is a stiff price, but it was noted in amici supporting HHS that the $26 million annual penalty is actually less than the average cost of providing health insurance. The HHS thus provides businesses run by faithful Christians three choices: (1) deny your faith and follow our mandate; (2) refuse to follow our mandate and be forced out of business by ruinous fines; (3) avoid such fines by dropping employee insurance altogether. The Court majority opined that the third option ignores the fact that religious owners of companies “have religious reasons for providing health-insurance coverage for their employees. Before the advent of ACA, they were not legally compelled to provide insurance, but they nevertheless did so—in part, no doubt, for conventional business reasons, but also in part because their religious beliefs govern their relations with their employees”.

The Court also ruled that the HHS claim that Hobby Lobby has to provide abortifacients does not hold because the government has less restrictive means for employees to access them. These means include government provision of contraceptives, tax credits, or other financial support for those who want them. Justice Alito summed up the majority opinion in a way that shows that he and four of his colleagues still respect religious liberty: "We doubt that the Congress that enacted RFRA—or, for that matter, ACA—would have believed it a tolerable result to put family-run businesses to the choice of violating their sincerely held religious beliefs or making all of their employees lose their existing healthcare plans". Senator Ted Cruz characterized the Court's decision as a repudiation of the Obama Administration's ongoing onslaught against people of faith being forced to comply with statutory mandates that violate constitutional protections: "The right to religious liberty, as enshrined in the First Amendment, remains under an incredible assault by this [Obama] Administration on a variety of fronts" (2014, np). Do not clap too loudly though, the Biden administration threatens to continue Obama's "incredible assault" on religious liberty. On Biden's campaign website, we find that his administration promises to: "Restore the Affordable Care Act's contraception mandate in place before the U.S. Supreme Court's *Hobby Lobby* decision" (2020, np).

Joanna Duka, Breanna Koski, and Brush and Nib Studio

We saw in *Hobby Lobby* that the Greens filed a motion for a preliminary injunction, which is a petition seeking to prohibit a party from enforcing an act which is in dispute until there is a final judgment on the matter in court. To file such a motion, the filing party must have standing. To have standing to bring a case to court, one must show "injury in fact". However, the claim of harm can be "actual or imminent". Thus, a plaintiff need not wait for an actual prosecution or enforcement action before challenging a law's constitutionality. The plaintiff can raise an issue of harm preemptively by seeking an injunction against a state statute or city ordinance because the plaintiff intends to engage in conduct proscribed by the statute or ordinance that he or she claims would abridge a constitutional right.

Such a preliminary injunction was filed against the enforcement of a city of Phoenix, Arizona, antidiscrimination ordinance by Joanna Duka and Breanna Koski, owners of Brush & Nib Studio, an art studio that specializes in hand-painting, hand-lettering, and calligraphy for weddings. Because they cater to weddings, and because they are devout Christians, they feared that they would have to use their artistic talents to promote same-sex marriages. According to the Phoenix ordinance, anyone not complying with its requirements faced up to six months of jail time, $2,500 in fines, and three years of probation for each day they failed to comply. The ordinance also forbids them from publicly expressing the Christian belief that requires them to create art celebrating only marriages between one man and one woman. The harm to free expression of religion and free speech were such an ordinance to be enforced is something one would expect to see in countries such as atheist China, not in the USA.

In an amicus brief by the Center for Religious Expression filed with the Arizona Court of Appeals, it is noted exactly what the city itself says what it would require Joanna and Breanna to do: "As Phoenix confirms in this litigation, Joanna and Breanna are obliged to author and design a specific message celebrating and promoting same-sex marriage using the same words and messages they author and design to celebrate and promote opposite-sex marriage" (Kellum & Clark, 2017, p. 5). That is, Joanna and Breanna would be compelled to write and paint the same words promoting same-sex weddings—indicating that God has joined together and blessed same-sex couples in marriage—as they would to promote opposite-sex weddings. Apparently, the city of Phoenix views an artist's hands of Joanna and Breanna as mere conduits for reproducing state-approved messages, however objectionable they may be to the artists.

Freedom for all Americans, a group that aggressively supports the LGBTQ cause, which concurrently means a group that aggressively opposes freedom of religion, presents the case thusly: "Brush & Nib owners Joanna Duka and Breanna Koski file suit against the city of Phoenix, seeking a religious exemption from the city's LGBTQ nondiscrimination ordinance and hoping to preempt them from *having to serve* LGBTQ customers" (2019, np; emphasis added). This group frames the issue as one involving discriminatory conduct based on a customer's status as gay or lesbian rather than on an event. This is a mischaracterization, and the folks at Freedom for all Americans know it. Their cynical and biased distortion of the facts does not reflect Duka and Koski's position because the record shows that they serve all customers regardless of their sexual orientation. However, Joanna and Breanna decline to create art promoting any kind of objectionable event or message for anyone regardless of their sexual orientation. Their Operating Agreement states that Brush & Nib will refuse to create "custom artwork that communicates ideas or messages.... that contradict biblical truth, demean others, endorse racism, incite violence, or promote any marriage besides marriage between one man and one woman, such as same-sex marriage". In every such case, the decision to refuse is related to the message requested, not to the individual requesting it.

The trial court denied the motion for a preliminary injunction filed by Brush & Nib and granted the city's motion to dismiss, concluding that the ordinance did not violate the Plaintiffs' rights to free speech or free exercise of religion. Duka and Koski then filed their motion in the court of appeals which also held that the ordinance did not violate Duka and Koski's freedom of speech or substantially burden their free exercise rights. Judges are not in the business of deciding when a person's ability to comply with the dictates of faith, as *the person* understands those dictates, have been impaired, although they believe they are. The case then went before the Arizona Supreme Court, which overruled the lower courts and granted Duka and Koski their injunction. In delivering the majority opinion in *Brush & NIB Studio, LC v. City of Phoenix* (2019), Justice Gould revealed that he had actually read the plain words of the Constitution, and acknowledged that it is a document to which judges must adhere, when he wrote:

> The rights of free speech and free exercise, so precious to this nation since its founding, are not limited to soft murmurings behind the doors of a person's home or church, or private conversations with like–minded friends and family. These guarantees protect the right of every American to express their beliefs in public. This includes the right to create and sell words, paintings, and art that express a person's sincere religious beliefs.

True to those words, Arizona Supreme Court ruled the city of Phoenix cannot force Joanna and Breanna to design and create custom wedding invitations expressing messages that conflict with their core beliefs. The court held that doing so would violate the fundamental principle that "an individual has autonomy over his or her speech and thus may not be forced to speak a message he or she does not wish to say". The court also distinguished between serving and participation. Noting that serving homosexuals is not an issue, since Brush & Nib have done so on numerous occasions, the court wrote: "the Ordinance forces Plaintiffs to *personally* write, paint and create artwork celebrating a same–sex wedding. Additionally, it requires them to design and create invitations that enable and facilitate the attendance of guests at a same–sex wedding".

The dissenting Justices focused solely on the anti-discrimination purpose of the ordinance and dismissed free exercise and free speech claims totally. They made the false claim that Joanna and Breanna were discriminating against same-sex couples based on the couple's status and not on the message they want Brush & Nib to convey: "Our constitutions and laws do not entitle a business to discriminate among customers based on its owners' disapproval of certain groups". This argument was demolished in the majority opinion, and such a claim was not even made by the city of Phoenix. These Justices, as well as the city of Phoenix, inevitably played the race card, but the majority opinion scorned this tactic and issued a warning about government enforced conformity:

> The enduring strength of the First Amendment is that it allows people to speak their minds and express their beliefs without government interference. But here, the City effectively cuts off Plaintiffs' right to express their beliefs about same–sex marriage by telling them what they can and cannot say. And to justify this action, both the City and the primary dissent claim that if we dare to allow Plaintiffs to express their beliefs, we, in essence, run the risk of resurrecting the Jim Crow laws of the Old South. But casting Plaintiffs' free speech and exercise rights in such a cynical light does grave harm to a society. As Justice Jackson observed in Barnette, "[s]truggles to coerce uniformity of sentiment in support of some end thought essential to their time and country have been waged by many good

as well as by evil men," but, inevitably "those bent on its accomplishment must resort to an ever-increasing severity." We would be wise to heed his warning about government efforts to compel uniformity of beliefs and ideas.

Blaine Adamson and Hands on Originals

Lexington-Fayette Urban County Human Rights Commission v. Hands On Originals (2019) is a case that began in 2012 and concerns a promotional printing company that refused to print t-shirts for a Kentucky LGBTQ organization, the Gay and Lesbian Services Organization (GLSO), promoting the annual Lexington Pride Celebration. The message GLSO wanted on the t-shirts was contrary to the religious beliefs of Blaine Adamson, the owner of Hands On Originals. Lexington-Fayette County has a nondiscrimination ordinance on the books that prohibits sexual orientation and gender identity discrimination by public accommodations. However, the issue for Adamson was the shirt's message promoting homosexuality, and not the customer's homosexual identity. In fact, he printed materials for a lesbian musician—promoting her, not her sexuality—who performed at the 2012 event. In fact, Adamson refuses the business of anyone requesting any kind of morally offensive message, as Judge David Buckingham noted in his concurring decision in *Hands On*: "Hands On declined thirteen orders on the basis that it believed the designs to be offensive or inappropriate, including refusal to print shirts promoting adult entertainment establishments, pens promoting a sexually explicit video, and shirts containing a violence-related message."

Adamson claimed that his refusal to print the t-shirts is exempt from the county ordinance because being required to print them would violate his First Amendment religious beliefs and freedom of speech. He also noted that he had offered to connect GLSO to another printer that would produce the shirts for the same price. This is surely "the least restrictive means" for the organization to acquire its needs, but GLSO decided to file a complaint, despite receiving the shirts free from another printer. This vindictiveness once again displays that the issue of obtaining services for LGBTQ individuals is not about obtaining services obtainable elsewhere, but rather it is about taking every opportunity to use the powerful arm of the state to demean and destroy the livelihoods of Christians who will not bend a knee to their demands. Such bullying disgusts some in the LGBTQ community, such as Kathy Trautvetter and Diane DiGeloromo, a lesbian couple who own a t-shirt business and who support Blain's actions: "We feel this really isn't a gay or straight issue. This is a human issue. No one really should be forced to do something against what they believe in. It's as simple as that" (in Jonathan, 2015, np). Indeed, it really is as simple as that.

The Lexington-Fayette Human Rights Commission, ignoring the least restrictive means test totally, ordered Adamson to comply with GLSO's request and to participate in mandatory "diversity training" conducted by the Commission. So, not only was he ordered to labor involuntarily, like Phillips in the *Masterpiece* case, he was ordered to attend indoctrination classes designed to show him that his beliefs were wrong! Adamson refused this egregious misuse of state power, and in 2014 the Commission issued him a final ruling stating that Hands On Originals violated its ordinance by discriminating against the LGBTQ organization, and that it must comply or face legal consequences. Adamson then filed an appeal to the Kentucky Court of Appeals, which overturned the Human Rights Commission's ruling. One judge concluding that Adamson's right to free speech, but not his religious freedom, was compromised, another concluded that his religious freedom was violated. A third judge dissented, amazingly finding that neither of Adamson's constitutional rights had been violated and found for the Commission. The Kentucky Human Rights Commission then appealed to the Kentucky Supreme Court.

Handing a victory to Hands On Originals, in 2019 the Kentucky Supreme Court said that the festival sponsor on behalf of GLSO lacked statutory standing to sue Adamson because only individuals, not groups, have the right to bring such claims. While the ruling is legally correct, it sidestepped the important First Amendment issues of free exercise and free speech in the case, as the courts in LGBTQ cases have an infernal tendency to do. However, Senior Counsel for Alliance Defending Freedom, Jim

Campbell, who argued the case on Adamson's behalf, noted that one concurring judge did express the notion that First Amendment rights were the unnoticed gorilla in the corner in this case. Campbell wrote:

> Today's decision makes clear that this case never should have happened. For more than seven years, government officials used this case to turn Blaine's life upside down, even though we told them from the beginning that the lawsuit didn't comply with the city's own legal requirements. The First Amendment protects Blaine's right to continue serving all people while declining to print messages that violate his faith. Justice David Buckingham recognized this in his concurring opinion, and no member of the court disagreed with that.

Carl and Angel Larsen and Telescope Media Group

Carl and Angel Larsen, the owners of Telescope Media Group, make commercial videos for a variety of customers, believing that their company exists to glorify God. In 1916, the Larsens decided they wanted to expand their business to include wedding videos, but because of their religious beliefs, they would not do so if they would be required to make videos for same-sex weddings. Anticipating that a refusal to do so would conflict with Minnesota's Human Rights Act (MHRA), they filed a preliminary injunction in federal district court seeking a ruling that they had a right to refuse such business. They argued that making wedding videos is an expressive activity protected by the First Amendment under a hybrid free exercise/free speech claim. The penalties they faced for violating the MHRA include triple compensatory damages to a refused same-sex couple, punitive damages of up to $25,000; a criminal fine of up to $1,000, and up to 90 days in jail. These penalties are particularly galling since Minnesota law treats other ordinance violations as petty misdemeanors and prescribes a maximum fine of $300. It is clear that the Larsens faced a credible threat of enforcement since Minnesota publicly announced that the MHRA relating to same-sex wedding would be enforced, even employing the Gestapo-like tactic of employing "testers" to target noncompliant businesses for prosecution.

It is a matter of constitutional law that wedding videos are a form of speech, and videographers have a First Amendment right under the Free Speech Clause to make them for opposite-sex weddings and cannot be compelled to make them for same-sex couples against their religious consciences. The First Amendment is relevant whenever the government compels speech, regardless of who writes the script and in what form and regardless of whether they are expressing their views through a for-profit enterprise. Nevertheless, a district court granted Minnesota's motion to dismiss and denied the Larsens' request for a preliminary injunction because it had already dismissed their lawsuit. The district court also dismissed the Larsens' free-speech claim law because it said that the MHRA serves a compelling governmental interest, and that the MHRA did not violate any of the Larsen's constitutional rights. This despite the United States Supreme Court itself recognizing that the government compels speech when a law has the effect of foisting a third party's message on a speaker.

The Larsens then appealed to the United States Court of Appeals for the Eighth Circuit, which granted an injunction preventing Minnesota from enforcing the law against the Larsens. Writing for the majority, in *Telescope Media Grp. v. Lucero* (2019), Judge Stras noted:

> The First Amendment, which applies to the states through the Fourteenth Amendment, prohibits laws "abridging the freedom of speech." It promotes the free exchange of ideas by allowing people to speak in many forms and convey a variety of messages, including those that "invite dispute" and are "provocative and challenging." It also prevents the government from "[c]ompelling individuals to mouth support for views they find objectionable." As the Supreme Court has made clear, "[t]here is no room under our Constitution for a more restrictive" approach because "the alternative would lead to standardization of ideas ... by legislatures, courts, or dominant political or community groups."

This is a straightforward understanding of the Constitution's prohibition of governmental restrictions on free speech and freedom in general. Despite the appalling MHRA threats of draconian penalties for anyone daring to exercise those rights, dissenting Judge Kelly saw fit to employ a slippery slope argument and once again dealt the race card: "And what may start in the wedding business—"we don't do interracial weddings," "we don't film Jewish ceremonies," and so on—likely will not end there. Nothing stops a business owner from using today's decision to justify new forms of discrimination tomorrow". This is a totally bogus argument, and Kelly must know it. We can turn the slippery slope argument 180 degrees and say that if Minnesota can force the Larens to celebrate messages about marriage they disagree with, nothing stops it from compelling other speech as well, such as forcing Muslim videographers to produce videos promoting Christianity because they do so for Islam. Thus, the threat to the Larsens is a threat to all beliefs and views; the same principles that protect the Larsen's freedom protects everyone's.

Then there is Kelly's racial argument. As pointed out before, it is spurious because no one would bring a religious liberty claim against having to serve blacks, Jews, or interracial couples since there is absolutely no biblical underpinning for bringing such a claim. Wedding vendors could, however, hypothetically bring free speech claims in refusing to host such ceremonies. No one has, or is likely to, make such a claim. Their refusal to speak in favor of such weddings could only be based on racist ideology, and never on solid moral grounds. Anyone making such a claim would be driven from out of business by normal free-market pressures long before it would reach the steps of a courthouse. Anyway, it is extremely unlikely that a racist vendor would be willing risk state prosecution for the sake of his or her views the way Christian vendors are willing to risk all for their devotion to their religious principles.

Expressing her disagreement with the decision in this case, Teresa Nelson of the ACLU of Minnesota made the following argument: "While freedom of speech and religion are among our most fundamental rights, those freedoms do not give any of us the right to harm other people or to impose our beliefs on others. Discrimination has no place in our

Constitution, and businesses can't put up signs saying 'your kind not served here'" (2019, np). Although Nelson agrees that freedom of religion and speech rights are most fundamental, she believes that they must give way to mere local ordinances. Fundamental rights can never be sacrificed to statutes or ordinances; this is Constitutional Law 101. Nelson, however, claims that constitutional rights must be subservient if exercising them harms other people. As we discussed in Chapter Eight, the only harm that persons being denied access to the labor of others is dignitary harm, which can be easily avoided by not approaching devout Christian vendors requesting their services in the first place. According to Nelson, because someone is offended the offender must surrender his or her constitutional rights. This would be an egregious harm far exceeding the harm suffered by any same-sex couple refused access to the Larsen's talents. Nelson illustrates the hypocritical nature of the thorough-going leftist ACLU, an organization that claims to protect our liberties.

Nelson also argues that a vendor refusing to facilitate or participate in a same-sex wedding amounts to the vendor imposing his or her beliefs on others. She has it backwards. The Larsens did not plan on showing up on a same-sex couple's home or wedding ceremony quoting Leviticus. They simply want to go about their lives and earn a living without state interference, but Minnesota was planning to impose its beliefs on them, or if it could not, it would drive them out of business and into bankruptcy. Nelson also writes that businesses can't put up signs saying "your kind not served here". Did she even read the various amici supporting the Larsens? It is a matter of record that the Larsens will, and have, serviced lesbians and gays. They will video their graduations, birthday parties, Christmas parties, sporting events, or any other occasion, but they will not video a same-sex wedding. Nelson views this one exception as a blanket refusal to serve LGBTQ folks. She knows that this is untrue, but persists in conflating refusal to *serve* based on sexual orientation status with refusal to participate in an *event* the Larsens deem contrary to their religious beliefs.

TRINITY LUTHERAN CHURCH OF COLUMBIA

Although the Trinity Lutheran Church case is not one involving an LGBTQ issue, it is important from our point of view because it is a rare case in which the decision was guided by the almost forgotten Free Exercise Clause. In 2012, Trinity Lutheran Church of Columbia, Missouri, sought a competitively available state grant to install a rubberized surface on its preschool playground. Trinity's application ranked fifth out of 44 applicants and would have received a grant, but the state's Department of Natural Resources belatedly realized that Trinity is a religious school, and denied it a grant. In 2017, the case found its way to the United States Supreme Court as *Trinity Lutheran Church of Columbia, Inc. v. Comer* (2017). In a 7-2 decision, the Court ruled that the state's action violated the Free Exercise Clause by denying a public benefit to an otherwise eligible school solely on the basis of its religious status. Chief Justice Roberts called it "odious to our Constitution" to exclude Trinity from the grant program. In his majority opinion, Justice Roberts stated:

> Like the disqualification statute in *McDaniel* [a minister disqualified from serving as a legislator because of his ministerial status], the Department's policy puts Trinity Lutheran to a choice: It may participate in an otherwise available benefit program or remain a religious institution. Of course, Trinity Lutheran is free to continue operating as a church, just as McDaniel was free to continue being a minister. But that freedom comes at the cost of automatic and absolute exclusion from the benefits of a public program for which the Center is otherwise fully qualified. And when the State conditions a benefit in this way, *McDaniel* says plainly that the State has punished the free exercise of religion: "To condition the availability of benefits ... upon [a recipient's] willingness to ... surrender his religiously impelled [status] effectively penalizes the free exercise of his constitutional liberties.

Consistent with progressivism's hostility toward religion, the two most liberal Justices on the Court, Sotomayor and Ginsburg, strongly dissented from the majority, and asserted the priority of the Establishment Clause over the Free Exercise Clause. Justice Sotomayor wrote: "The Establishment Clause does not allow Missouri to grant the Church's funding request because the Church uses the Learning Center, including its playground, in conjunction with its religious mission". If one were to ask Justice Sotomayor where exactly in the Establishment Clause does it say church schools must be barred from a public program, she could not. Once more, it plainly and simply states that Congress should not establish a state religion. Her argument that the Exercise Clause trumps the Free Exercise Clause was rejected by the majority in this case and may signal a return of the kind of respect for the Free Exercise Claus that the founders meant it to have. It is therefore refreshing to see Justice Roberts' assertion that to deny a public benefit to a school based solely on the fact that it has a religious mission is "odious to our Constitution"

As for Missouri's discrimination against Trinity and the Free Exercise Clause, Sotomayor writes: "If the denial of a benefit others may receive is discrimination that violates the Free Exercise Clause, then the accommodations of religious entities we have approved would violate the free exercise rights of nonreligious entities". Just how would providing a grant to resurface a playground violate the free exercise rights of a nonreligious entity? To talk about the free exercise rights of nonreligious entities does not make sense since they claim no such rights. If no rights are claimed, how can they be violated? The grants in question were competitively available to any school that showed a need. If a religious school showed a greater need than a secular school and received the grant, it is certain that the secular school would not claim their free exercise rights had been violated. To deny a generally available public benefit based solely on religious grounds is to fence out religious persons or entities from public life as pariahs. Sotomayor's puzzling logic notwithstanding, it is heartening to see the Supreme Court resurrecting the Free Exercise Clause in this case. We shall see if it remains alive in the next religious liberty versus a public accommodation case that comes before it.

Chapter 12

BIG GOVERNMENT AND FREEDOM

SOCIALISM: THE FRIEND OF BIG GOVERNMENT

Ever since the signing of the signing of *Magna Carta* on June 15, 1215, there has been an evolving principle in Anglo-Saxon law that the people have the right to limit the power of the government to constitutionally prescribed duties. Although the rights expounded in the *Magna Carta* applied only to freemen, it supplied the trajectory for those freedoms to be extended eventually to everyone in the Western world. Advocates of limited government are not hostile to government, but they are hostile to the concentration of coercive state power. History reminds us of the dangers of unconstrained government, thus the struggle for limited government; one powerful enough to protect inalienable rights, but not powerful enough to take them away. Only if we recognize that there is a power greater than the state can we have such a government. That is why the foundering fathers of America attached it to God the Creator and not to the state.

Limiting government's natural expansive inclinations requires strong intermediary institutions. The family and the Christian faith are the two epicenters of Western morality and conservatism, which is why Karl Marx knew that for socialism to be successful in the West it must first spiritually disarm the people by destroying these barriers to the success of socialism.

In his *Feuerbach Thesis # 4*, Marx wrote: "Once the earthly family is discovered to be the secret of the heavenly family, the former must be destroyed in theory and in practice" (in Jal, 2010, p. 136). Marx also noted that: "communism begins where atheism begins" (in Sheen, 1948, p. 69). Historians Will and Arial Durant agree: "Heaven and utopia are buckets in a well: when one goes down the other goes up; when religion declines Communism grows" (1968, p. 51).

Americans who value their hard-won freedoms should tremble at the resurgence of socialist thought in our country and at the Democratic party's willingness to embrace it. Witness Joe Biden and an endless stream of politicians, sports teams, and entertainment celebrities signaling their virtue by kneeing for Black Lives Matter (BLM). BLM leaders openly declare that they are "trained Marxists," and BLM's publicly available agenda clearly toes the Marxist line. It may be politically expedient and socially "cool" to kneel for BLM, because the more the mob professes to hate imagined evil, the more it showcases its imagined goodness. For those who kneel only for God, the destructive riots of the 2020 mob have troublesome undercurrents for liberty.

As government's role in our lives continues to expand, an increasingly important question is: "Does a person's life belong to his or herself or to the state"? By definition, the socialist is a believer in collectivism; the notion that the individual's life belongs to the communal whole, and that individuals have no rights except those the state permits. All private needs are subordinate to the needs of the state, and the individual is of value only insofar as he or she serves it. Collectivism emphasizes the embeddedness of individuals in society, encourages conformity, and discourages dissent and personal autonomy. The idea of collectivism was revealed in the National Socialist Party slogan "*Du bist nichts, dein Volk ist alles*" ("You are nothing, your nation is everything"). As Millennials lurch to the left in America and elsewhere, they remain largely ignorant of socialism's role in the greatest catastrophes in human history.

Individualism, on the other hand, is the idea that individuals' lives belong to themselves, and that they have the inalienable right to live, believe, and practice, according to their own consciences under a government that recognizes and protects those rights. This is the ideal that the founders set forth and sought to establish in the Declaration and the Constitution. Personal autonomy is paramount to individualism, and its ideal was well stated by Winston Churchill in 1936: "I rank the citizen higher than the State, and regard the State as useful only insofar as it preserves his inherent rights" (2012, p. 740). Unfortunately, we are living in a time when the state believes that it can divest people of faith of their precious First Amendment rights.

This is why we should dread Godless socialism, now mainstream among the leadership of the Democratic party. Socialism extinguishes all freedoms and grants the state all power. Eugenicist and mathematician Karl Pearson illustrates its totalitarian nature in his *The Moral Basis of Socialism*: "The legislation or measures of police, to be taken against the immoral and antisocial minority, will form the political realization of Socialism. Socialists have to inculcate that spirit which would give offenders against the State short shrift and the nearest lamp-post. Every citizen must learn to say with Louis XIV, *L'etat c'est moi*!" (Paul, 1984, p. 573). Socialist states have always given their dissidents "short-shrift and the nearest lamp-post". The concepts of individual rights and procedural limitations on state power only have purchase as long as the state and the individual are distinct entities. In Marxist theory, whatever is to be construed as the "state" will become one and inseparable with the individual (*L'etat c'est moi!).* If you are the state and the state is you, then all individuality is extinguished, and you cannot even claim ownership of yourself. If you dare to do so, a lamppost awaits.

American advocates of socialism are not yet calling for the nearest lamppost for their dissenters. Most are doubtless well-meaning people who simply lack historical insight, but in the political realm, well-meaning people are often more dangerous to our liberties than those that are openly hostile. Justice Louis Brandeis long ago noted this in his opinion in *Olmstead v. United States* (1928): "Experience should teach us to be most on our guard to protect liberty when the Government's purposes are beneficent. Men born to freedom are naturally alert to repel invasion of their liberty by evil minded rulers. The greatest dangers to liberty lurk in insidious encroachment by men of zeal, well-meaning but without understanding". Malcolm X also saw the perfidious nature of liberal do-gooders who keep African Americans in bondage to the welfare system so that they consistently vote Democrat despite the horrific state of their cities:

> The white liberal differs from the white conservative only in one way: the liberal is more deceitful than the conservative. The liberal is more hypocritical than the conservative. Both want power, but the white liberal is the one who has perfected the art of posing as the Negro's friend and benefactor; and by winning the friendship, allegiance, and support of the Negro, the white liberal is able to use the Negro as a pawn or tool.... (1963, np).

Socialism, by definition, is big government. Big government is like a balloon, the more wind we put into it the bigger it grows, and the bigger it grows the more power it grabs from intermediary social institutions. LGBTQ activism is blowing hard into the balloon as it demands that the state crush those who refuse to endorse its agenda, which weakens religion—the major institutional bulwark against socialism. LGBTQ activists who appeal to government and to the leftist intelligentsia for support in their efforts to destroy religious dissenters should be made aware that socialist governments, once in power, have traditionally persecuted homosexuals. They should thus be just as concerned as religious people about weakening religion. If the church is enfeebled, what other institution exists to protect us from the increasing encroachment of government? Michael McConnell notes the importance of the church in this regard: "The political importance of churches is even more evident on the world scene. In many countries (Poland, South Africa, and Nicaragua come immediately to mind) the church is virtually the only institution strong enough to stand up to the state. Traditions of church autonomy thus constitute one of the last protections against the all-powerful state" (2017, p. 201).

Freedom to own yourself requires a moral foundation to sustain a free state that only Christianity can supply. The American Humanist Association motto, "Good without God", assumes that an atheistic value system can supply the government with moral foundations, but "Good without God" will only last as long as society has a cadre of people nourished on Judeo-Christian values remaining on Earth; after they have gone to their reward and we have only citizens raised in a society that has given God the boot, watch out! As Robert Winthrop cogently put it: "Men… must necessarily be controlled, either by a power within them, or by a power without them; either by the Word of God, or by the strong arm of man; either by the Bible, or by the bayonet" (1852, p. 172). When we are ruled by the bayonet our freedoms are gone. In an article in Britain's *Daily Mail* Peter Hitchens, who shared his brother Christopher's socialism and atheism until his tenure as a Moscow news correspondent turned him to God, notes how leftism is bound to lead either to anarchy or to a police state ruled by Winthrop's bayonet:

> The left's real interests are moral, cultural, sexual and social. They lead to a powerful state.... Many leftists fondly imagine they are rebels against authority, and liberators of mankind. It is because the left's ideas— by their nature—undermine conscience, self-restraint, deferred gratification, lifelong marriage and strong, indivisible families headed by authoritative fathers. Without these things, society becomes anarchic, chaotic, lustful and violent – unless it is very heavily policed and supervised" (2012, np).

Socialism has failed in countries around the world; producing economic impoverishment and political authoritarianism everywhere it has been tried. When this becomes apparent, socialists cry like the man in the dock that someone else did it; "It wasn't really socialism, real socialism has never been tried" (Cox, 1991, p. 170). Slovenian communist philosopher Slavoj Zizik writes that Venezuelan socialism failed because it didn't go far enough. What it should have done he says, is to utterly gut the old habits and customs and impose and enforce new ones, or new "proverbs" as he calls them (2017). Socialism cannot work unless an intelligentsia is recruited to manage a central planning system and the state abolishes all private property, shatters all individualism, and whole new norms of thinking are imposed, then we will see real socialism. The answer to socialist failure, then, is more of the same, but trying the same thing over and over again expecting a different result is Einstein's definition of insanity.

Socialists blame everything from the flawed personalities of Stalin and Mao to the flawed remnants of capitalism for its failure; they never attribute the failure to a flawed ideology. The former Marxist and atheist, Eugene Genovese, who became a conservative and a Christian, knew that the evils of socialism are inherent in its philosophy, and that you cannot plan a whole economy and enforce new "parables" without imposing dictatorship:

> The horrors did not arise from perversions of radical ideology but from the ideology itself. We were led into complicity with mass murder and the desecration of our professed ideals not by Stalinist or other corruptions of high ideals, much less by unfortunate twists in some presumably objective course of historical development, but by a deep flaw in our very understanding of human nature—its frailty and its possibilities—and by our inability to replace the moral and ethical baseline long provided by the religion we have dismissed with indifference, not to say contempt (1994, p. 374).

As Genovese knew, socialism and atheism are birds of a feather, and together they destroy cultures by gnawing at their souls. Nobel Prize winner for literature, Aleksandr Solzhenitsyn, knows that Russia became a dystopian nightmare because it forgot God:

> More than half a century ago, while I was still a child, I recall hearing a number of older people offer the following explanation for the great disasters that had befallen Russia: Men have forgotten God; that's why all this has happened…I have read hundreds of books, collected hundreds of personal testimonies, and have already contributed eight volumes of my own toward the effort of clearing away the rubble left by that upheaval. But if I were asked today to formulate as concisely as possible the main cause of the ruinous Revolution that swallowed up some sixty million of our people, I could not put it more accurately than to repeat: Men have forgotten God; that's why all this has happened (2006, p. 577).

Limited Government and Its Friend: Christianity

As all true Marxists know, ultimately only Christianity champions the individual conscience against the collective will. Over the centuries, Christianity has paved the way for such ideas as human dignity (made in the image of God), social, civil, and political rights, and democracy. Any number of historians will attest to the fact that Christianity is the only religion that serves as a standard-bearer of the value of the individual. The Freedom House's survey of freedom in the world strongly supports this thesis. In its 2018 *Freedom in the World Index* (2018), based on 25 indicators of political and civil rights, only 82 of 210 nations (39%) are designated "free". All but 5 (India, Japan, Mongolia, South Korea, and Taiwan) are Christian nations, but except for Mongolia, all have been heavily influenced by the West. Some nations with largely Christian populations such as Mexico, are designated "partly free", and the only nations with majority Christian population designated "unfree" are those scarred by socialism, such as Cuba and Venezuela. That 77 out of 82 (90.6%) of the world's free nations are Christian makes it difficult to deny that Christianity is the major force behind sociopolitical freedom in the Western world.

The Christian belief that God is a God of reason who wants us to get to know him through his creation shapes motives, and motives produce actions that evolve over time. From the very earliest days of Christianity, it was taught that reason is a unique gift of God. In the second century AD, the founder of Western theology, Quintus Tertullian of Carthage, preached that: "Reason is a thing of God, inasmuch as there is nothing which God the Maker of all has not provided, disposed, ordained by reason—nothing which He has not willed should be handled and understood by reason" (in Coyne & Heller, 2008, p. 42). The Church founded the first true university (as opposed to earlier Islamic purely religious schools)—the University of Bologna—in 1088, and made mathematics and natural philosophy (science) compulsory for those wanting to study theology (Stark, 2005). Christianity thus created fertile intellectual soil for science to grow, from which grew the technology and capitalism that made the West preeminent in the world. Christianity, reason, science, and capitalism would eventually lead to democracy, civic and social equality, and individual freedom in the West. Historian and sociologist of religion Randy Stark draws a straight line from Christianity to moral equality, capitalism, and science:

> To put it simply, Christianity created Western societies. Without a theology committed to reason, progress, and moral equality, today the entire world would be about where non-European societies were in, say, 1800: A world with many astrologers and alchemists, but no scientists. A world of despots, lacking universities, banks, factories, eyeglasses, chimneys, and pianos. A world where many infants do not live to the age of five, and many women die in childbirth—a world truly living in "dark ages." (2006, p. 19).

Western scholars are not alone in this observation. David Aikman cites the words of a research team from the Chinese Academy of Social Science appointed by the government to investigate the secret of Western success. The team reached the following conclusion:

> One of the things we were asked to look into was what accounted for the success, in fact, the preeminence of the West all over the world. We studied everything we could from the historical, political, economic, and cultural perspective. At first, we thought it was because you had more powerful guns than we had. Then we thought it was because you had the best political system. Next, we focused on your economic system. But in the past twenty years, we have realized that the heart of your culture is your religion: Christianity. That is why the West is so powerful. The Christian moral foundation of social and cultural life was what made possible the emergence of capitalism and the successful transition to democratic politics. We don't have any doubt about this (2012, p.5).

It would be centuries before it was recognized that all people are equally entitled to all political and civil rights. These rights are recognized in Western Christian societies (however secularized they may have become) and are yet to be seen in the vast majority of non-Christian societies. The United Nations framed its 1948 *Declaration of Human Rights* in the fervent hope that human rights would be universalized. Its primary purpose was to protect the individual from arbitrary state power by recognizing that the fundamental requirement of justice is that government should exist for the benefit of its citizens, and not vice versa. The *Declaration* is so patently based on Judeo/Christian principles that many Islamic nations refused to sign it on the grounds that it conflicted with Sharia law. Islamic nations formulated their own *Cairo Declaration on Human Rights in Islam* in 1990, but stipulated in Article 24 that: "All the rights and freedoms stipulated in this Declaration are subject to the Islamic Sharia". Sharia law lacks anything remotely resembling religious or political freedom, even prescribing death for apostasy, thus the whole Islamic *Declaration* is rendered impotent. Atheist philosopher Jurgen Habermas is among those who acknowledge that true human rights took root *only* in the Judeo/Christian tradition:

> Egalitarian universalism, from which sprang the ideas of freedom and social solidarity, of an autonomous conduct of life and emancipation, of the individual morality of conscience, human rights and democracy, is the direct heir of the Judaic ethic of justice and the Christian ethic of love...To this day, there is no alternative to it. And in light of the current challenges of a postnational constellation, we continue to draw on the substance of this heritage. Everything else is just idle postmodern talk (2006, pp. 150-151).

None of the freedoms found in modern Christian nations were remotely envisioned by early Christians, but as Habermas noted, they are inherent in the values and beliefs of the Judeo/Christian tradition. The idea of the equality of all people is stated by Paul in Galatians 3:28: "There is neither Jew nor Greek, there is neither bond nor free, there is neither male nor female: for ye are all one in Christ Jesus". Paul did not mean this as a call for voting booths and bicameral parliaments; nor did he mean that secular distinctions among people can or should be disregarded. He meant that whatever secular distinctions exist, all people are God's creations, and equally deserving of His love. All humans share the same origin, the same nature, and the same ultimate destiny regardless of their earthly status, and thus are all deserving of the same rights.

How Christianity Both Constrains and Aids the State

The free and independent institution of religion is a bulwark against state power, but at the same time it aids in the state's success in making its people free, happy, and prosperous; and in its effective operation. As David Bleich contends: "Freedom of religious practice.... enables a government to govern effectively. A populace that perceives its religious principles to be thwarted by the government will harbor deep resentment and disrespect for the ruling authority. Consequently, the government will be delegitimized in the eyes of those whose religious liberties are denied, thereby compromising respect for the government and its laws" (2002, p. 249).

Religion aids the state by providing it with moral principles. Martin Luther King, Jr. once said that religion "is not the master or the servant of the state, but rather the conscience of the state" (1986, p. 501). A state without a conscience cannot long endure. As Pope John Paul II noted: "if there is no ultimate truth to guide and direct political activity, then ideas and convictions can easily be manipulated for reasons of power. As history demonstrates, a democracy without values easily turns into open or thinly disguised totalitarianism" (2000, np). All governments are administered by flawed human beings whose power will certainly expand and corrupt unless other institutions have the power to place limits on its rulers. Religious liberty is the foundation stone of all free societies, which is why James Madison said it is was: "enshrined it in our Constitution, and so etched in our national consciousness, a principled and practical commitment to that liberty that has helped us to remain a free society ever since" (in Levin, 2010, p. 30).

Only in society under the rule of law can people freely speak their conscience. This freedom enshrined in the First Amendment recognizes that in the domain of moral conscience, there is a power higher than the state that grants us inalienable rights. As Justice Douglas wrote in *Girouard v. United States* (1946): "The struggle for religious liberty has, through the centuries, been an effort to accommodate the demands of the State to the conscience of the individual. The victory for freedom of thought recorded in our Bill of Rights recognizes that, in the domain of conscience, *there is a moral power higher than the State*". With their God-given rights, people in democracies are free to criticize their government and its leaders without fear, which the vast bulk of humankind could not do throughout history, and cannot do today. For instance, Article 22 of the *Cairo Declaration on Human Rights in Islam,* state that: "Everyone shall have the right to express his opinion freely in such manner as would not be contrary to the principles of the Sharia". Muslims are thus free to speak as long as they speak the orthodoxies of Sharia, which means that they cannot criticize their governments because Sharia law supplies their foundation. This amounts to a religious version of *L'etat c'est moi!* Freely exercising the right to publicly disagree with the orthodoxies of society becomes problematic if no higher power than the state is recognized. As the great British writer and philosopher, G. K. Chesterton, put it:

> But the truth is that it is only by believing in God that we can ever criticise the Government. Once abolish the God, and the Government becomes the God. The fact is written all across human history; but it is written more plainly across that recent history of Russia.... There the Government is the God, and all the more the God, because it proclaims aloud in accents of thunder, like every other God worth worshipping, the one essential commandment: "Thou shalt have no other gods before Me." The truth is that Irreligion is the opium of the people. Wherever the people do not believe in something beyond the world, they will worship the world. But, above all, they will worship the strongest thing in the world (2001, p. 57).

The truth of Chesterton's words was written in the blood of the 20th century when Godless state worship washed the world in tears. The vile immoral ideologies of communism and Nazism were worshiped with almost evangelical fervor by its followers because God had been dethroned. Thomas Jefferson warned of the fate awaiting nations that give God his walking papers: "And can the liberties of a nation be thought secure when we have removed their only firm basis, a conviction in the minds of the people that these liberties are of the gift of God? That they are not to be violated but with his wrath?" (in Coates, 2012, np). If we value freedom and a moral society, we must value its Christian origins and acknowledge that without God we will become slaves of the state. If the state is transcendent, then we look to it to provide all our needs and wants in in a socialist utopia in exchange for subservience. Utopia is unattainable on earth, but the yoke of subservience is difficult to cast off once applied.

THE STATE AND MORALITY

The "Jeffersonian maxim" states: "That government is best which governs least, because its people discipline themselves" (Peterson. 1960, p. 79). But how are people able to discipline themselves without a sound basis of objective morality? To be virtuous it is necessary to curtail our natural appetites. Robert Winthrop told us that if we are not ruled by our moral consciences, we will be ruled by the strong arm of the state, and Benjamin Franklin noted: "Only a virtuous people are capable of freedom. As nations become more corrupt and vicious, they have more need of masters" (in Boyack, 2012, p. 235). Democratic governments provide a wide space for personal freedom, but they also require equally high standards of moral self-governance.

A free society is held together by the voluntary obedience of its citizens to moral rules. We get these rules from others with our best interests in mind, but ultimately, they come from God's commandments. These are the rules of any decent society that we sense intuitively. It was this sense of intuitive morality that moved C.S. Lewis to abandon atheism for Christianity. Lewis (2001) argued that because there is this pressing moral law there must be a moral law giver and that God has reasons for imbuing humans with moral awareness. Only God can provide a coherent foundation for objective moral values and duties because without God we do not have an objective basis by which to make moral judgments, and are left with moral relativism that asserts that what is "good" and "bad" depend on culture or on whom you ask.

It is assumed that most atheists subscribe to the universality of human rights and are decent people who care about others, care about justice, value the good, and denounce evil. However, they cannot provide the ultimate justification necessary for a universal objective morality by which good and evil are clearly delineated and understood. As a worldview, atheism provides no basis for affirming objective moral values, nor can it. In this nihilistic outlook which views human beings are mere byproducts of pitiless nature that have evolved on an insignificant rocky planet in a hostile, mindless, and accidental universe just waiting for death and oblivion. In this view, why should human beings have any more moral worth than cockroaches?

Any number of atheist philosophers affirm that without God there is no objective morality. German philosopher Friedrich Wilhelm Nietzsche made no bones about the fact that he wanted to rid the world of morality, and that to do so we have to get rid of God. He considered morality humankind's greatest weakness and that good and evil are mere social constructions plastered over the moral neutrality of nature. He recognized that the reality of good and evil leads to the development of a conscience, which he abhorred as inhibiting the greatness of the *ubermensch* ("supermen"). If God is dead, meaning, morality, and reason die with him, and all that is left is the relentless "will to power" of the *ubermensch.* Nietzsche candidly acknowledged the Christian origin of Western morality:

> When one gives up Christian belief one thereby deprives oneself of the right to Christian morality… Christianity is a system, a consistently thought out and complete view of things. If one breaks out of it a fundamental idea, the belief in God, one thereby breaks the whole thing to pieces: one has nothing of any consequence left in one's hand… Christian morality is a command: its origin is transcendental… it possesses truth only if God is truth – *it stands or falls with the belief in God* (1990, pp. 80-81; emphasis added).

Philosopher Joel Marks admits that his atheism implies amorality "The long and the short of it is that I became convinced that atheism implies amorality; and since I am an atheist, I must therefore embrace amorality... without God, there is no morality" (2012, p. 2). In this view, since universal morality can only issue from God, and since there is no God, there is no objective morality. If there is no morality, what right do we have to judge anyone in our hedonistic culture in which the number one song at the time of writing is *WAP* (wet a** p***y), full of every vulgar word in the book and sung by two scantily dressed women groping one another? Aldous Huxley warned us in his *Brave New World*: "As political and economic freedom diminishes, sexual freedom tends compensatingly to increase" (1946, p. xix). I do not mean this as a call for state censorship, a practice that only advances state power. In a moral nation where most people are dedicated to God, and whose consciences serve as personal censors, such displays of vulgarity in the public square would be inconceivable.

The only displays in the public square that are censored by the state today are displays that remind us of our duty to the Creator. Christians are increasingly being targeted by the state for doing so. Citing events that occurred from 2012 to 2015, the International Christian Concern (ICC) *Hall of Shame Report* included the United States for the first time among the nations persecuting Christians. The report stated that the: "ICC sees these worrying trends as an alarming indication of the decline in religious liberty in the United States" (2017, p. 11). A report from the First Liberty Institute (Shackelford, 2017) documents 1,400 incidents from 2005 to 2016 of people in the USA being persecuted for exercising what used to be called religious freedom.

Among these incidents is a high school football coach fired for kneeling in prayer after games; if he had kneeled for BLM he would have been lauded. Among other incidents was an air force veteran manhandled off the stage for daring to use the word "God" in his speech at a friend's retirement ceremony; the Department of Veteran's Affairs banning prayers at funerals containing the words "Jesus" or "God," and a navy chaplain disciplined for counseling sailors using biblical wisdom. These attacks are aided by far-left organizations such as the Southern Poverty Law Center (SPLC) which labels organizations that support religious or traditional family issues as "hate groups". Included in such groups are the Alliance Defending Religious Freedom, First Liberty Institute, the American Family Association, and the Association of American Physicians and Surgeons, along with true hate groups such as the KKK and the American Nazi Party. While Christian ministries are on the SPLC's hate map, violent leftist groups such as Antifa and Black Lives Matter are nowhere to be found. The SPLC, which has publicly pledged to "destroy" any organization with whom it disagrees, is surely itself a hate group.

We appear to have absentmindedly agreed to a collective Faustian bargain, trading our souls and moral integrity for mindless hedonism. Having made such a bargain, can we survive for very long as a free society? Eminent historian Will Durant didn't think so, and noted that: "Conduct, deprived of its religious supports, deteriorates into epicurean chaos; and life itself, shorn of consoling faith, becomes a burden alike to conscious poverty and to weary wealth. In the end a society and its religion tend to fall together, like body and soul, in a harmonious death" (1935, p. 71). In another work with Ariel Durant, they made the observation that: "*There is no significant example in history... of a society successfully maintaining moral life without the aid of religion* (1968, p. 51; emphasis added).

The gravest threat to religious freedom, and therefore to freedom generally, today is the radical LGBTQ agenda that wants to assert its rights and to destroy faith-based to affirm their demands. It is a dire threat because it provides multiple inroads for the state to trample on other rights our forefathers considered inalienable. If it can deny us these rights, it can deny us anything. There can only be one ultimate master: God or the state. If one abandons God, life becomes shorn of any real purpose or ultimate meaning, and one may then, as Chesterton observed, turn to the worship of the state. When enough people do this, then it will not be long before Western societies lose all freedoms and rights bequeathed to us by our Christian forefathers. In his farewell address to the nation upon leaving his second term as President of the United States, George Washington warned the nation that freedom, morality, and prosperity cannot be maintained without God:

> Of all the dispositions and habits which lead to political prosperity, Religion and Morality are indispensable supports. In vain would that man claim the tribute of Patriotism who should labor to subvert these great

> Pillars of human happiness-these firmest props of the duties of Men and citizens... Let it simply be asked, Where is the security for property, for reputation, for life, if the sense of religious obligation desert the oaths, which are the instruments of investigation in Courts of Justice? And let us with caution indulge the supposition that morality can be maintained without religion. Whatever may be conceded to the influence of refined education on minds of peculiar structure, reason and experience both forbid us to expect that National morality can prevail in exclusion of religious principle (1796, np).

President Calvin Coolidge echoed this insight in his speech in the 150th anniversary of the Declaration of Independence; when he remarked that our rights "have their source and their roots in the religious convictions. ...Unless the faith of the American people in these religious convictions is to endure, the principles of our Declaration will perish" (in Dyer, 2015, p. 118). These presidential warnings have been ignored as various administrations, especially the Obama administration, have run roughshod over our religious convictions. The courts, at all levels, have also been complicit in this. In an attempt to stem the tide, Congress responded with the First Amendment Defense Act (FADA), and President Trump signed it into law in 2019. The Act puts guardrails in place for judges to ensure they rule in accordance with First Amendment rights. The founding fathers would be shocked to hear that a Congressional act to protect a First Amendment right would be necessary in 21st century America. When a Constitutional right requires a Congressional act to back it up, you know religious freedom is in trouble. The Act reads in part:

> Protecting religious freedom from government intrusion is a government interest of the highest order. Legislation advances this interest by remedying, deterring, and preventing government interference with religious exercise in a way that complements the protections mandated by the First Amendment to the Constitution of the United States.
>
> Laws that protect the free exercise of religious beliefs and moral convictions about marriage will encourage private citizens and institutions to demonstrate tolerance for those beliefs and convictions and therefore contribute to a more respectful, diverse, and peaceful society.

Not surprisingly, Democratic politicians, the ACLU, and various other anti-Christian groups mounted a campaign against the Act. One wonders if the Supreme Court will treat it as it did the RFRA by ruling that it does not apply to the states, or if the Biden administration will treat it as null and void. Unlike the practically unanimous bipartisan vote for the RFRA, 14 Democrats voted against FADA in the Senate and only *one* Democrat voted for it in the House. This makes it crystal clear that the great majority of Democratic lawmakers today are hostile to religious freedom.

The wide difference between support for the RFRA and the FADA is doubtless the result of the advent the LGBTQ movement in the 26 years between the two Acts. Perhaps the greater atheism among liberal democrats also played a large role. There are theistic liberal Democrats, just as there are atheistic conservative Republicans, but atheism is found mostly among those on the left-wing of American politics. According to the Pew Research Center, 4% of Americans identify as atheists. Of that 4%, 69% who identify themselves as atheists identify politically as liberal Democrats while only 10% of self-identified atheists identify politically as conservative Republicans (Lipka, 2016). Moreover, the religious freedom attitude of the respective Republican and Democratic lawmakers is mirrored in the general population. When asked by researchers from the Pew Research Center (2016) if wedding vendors should be required to serve same-sex marriage, 27% of Republicans and 67% of Democrats said that they should. When asked if vendors should be able to refuse, 71% of Republicans and 30% of Democrats said they should be able to refuse.

The ultimate proof of the value of Christianity is that freedom, human rights and democracy are, with rare exceptions, only found in nations founded on Christian principles. Religion is a uniquely valuable check on government abuse of power because it recognizes a source of transcendental authority above the state. Socialists know that complete subjugation of the individual to the state can only occur if Christianity is destroyed and that there can only be one ultimate master: God or the state. If one abandons God, life becomes shorn of any real purpose or ultimate meaning, and one may then turn to the worship of Big Government. When enough people do this, then it will not be long before Western societies lose the freedoms and rights hard fought for and won by our Christian forefathers.

Chapter 13

CONCLUDING REMARKS ON THE BATTLE FOR RELIGIOUS LIBERTY

THE POLITICAL LEFT AND SUBVERSIVE RELIGION

David Horowitz, agnostic Jew and former communist turned conservative, has noted that:

"Since its birth in the fires of the French Revolution, the political left has been at war with religion and with the Christian religion in particular" (2019, p. 3). The experience of the French Revolution could well be a precursor to what may happen closer to home if we are not vigilant. Religious liberty is one of the reasons that has made America great, but so far it appears to be losing its battle with American Jacobins trying to destroy it. Principled men and women know that America's religious conscience is precious, and are willing to risk everything to preserve it. As a community of the faithful with a strong tradition of transmitting values of meaning across the generations, Christianity serves our nation by providing it with an independent moral voice. Religious adherents have bona fide claims of allegiance to a power greater than the state, and because of this challenge to the state's claim of ultimate power, it weakens its control over our lives. Religious people look to their religious traditions for moral guidance, which may lead them to refuse to accept the will of the

> state when they see it as unjust. The nature of religion is not just to believe, but to act, and to act at times without regard to what the state, and perhaps most of its members, consider a settled moral truth. This may be considered subversive, but subversion has served American democracy well from the Revolution to the Civil Rights movement. Subversion in defense of liberty is exactly why we have a First Amendment.

It is this subversive nature of religion that leads America's political left to be suspicious of religious belief, and to scorn religious liberty. "Religion poses a threat to the intellectual world of the liberal tradition because it is a form of social life that mobilizes the deepest passions of believers in the course of creating institutions that stand between individuals and the state." (Tushnet, 1988, p. 248). As strong believers in the ultimate supremacy of the state, to the leftist the idea of any group refusing to bow to the law, or to even what they may call reason, simply cannot be tolerated. Thus, the left's enmity toward the Christian values that shaped America is deep and strong. As Historian Joseph Loconte remarks: "There are a lot of people on the cultural left who think that political liberalism is, and ought to be, the enemy of traditional religion. And they're happy about that. I think many on the left want their particular vision of liberalism to render religious belief irrelevant and to keep people of faith confined to their little sanctuaries" (2019, p. 9). It is of no concern to the cultural left that governments which respect religious liberty tend to respect all freedoms, and that respect is strongly related to economic freedom and prosperity. Because many on the left support socialism, which only respects the state, they yearn for a quiet spot in the middle of the herd. The frightening trend toward socialism in America is revealed in a Pew Research study (2019) which showed that 65% of Democrats have a favorable view of socialism, and even among Republicans, 9% had a favorable view of it.

Not all leftists, of course, are anti-Christian, and some are even good and moral Christians as they view Christian morality. There is even an organized Christian left represented by the Sojourners, but the bulk of their literature reveals that they are more left than Christian. Charles Hall (1997) notes that over 50% of the *Sojourner* magazine is devoted to critiques of American institutions and practices and the promotion of alternative lifestyles. In one of its editions, none of its five major articles were strictly religious. They were politically correct offerings, such as one asserting that engaging in a culture practice different from one's own is "appropriating" that culture. Another article written by Jamar Boyd, a theology graduate, comments that: "America is still led by an apathetic majority void of compassion, empathy, and sympathy. A majority unable and unwilling to confess their biases, hate, phobia, and toxicity" (2018, np). This is the kind of anti-American rhetoric that is typical of the left, even from the Christian left.

Living in a society where objective truth does not exist and morals are relative, the Sojourners seek to apply this secular worldview to the spiritual realm of Christianity. According to Hall: "Eschatologically, Sojourners envisions an ideal world where social structures and institutions will no longer be necessary—a complete destruction of the old order, characteristic of transformative movements" (p. 29). Christian eschatology, on the other hand, is unconcerned with this life; it is about the fulfillment of God's promises and purposes, the second coming of Jesus Christ, and everlasting life with God. The Sojourner's theology is human-centered, with the core tenets of tolerance, self-acceptance, and personal fulfillment. These are healthy goals, but they hollow out the spiritual core of Christianity. Sojourners view Christianity as providing *situational* ethics rather than universal morality as their guide to right behavior, but the guide is changeable dependent on circumstances. On the other hand, conservative Christians view Christianity as providing universal and timeless moral truths that tell us what we should do regardless of circumstances.

ALIENATION AND "CLEVER SILLINESS" IN ACADEMIA

The attack on America's Judeo/Christian heritage is part of a larger attack on all things white and Western. Leading the charge are the intellectuals of academia who pride themselves in open mindedness. Freed by lifelong tenure, they are able to pursue whatever nonsense they can think up. Abstract thinking outside the box may lead to new and useful developments in the physical sciences where practitioners can explore counter-intuitive phenomena, but when social science and humanities types and get into abstractions about human conduct political and socioeconomic issues it's a different story altogether. Humans have brains with built-in biases for certain kinds of social relationships and practices, how to get along within them, and how social intuitions should work. When intellectuals in the social sciences involve themselves in abstractions about such things they run up against our built-in biases. Physician and evolutionary psychologist Bruce Charlton calls these intellectuals "clever sillies" who over think social phenomena to the point of utter confusion in matters where common sense would better suffice. He says that they embrace ideas "about social phenomena that are not just randomly inaccurate (due to inappropriately misapplying abstract analysis) but are *systematically* wrong" (2009, p. 869). Clever silliness springs from what he calls "IQ-advertising", and it amounts to the rejection of the wisdom of ages, traditional morality, religion, universal truths, and the allure of the dreams of the should and ought. Charlton defines clever silliness as a:

> ... somewhat tragic state; because it entails being cognitively trapped by compulsive abstraction; unable to engage directly and spontaneously with what most humans have traditionally regarded as psycho-social reality; disbarred from the common experience of humankind and instead cut-adrift on the surface of a glittering but shallow ocean of novelties: none of which can ever truly convince or satisfy. It is to be alienated from the world; and to find no stable meaning of life that is solidly underpinned by emotional conviction (p. 869).

The American intellectual views it as a sacred duty to be against anything that most Americans revere. For leftist True Believers, the United States is the moral equivalent of a leper wrapped in the putrid rags of racism, sexism, bigotry, homophobia, xenophobia and hatred and thus its foundational values and institutions, to steal a Barack Obama's infamous phrase once more, must be "fundamentally transformed". Jean Elshtain has remarked that "to be an intellectual, you have to be *against* it, whatever *it* is. The intellectual is a negator. Affirmation is not in his or her vocabulary. In our view, anti-Americanism is a central part of this wider moral order" (in

Fleming, & O'Carroll, 2004, p. 2). To get the attention of unconventional folks attracted to faddish abstractions something radical, idealistic, and challenging is needed, and socialism fits the bill nicely. Gustave LeBon, perhaps the smartest Frenchman of the 19th century, noted how discontented and alienated academics become the intellectual spearheads of socialism.

> It is from the ranks of the demi-savant [people whose knowledge comes only from books; never the real world], and notably from the ranks of unemployed licentiates [a degree between master and doctor in some European countries] and bachelors of the universities, outcasts from society whom the State has been unable to place, ushers discontented with their lot, university professors who find their merits overlooked, that the most dangerous disciples of Socialism are recruited (2001, p. 46).

Intellectuals in the humanities and social sciences are a subset of people of intelligence. They are not the smartest subset, but they are the influential keyboard commandos who shape the cultural narrative by controlling the flow of ideas in their academic writings and classroom instruction. They are the intellectual wordsmiths who craft the narratives and teach the classes that help to shape public views. Their ideas trickle down to others outside academia who are not intellectuals but who share the intellectual's sense of alienation. This trickle-down effect was manifested for a good portion of 2020 as BLM and Antifa thugs rampaged across America's Democrat controlled cities, pillaging, looting, vandalizing, and burning. This is not just random vandalism; it is the deliberate repudiation of the principles of the Constitution and the Declaration of Independence. In a July, 4th, 1926, speech, Calvin Coolidge issued a warning about allowing the Christian roots of the Declaration of Independence to wither: "Unless the faith of the American people in these religious convictions is to endure, the principles of our Declaration will perish. We cannot continue to enjoy the result if we neglect and abandon the cause" (in Humes, 2016, p. 61). Leftists are not merely neglecting or abandoning the cause, they are actively engaged in destroying it. They are not only attacking our religious roots, they are attacking our secular historical roots by vandalizing or demolishing any statue of great Americans in sight as leftist-appeasing mayors ordered the police to stand down and give the rioters "space to destroy".

Noting with undisguised relish that BLM and Antifa rioters tore down the Francis Scott Key monument in San Francisco's Golden Gate Park, *LA Times* columnist Jody Rosen wrote an op-ed piece calling for removing the Star-Spangled Banner as our national anthem. Alternatives such as America the Beautiful or God Bless America, just won't do, because they reflect "uncomplicated patriotism" which Rosen says "doesn't wash in 2020." These songs celebrate love of country, which Rosen evidently despises. His choice for our national anthem is Bill Withers' *Lean on Me*, because it is a song that doesn't lift our gaze toward God. He opines that *Lean on Me* "represents the very best of this country. Not only is Black music the finest American thing, the greatest gift that the United States has given to world culture, it is one of the deepest, most truthful repositories of American history" (2020, np). Rosen's article would be hilarious if it did not so tragically reflect the atheistic left's true attitude toward their country.

Perhaps Rosen's comments were inspired by *The New York Times Magazine's* "1619 Project", which aims to reframe the country's history by replacing July 4th, 1776 with August 20th, 1619, when the first slaves landed on our shores, as the true founding of America. The 1619 Project is a collection of essays aimed at rewriting American history, with the partial title of the opening essay revealing its steep leftist slant: "Our democracy's ideals were false when they were written" (Hannah-Jones, 1919, p.14). Among the essays are claims such as the American Revolution was fought to preserve slavery, the Constitution is a racist rich white man's document, black Americans forged our democracy, and America was built on slavery. The same rhetorical move is made over and over again in these essays: The United States is downright evil. Slavery is not just a long-dead odious practice, for these ink slingers its legacy is felt today in the treatment of prisoners, excess sugar consumption, the lack of universal health care, and even traffic jams; yes, traffic jams! You will have to read these scribblers for yourself to see how they manage to make their tenuous connections. Thousands of extra copies of the *New York Time Magazine* were printed and distributed to schools, and it is now part of the curriculum. Democratic presidential hopeful Beto O' Rourke endorsed the 1619 Project in a primary debate, which met with nods of approval from others on the stage. When the nation's largest newspaper and leading Democrats endorse the Project, and with it in the curriculum of many high schools, the integrity of the Union is threated by denial of the noble principles on which it was founded.

Historian Jamie Glazov, whose family fled the tyranny of the Soviet Union, argues that many hard leftist intellectuals in America bitterly lament the fall of the Soviet Union as the alternative to American capitalism were rejuvenated by 9/11, which they saw as another opportunity to vindicate their opposition to everything American. Because the communist revolution has, he says, lost its momentum, other causes must be found, and the Islamist cause fits the bill. The enemies of both the hard left and radical Islam are America, freedom, and Christianity. Glazov nicely analyzes the totalitarian streak, alienation, self-loathing, and character flaws of rife among radical left intellectuals and why they long for socialist collectivism:

> The believer's totalitarian journey begins with an acute sense of alienation from his own society—an alienation to which he is himself completely blind. In denial about the character flaws that prevent him from bonding with his own people, the believer has convinced himself that there is something profoundly wrong with his society... He fantasizes about building a perfect society he will, finally, fit in... Tortured by his personal alienation, which is accompanied by self-loathing, the believer craves a fairy-tale world where no individuality exists, and where human estrangement is thus impossible. The believer fantasizes about how his own individuality and self will be submerged within the collective whole (2009, pp. 6-7).

Anti-Americanism among the hard left often displays the most atrocious levels of callousness. After watching the airplanes flying into the Twin Towers and the Pentagon, history professor Richard Berthold remarked to his students: "Anybody who blows up the Pentagon gets my vote" (in O'Neil, 2008). Another American leftist gleefully clapping at the death and destruction of 9/11 was ethnic studies professor Ward LeRoy Churchill, likening the Twin Towers victims to the architect of the Holocaust, Adolf Eichmann, who deserved their fate:

> If there was a better, more effective, or in fact another way of visiting some penalty befitting their participation upon the little Eichmanns inhabiting the sterile sanctuary of the twin towers, I'd really be interested in hearing about it... No matter what its eventual fate, America will have gotten off very, very cheap. The full measure of its guilt can never be fully balanced or atoned for (2005, np).

ABOLISH WHITENESS

Dennis Prager has noted that: "Contempt for America is so central to leftism that there would be no leftism without it" (2018, np). There are programs in our universities that fly under the moniker of "whiteness studies" that are the quintessence of Prager's statement. Don't expect whiteness courses to celebrate white identity as black, women's, Chicano, ethnic, or queer studies courses celebrate those human categories. Students in such a class will hear that: "Whiteness is, variously, a metaphor for power, a proxy for racially distributed material benefits, a synonym for 'white supremacy,' an epistemological stance defined by power, a position of invisibility or ignorance, and a set of beliefs about racial 'Others' and oneself that can be rejected through 'treason' to a racial category" (Arnsen, 2001, p. 9).

Students in whiteness study classes will not hear that white Western civilization has been responsible for just about every advance in science, medicine, technology, democracy, the free market, and the rule of law. Rather, they will hear that the United States is the most warlike nation in history; that it practically invented slavery, that it exploits workers, women, children, and people of color, and that white people are relentlessly racist and sexist. Whiteness studies are guilt trips masquerading as education and taught by impeccably politically correct types who proclaim that whiteness is evil: "It is not merely that whiteness is oppressive and false", wrote David

Roediger, a self-proclaimed white "race traitor", it is that whiteness is *nothing but* oppressive and false" (1994, p. 13; emphasis added).

In whiteness studies, "whiteness" is the tendency of whites not to define themselves by their race and to be blind to the supposed privileges associated with it. They are quite right on this point; we don't see whites celebrating whiteness in the same way that we see blacks celebrating their race—a white pride parade replete with "White is Beautiful" slogans would be an unforgivably politically incorrect display of white supremacy. Whites are told that they must struggle against their privilege. Paula Rothenberg explains that her struggle against her privilege was difficult, and chastises whites who remain impervious to it, telling them that "decent people should know better" (2000, p. 8). Reading between the lines, she is saying: "I am wise enough to know that I'm poisoned by my white privilege and decent enough to renounce it".

Taking it one-step further is Noel Ignatiev's statement at a conference at UC Berkeley, on abolishing whiteness that: "The United States, like every capitalist society, is composed of masters and slaves" (1997, np). At the ultra-liberal UC Berkley, this was taken by the affluent slaves in the audience as just too cool not to be true, and it received a rousing applause of affirmation. Ignatiev and fellow Marxist John Garvey are quite serious about their contempt for their race. In 1993 they founded a journal actually *devoted* to race hatred called *Race Traitor.* The journal contains the following mission statement:

> RACE TRAITOR aims to serve as an intellectual center for those seeking to abolish the white race. It will encourage dissent from the conformity that maintains it and popularize examples of defection from its ranks, analyze the forces that hold it together and those that promise to tear it apart. Part of its task will be to promote debate among abolitionists. When possible, it will support practical measures, guided by the principle, Treason to whiteness is loyalty to humanity (1996).

Ignatiev was deadly serious about this, writing in Harvard University's magazine: "Make no mistake about it: we intend to keep bashing the dead white males, and the live ones, and the females too, until the social construct known as 'the white race' is destroyed—not 'deconstructed' but destroyed" (2002, p. 2). In the Orwellian atmosphere of the "Great Awokening" on campuses across America, Ignatiev's "Treason to whiteness is loyalty to humanity" motto has become almost sacred. Universities are actively promoting programs seeking to impose self-loathing on white students as a way of making non-white students feel better about themselves. The goal is to create racial shame in young white college students, and certainly not to create pride in their country and its Judeo/Christian values. Michael West echoes the self-loathing theme that animates such a strategy: "The failure of the socialist projects of the twentieth century led many on the left to give up any hope…we have become self-hating, deeming Western man as an agent merely of war, racism, slavery" (2005, p. 5).

The Anti-Christian Crusade of the New Atheists

There is a subset of academics who do not spew anti-American rhetoric but who go to great lengths to attack America's Christian heritage known as the new atheists. "New atheism is a loosely defined movement that has emerged over the past decade as prominent scholars and public intellectuals have made their opposition to religion public" (Schulzke, 2013, p. 780). The new atheists are led by the intellectually gifted "Four Horsemen" of atheism: Richard Dawkins, Daniel Dennett, Sam Harris, and Christopher Hitchens. These men are not classical atheists, they are anti-theists. In the hands of these clever wordsmiths, atheism has repackaged the old philosophical arguments as doctrinal commitment delivered in an aggressive and dogmatic way. The basic tenet of the movement is that religion is irrational, should not be tolerated, and must be robustly attacked by rational folk like themselves.

What is "new" about the new atheism movement is its scientism, its political activism, and its confrontational tone. Except during the French Revolution, pre-modern atheism rarely assumed an overtly political and anti-Christian character. The goal of the new atheism movement, stated forcefully in articles and best-selling books (Dawkins's *God Delusion*, for instance, remained on the *New York Times* best-seller list for 51 weeks), like the Jacobins of the French Revolution, is to delegitimize and extinguish religion. Its popularity among leftists stems from the fact that it can be linked to wider and more expansive political goals. Marcus Schulzke (2013) applauds new atheism as a political movement designed to spread the liberal/progressive/socialist worldview. Schulzke complains that traditional atheists are too willing to let their atheism coexist as separate discourses and keep their non-belief a private thing. New atheists don't want to accommodate such a notion and urge atheists to "come out of the closet" and let the world know what they think.

Richard Dawkins says that the "God hypothesis" should be treated as a falsifiable scientific hypothesis. Theism and atheism are thesis and antithesis, the latter exists only because the former exists. If atheists want theists to provide evidence for the existence of God, then they too should provide evidence that God does not exist if it is to be a valid antithesis. But like the prisoner in the dock, an atheist doesn't feel it necessary to defend his position since it is an entirely negative one of simply denying the evidence theists point to. Neither side, of course, can prove their position scientifically since God is by definition outside of the methods of science. Theistic scientists make the effort, however, by using the method of abductive reasoning. That is, by looking at multiple lines of evidence from all scientific endeavors and reasoning to the best explanation (Lipton, 2000). Abductive reasoning is not deductive certainty, but falling back on our courtroom metaphor, it engages the "beyond a reasonable doubt" test, while leaving open the possibility of a different explanation. When theistic scientists ponder the exquisite precision of the initial conditions of the Big Bang, and the mind-blowing fine-tuning of the laws for intelligent life, they see these things as evidence of a transcendent designer (Lennox, 2009, Walsh, 2020). Atheists simply dismiss all this out of hand as probability-defying coincidences. But as Wilkins and Moreland contend: "Like it or not, a significant and growing number of scientists, historians of science and philosophers of science see more scientific evidence now for a personal creator and designer than was available fifty years ago" (2010, p. 10).

God Bless the Atheist Civil Liberties Union

As dangerous as the academic left is, it can only persuade; it cannot force. The law, however, can. It does so when either the plaintiff or defendant triumphs in the courts and judges hand down rulings. When a religious liberty claim involving Christians comes before the courts, we inevitably see the mighty ACLU gearing up to oppose it. It is this legal power that is dangerous. The stated mission of the ACLU is "to defend and preserve the individual rights and liberties guaranteed to every person in this country by the United States Constitution". This is a statement of pure hypocrisy. We have seen how this has played out when Christian vendors have battled for their First and Thirteenth Amendment rights. The irony has been that those freedoms have needed to be defended by legal groups such as the Alliance Defending Freedom or the First Liberty Institute *from* the legal onslaughts of the ACLU. As the Alliance Defending Freedom points out: "Far from the noble protector of our constitutional rights many Americans believe it to be, the ACLU has from its earliest days deliberately and patiently chipped away at the legal, moral, and religious foundations of our Republic" (in Walsh & Hemmens, 2020, p. 21).

Philosopher Michael Novak aptly renames the American Civil Liberties Union "the Atheist Civil-Liberty Union" and provides a number of reasons for doing so.

> The American Civil Liberties Union has a public agenda, and that agenda appears to be this: to make the United States in all her public manifestations reflect an atheist's view of the nation's Founding and continuing existence. In item #84 on the ACLU's published agenda that calls for the elimination of "In G-d We Trust? from our coins" "Under G-d" must also be torn from the Pledge of Allegiance. The Commandments given Moses must never appear as public symbols under government auspices. This nation must so thoroughly appear to be atheist in public as to be, in fact, and for all practical purposes, atheist in all public spheres (2002, np)

The ACLU is not against all religion; it is only against religions falling under the umbrella of Judeo/Christian beliefs and values. For instance, when the University of North Carolina (UNC) established a requirement that all incoming freshmen read *Approaching the Qu'ran: The Early Revelations,* the North Carolina ACLU rushed to support the University in federal district court when it was challenged by concerned citizens (*Yacovelli v. Moeser*, 2002). UNC won their case and the subsequent appeal thanks to the ACLU's legal muscle. Imagine the ACLU's response had UNC mandated that incoming freshmen read the Bible or the Talmud. The ACLU has done everything it could to remove the last vestiges of Judeo/Christian teachings from our schools, but defends attempted Islamic indoctrination (students could later opt out of the requirement and substitute a one- or two-page paper outlining their objections). Islam represents the antithesis to everything our Constitution holds dear, particularly the rights found in the First Amendment. The anointed ones of the ACLU are well aware of this, but "the enemy of my enemy is my friend". The actions if the ACLU vindicates Jamie Glazov's view that the radical left has embraced Islam as the new champion of anti-Americanism.

The ACLU has finally acknowledged its left-wing bias. According to former Harvard law professor, liberal Democrat, and long-time ACLU member, Alan Dershowitz: "The director of the American Civil Liberties Union has now acknowledged what should have been obvious to everybody over the past several years: The ACLU is no longer a neutral defender of everyone's civil liberties. It has morphed into a hyper-partisan, hard-left political advocacy group" (2018, np). It has shown its true colors by advocating Marcuse's tolerance for speech from the atheist left but intolerance for Christian speech. It has stoutly defended pornography as free speech, but never defends Christian speech when it clashes with LGBTQ causes. The ACLU has been a major player in almost every court case on the side of the left's goal of purging religion from the public square. It has defended the Man/Boy Love Association that advocates "Sex before eight, or else it's too late", but has fought against the Boy Scouts holding their Jamborees on government property because they have the audacity to pray and swear an oath of duty to God (Boychuk, 2000). The ACLU is a destructive force engaged in undermining the Constitution and attempting to steal our Judeo/Christian heritage so it can steal our country.

What We Would Lose without Christianity

I have dipped my pen only briefly in some of the cases in which the ACLU has supported state bureaucrats or individuals seeking to undermine the works of Christian charities. People who, for whatever reason, cheer these efforts, may have no idea what their society would lose were these charities to disappear. Numerous books and countless scholarly articles attest to the practical value for society of that which the left labors to destroy and atheism cannot replace. Faith-based charities such as Feeding America, Lutheran World Relief, the Salvation Army, and many more, dispense as much as 75% of all charity in the United States (Richardson, 2017, np). According to the Pontifical Council for Pastoral Assistance to Health Care Workers: "the Catholic Church manages 26 percent of health care facilities in the world... the Church has 117,000 health care facilities, including hospitals, clinics, orphanages, as well as 18,000 pharmacies and 512 centers for the care of those with leprosy" (Catholic News Agency, 2017, np). Catholic Charities USA, supplemented by a panoply of other Catholic-affiliated groups, has "emerged as the largest private provider of social welfare services" (Degeneffe, 2003, p. 374). It serves millions of people each year regardless of their religion, sex, race, or sexual orientation. Numerous other Christian and Jewish groups cater indiscriminately to all manner of people in need.

Atheists and humanists claim they have charities, but they are utterly anemic compared to Christian charities. Ask your atheist friends where the nearest atheist- or humanist-based orphanage is. Without Christian charity the needs of the poor, sick, homeless, and helpless may go unmet. This was the conclusion of D. J. Taylor on noting that the city of Norwich topped the table for "no religious belief" in the British census. Taylor wrote: "my godless city is full of Christian charity. ...But it would be difficult to deny that, first, the church is still making its presence felt here in the Great Eastern

Land, and, second, were you to take it out of Norwich, or any other similarly sized city, you would create a gaping hole that no government agency—and certainly not the British Humanist Association—would ever be able to fill" (2012, np). If Christian charities step aside then government welfare will have to step in. Christian charities, however, aim to care for the whole person rather than simply handing out welfare checks, offering support and counseling to those they cater to. Moreover, only 25% of state tax dollars targeted for welfare programs go to the needy, and the rest going for administration. On the other hand, 75% of Christian charity monies go to the poor (Edwards, 2007).

As for private giving, there is a mountain of articles showing that practicing Christians live up to the "Love thy neighbor" command far more than atheists. An American national sample of 12,100 adults indicated that: "more frequent church attendance and greater participation in religious activities increase the levels and likelihood of both religious and/or secular giving" (Forbes & Zampelli, 2013, p. 2487). A study of 30,000 people from 50 different sites across the U.S. found that people who attend church once or more per week were 25% more likely to donate money, and 23% more likely to volunteer time than their secular counterparts (Brooks, 2003). Yet another study across 29 states found that practicing Christians give far more time and money, and far more often, to both religious and secular causes than secularists (Brooks, 2004). Journalist George Will summarized it bluntly: "America is largely divided between religious givers and secular nongivers" (2008, np).

David Campbell and Robert Putnam's (2010) sweeping look at contemporary American religion in *American Grace* provide a number of reasons why practicing Christians make better neighbors than their secular counterparts. They note that 40% of church attenders regularly volunteer to help the poor and elderly, compared with 15% of their secular counterparts. This was true for all kinds of services; giving money, donating blood, extending help to acquaintances experiencing hard times, such as unemployment, depression, or ill-health. The evidence that Christians live better, healthier, and longer lives, are happier with more stable and loving families, are much less likely to commit crimes and abuse mind-altering substances is unequivocal (Walsh, 2020). Most leftists are too smart to plead ignorance of the evidence, so they simply ignore it or look at it with such jaundiced eyes that their brains become so befuddled that they get things backwards. I have challenged atheist colleagues to produce one, just one, published peer reviewed article showing that Christians are less happy, more depressed, less healthy, more criminal, and less charitable than atheists—I'm still waiting.

CONCLUSION

We have witnessed a blizzard of legal persecutions of people who refuse to bow to state demands to violate their faith since the legalization of homosexual conduct in 2003, and many more are still winding their way in the legal system. Many small business owners have lost their livelihoods and have been subjected to the most egregious humiliation by agents of the state and by LGBTQ activists. Radical LGBTQ activists see Christianity as their enemy, although there are many good Christian gays and lesbians. Radical activists are intent on using the law to gain revenge for the suffering of previous generations of their peers by attempting to repeal what Thucydides, the father of history, called the "general laws of humanity" and what we call the rights granted to us by the Creator made manifest in the United States Constitution. To champion freedom of expression and conscience only for those who share your views while demanding that others be silenced, you may recall, is Herbert Marcuse's socialist goal of tolerating only views from the left. "Free speech for me but never for thee" is neither tolerant nor principled. In his *History of the Peloponnesian Wars,* describing the outbreak of civil war on the island of Corcyra in 427 BC, Thucydides makes this trenchant point:

> Indeed, it is true that in these acts of revenge on others men take it upon themselves to begin the process of repealing those general laws of humanity which are there to give a hope of salvation to all who are in distress, instead of leaving those laws in existence, remembering that there

> may come a time when they, too, will be in danger and will need their protection (1971, p. 245).

Every American should be free to peacefully live and work consistent with their beliefs, without government coercion. Expressive freedom belongs to all; it belongs to the conservative and the liberal, to the black and to the white, to the theist and the atheist, and to the gay and the straight. If, in this seemingly endless battle between religious liberty and LGBTQ rights, we strip away the rights contained in the First Amendment for one group, all other groups are in danger of losing them. We are all in danger of losing them when our Christian beliefs and values that have contributed immeasurably to our freedom and prosperity are labeled as intolerable. A truly tolerant society is one that is supposed to welcomes diverse beliefs rather than laboring aggressively to homogenize them in line with government approved orthodoxy. If we truly value freedom of expression and belief we must take pains to protect them and not try to cast religious dissenters as bigots and destroy them. The freedom of LGBTQ individuals to live their lives openly in the public square is a positive development in the evolution of American culture, but it must not be at the expense of religious liberty. Judeo/Christian values are at the very root of the American republic; kill them and all of our freedoms will perish.

REFERENCES

Abraham, K., & White, G. (2018). The puzzle of the dignitary torts. *Cornell Law Review, 104:* 317-380.

ACLU (2013). *Masterpiece Cakeshop.* ACLU http://aclu-co.org/court-cases/masterpiece- cakeshop/

Ahend, G., Connelly, J. & Waggoner, K (2019). Amicus b*rief. State of Washington v. Arlene's Flowers Inc, Arlene's Flowers and Gifts, and Barronelle Stutzman.*

Aikman, D. (2012). *Jesus in Beijing: How Christianity is transforming China and changing the global balance of power.* New York: Regnery.

Alliance Defending Freedom (2015). Wash. floral artist's home, savings at risk of state seizure after court ruling. http://www.alliancedefendingfreedom.org/News/Detail?ContentID=83837

Alliance Defending Freedom (2017). *Petition for a Writ of Certiorari to the United States Supreme Court.* https://www.scotusblog.com/wp-content/uploads/2017/08/17-108-petition.pdf

American Thinker (2008). Obama 2001: Scrap the Constitution, spread the wealth. *American Thinker*, October, 27th http://www.americanthinker.com/blog/2008/10/obama_2001_scrap_the_constitut.html

Anderson, R. (2014). *Marriage, reason, and religious liberty: Much ado about sex, nothing to do with race.* Backgrounder No. 2894.

Anderson, R. & Ford, L. (2014). Protecting religious liberty in the state marriage debate. *Backgrounder,* No. 2891.

Antieau, C. J., Downey, A. T., & Roberts, E. C. (1964). *Freedom from Federal Establishment: Formation and Early History of the First Amendment Religion Clauses* (No. 1). Milwaukee, WI: Bruce Publishing Company.

AP VoteCast Survey (2020). *Understanding the 2020 electorate.* https://www.npr.org/2020/11/03/929478378/understanding-the-2020-electorate-ap-votecast-survey

Arias, M. (2020). *"I stood up for that": Pope Francis voices support for same-sex civil unions.*

Axios, October 20th. https://www.axios.com/pope-francis-advocate-civil-union-same-sex-couples-new-documentary-354239b9-4f27-47be-a8e0-e1c56a850bd3.html.

Arnesen, E. (2001). Whiteness and the historians' imagination. *International Labor and Working-Class History, 60:* 3-32.

Backholm, J. (2015). Arlene's Flowers response to Attorney General's settlement offer. *Family Policy Institute.* February 20. http://www.fpiw.org/blog/2015/02/20/barronelle-stutzmans-repsonse-attorney-general/

Bacon, F. (1889). *Of atheism. Essays, civil and moral. Book XVI. London: Cassell & Company.*

Bailey, Cynthia (1995) Workfare and involuntary servitude--What you wanted to know but were afraid to ask. *Boston College Third World Law Journal,* 15: 285-321.

Barton, D. (2016). America's most Biblically-hostile U.S. President. *Wallbuilders.* http://www.wallbuilders.com/libissuesarticles.asp?id=106938

Baskerville, S. (2011). The sexual agenda and religious freedom-challenges in the Western world. *International Journal for Religious Freedom, 4:* 91-105.

Bastiat, F. (2006). *The law.* Minneapolis, MN: Filiquarian.

Bean, T., & Wilson, R. (2020). The administrative state as a new front in the culture war: Little Sisters of the Poor Saints Peter and Paul Home v. Pennsylvania. *Cato Supreme Court Review,* 229-261.

Beitzinger, A. (2011). *A history of American political thought*. Eugene, OR: Resource Publications.

Benkof, D. (2008). Why California gays shouldn't celebrate state court ruling. *Seattle Post-Intelligencer.* http://www.seattlepi.com/local/opinion/article/Why-California-gays-shouldn-t-celebrate-state-1273942.php

Berg, T. (2010). What same-sex marriage and religious-liberty claims have in common. *Northwestern Journal of Law and Social Policy*, 5:206-35.

Bernstein, D. (2003). Defending the First Amendment from antidiscrimination laws. *North Carolina Law Review*, 82: 1-32.

Bleich, D. (2002). The physician as a conscientious objector. *Fordham Urban Law Journal, 30:* 245-265.

Berger, P. (1967). *The sacred canopy: Elements of a sociological theory of religion*. Garden City, NY: Doubleday.

Biden Campaign Staff. (2020). *The Biden Agenda for women*. https://joebiden.com/womens-agenda/#.

Bonventre, V. (2018). Religious liberty: Fundamental right or nuisance. *University of St. Thomas Law Journal, 14:* 650-692.

Botham, F. (2009). *Almighty God created the races: Christianity, interracial marriage, and American law.* Chapel Hill, NC: University of North Carolina Press.

Boyack, C. (2012). *Latter-Day Responsibility: Choosing Liberty Through Personal Accountability*. Springer Fork: UT: Cedar Fork.

Boychuk, B. (2000). *The ACLU versus freedom of assembly. Claremont Review of Books.* September 29th. https://claremontreviewofbooks.com/digital/the-aclu-versus-freedom-of-assembly/.

Boyd, J. (2018). The deadly apathy of white America, *Sojourners*, October 10th. https://sojo.net/articles/deadly-apathy-white-america.

Brown, B. (1992). Pornography and feminism: is law the answer? *Critical Quarterly, 34:*72-82.

Brown, S. (1912). *The Secularization of American Education: As Shown by State Legislation, State Constitutional Provisions, and State Supreme Court Decisions* (No. 49). Teachers College, Columbia University.

Buden, B. (2018). To make the long march short: A short commentary on the two long marches that have failed their emancipatory promises. *Crisis & Critique*, 5 :129–41.

Burk, R. (2014). Cardinal Burke on faith, the right to life, and the family: English exclusive. *Lifesite.* https://www.lifesitenews.com/news/english-exclusive-cardinal-burke-on-faith-the-right-to-life-and-the-family

Burke, E. (1841). *The works of the Right Hon. Edmund Burke: With a biographical and critical introduction* (Vol. 1). London: HG Bohn.

Butler, P. & Scanlan, A. (1961). Wall of Separation--Judicial gloss on the First Amendment. *Notre Dame Law Review, 37:* 288-308.

Catechism of the Catholic Church (nd). *Matrimony.* http://www.vatican.va/archive/ccc_css/archive/catechism/p2s2c3a7.htm

Catholic News Agency (2017). *Catholic hospitals comprise one quarter of world's healthcare, council reports.* February 10th. https://www.catholicnewsagency.com/news/catholic_hospitals_represent_26_percent_of_worlds_health_facilities_reports_pontifical_council.

Campbell, D. & Putnam, R. (2010). Religious people are 'better neighbors.' *USA TODAY.* November 15th. http://www.usatoday.com/news/opinion/forum/2010-11-15-column15_ST_N.htm

Campbell, J. (2019). KY Supreme Court rules in favor of print shop owner who stood for free speech. Alliance Defending Freedom, October, 31st. http://www.adfmedia.org/News/PRDetail/9254.

Charlton, B. (2009). Clever sillies: Why high IQ people tend to be deficient in common sense. *Medical Hypotheses*, 73:867-870.

Chesterton, G. (2001). *The Collected Works of G.K. Chesterton, Vol. 20.* San Francisco: Ignatius Press.

Churchill, W. L. (2005) "Some people push back": On the justice of roosting chickens. *Democracy Now*, February 18. http://www.kersplebedeb.com/mystuff/s11/churchill.html.

Churchill, W. S. (2012). What good's a Constitution. Hillsdale College Political Science Department (Ed.), *The US Constitution: A reader*, pp. 737-743.

Cairo Declaration on Human Rights in Islam (1990). *University of Minnesota Human Rights Library.* http://hrlibrary.umn.edu/instree/cairodeclaration.html.

Clarkson, J., Chambers, J., Hirt, E., Otto, A., Kardes, F., & Leone, C. (2015). The self-control consequences of political ideology. *Proceedings of the National Academy of Sciences of the United States of America, 112:* 8250-8253.

Coates, T. (2012) Thomas Jefferson was more than a man of his times. *The Atlantic*, December 4th. https://www.theatlantic.com/national/archive/2012/12/thomas-jefferson-was-more-than-a-man-of-his-times/265850/

Cogan, N. (2015). *The complete Bill of Rights: The drafts, debates, sources, and origins*. New York: Oxford University Press.

Colby, K. (2013). *Peaceful coexistence? Reconciling non-discrimination principles with civil liberties.* United States Commission on Civil Rights Briefing. Center for Law & Religious Freedom of the Christian Legal Society.

Conkle, D. (2001). The Free Exercise Clause: How Redundant, and Why. *Loyola University Chicago Law Journal, 33:* 95-119.

Coolidge, C. (1926). *Speeches as president (1923-1929): The inspiration of the Declaration of Independence,* July 5, 1926. Calvin Coolidge Presidential Foundation. https://www.coolidgefoundation.org/resources/speeches-as-president-1923-1929-7/

Cooper, J. (2013). Modern day segregation: States fighting to legally allow businesses to refuse service to same-sex couples under the shield of the first amendment. *Rutgers Journal of Law & Religion, 15:* 413-432.

Corbin, C. (2015). Speech or conduct? The free speech claims of wedding vendors. *Emory Law Journal, 65:* 241-302.

Coyne, G. V., & Heller, M. (2008). *A comprehensible universe: The interplay of science and theology*. New York: Springer-Verlag.

Cox, R. (1991). 'Real socialism' in historical perspective. *Socialist Register*, 27:169-193.

Crossland, K. (2013). Baker must cater to same-sex weddings, or else. *The World.* http://www.worldmag.com/2013/12/baker_must_cater_to_same_sex_weddings_or_else

Cruz, T. (2014). Supreme Court strikes down Obama Care abortion mandate, *Bay Area News.* June 30th. http://www.yourhoustonnews.com/bay_area/news/supreme-court-strikes-down-obamacare-abortion-mandate/article_bde716e9-2747-51c1-ab5f-63aef1e13353.html

Curry, J. & Battistoni, R. (2000) *The American Constitutional experience: Selected readings & Supreme Court opinions.* Dubuque, IA: Kendall/Hunt.

Degeneffe, C. (2003). What is Catholic about Catholic charities? *Social Work, 48:*374-383.

Dent Jr, G. (2007). Civil Rights for Whom?: Gay Rights Versus Religious Freedom. *Kentucky Law Journal, 95:*553-647.

DePlato, J. (2019). *The United States Supreme Court and Politics: Judicial Retirements, the Docket, and the Nomination Process.* Lanham, MD: Lexington Books.

Dershowitz, A. (2018). The final nail in the ACLU's coffin. *The Hill*, June 6th. http://thehill.com/opinion/civil-rights/391682-the-final-nail-in-the-aclus-coffin.

De Toledano, R. (2002). What the ACLU doesn't want you to know. *Insight on the News*, July 1.

Dewart, D. (2012). *On Writ of Certiorari to the United States Court of Appeals for the Ninth and Second Circuits: Brief of Liberty, Life and Law Foundation, and North Carolina Values Coalition as amici curiae in support of Hollingsworth and bipartisan legal advisory group addressing the merits and supporting reversal.* American Bar Association. thttps://www.glad.org/uploads/docs/cases/windsor-v-united-states/amicus-brief-of-liberty-life-and-law-foundation.pd.

Dolan, T. (2012). *Wall Street Journal op ed on religious freedom.* http://www.usccb.org/about/media-relations/resources/wall-street-journal-op-ed-on-religious-freedom.cfm

Donohue, W. (1985). *The politics of the American Civil Liberties Union.* New Brunswick, NJ: Transaction.

Dreher, R. (2015). Traditional Christians under siege. *Time Magazine*, April 13, 185:13.

Drescher, S. & Engerman, S. eds. (1998). *A Historical Guide to World Slavery. N*ew York: Oxford University Press.

Duncan, R. (1994). Who wants to stop the Church: Homosexual rights legislation, public policy, and religious freedom, *Notre Dame Law Review*, 69: 393-445.

Duncan, R. (2001). Free Exercise is dead, long live Free Exercise: *Smith, Lukumi* and the general applicability requirement. *University of Pennsylvania Journal of Constitutional Law 3:* 850-884.

Duncan, R. (2016). Justice Scalia and the rule of law: originalism vs. the living constitution. *Regent University Law Review*, *29:* 9-34.

Durant, W. (1935). *Our Oriental Heritage*. New York: Simon & Schuster.

Durant, W. & Durant, A. (1965). *The Age of Voltaire*. New York: Simon and Schuster.

Durant, W. & Durant, A. (1968) *The Lessons of History,* New York: Simon and Schuster.

Dyer, J. (Ed.). (2015). *American soul: the contested legacy of the Declaration of Independence*. Lanham, MD: Rowman & Littlefield.

Edwards, J. (2007). The costs of public income redistribution and private charity. *Journal of Libertarian Studies*, *21:* 3-20.

Ekins, E. (2019). *Poll: What Americans think cause wealth and poverty.* Cato Institute. https://www.cato.org/blog/poll-what-americans-think-cause-wealth-poverty.

Easton, J. (2005). Survey on physicians' religious beliefs shows majority faithful. *Medical Center Public Affairs,* University of Chicago Chronicle. July 14th.

Esbeck, C. (2011). Uses and abuses of textualism and originalism in Establishment Clause interpretation. *Utah Law Review,* 5*:* 489: 683.

Favocci, C. (2020). Even liberals are blasting this Biden team leader for refusing to defend the Bill of Rights vs. Islamic values. *The Federalist Papers*, November 17th. https://thefederalistpapers.org/us/even-liberals-blasting-biden-team-leader-refusing-defend-bill-rights-vs-islamic-values.

Federer, W. (1994). *America's God and Country: Encyclopedia of Quotations.* St. Louis, MO: Amerisearch, Inc.

Fleming, C., & O'Carroll, J. (2004). Understanding Anti-Americanism. *Anthropoetics*, *9:*1-20.

Flynn, T. (2010). Clarion call or false alarm: Why proposed exemptions to equal marriage statutes return us to a religious understanding of the public marketplace. *Northwestern Journal of Law & Social Policy, 5:* 236-259.

Forbes, K., & Zampelli, E. (2013). The impacts of religion, political ideology, and social capital on religious and secular giving: evidence from the 2006 Social Capital Community Survey. *Applied Economics*, *45*(17), 2481-2490.

Free Legal Dictionary (nd). http://legal-dictionary.thefreedictionary.com/Involuntary+Servitude. Legal Information Institute of Cornell University (nd). https://www.law.cornell.edu/uscode/text/22/7102

Freedom for all Americans (2019). *Brush & Nib Studio v. City of Phoenix.* September 19th. https://www.freedomforallamericans.org/brush-nib-studio-v-city-of-phoenix/

Freedom House (2018). *Freedom in the World Index.* https://freedomhouse.org/sites/default/files/2020-02/FH_FIW_Report_2018_Final.pdf

Friedersdorf, C. (2015). Should mom-and-pops that forgo gay weddings be destroyed? *The Atlantic.* http://www.theatlantic.com/politics/archive/2015/04/should-businesses-that-quietly-oppose-gay-marriage-be-destroyed/389489/

Gallagher, M. (2010). Why accommodate-reflections on the gay marriage culture wars. *Northwestern Journal of Law and Social Policy, 5:* 260-273.

Garry, P. (2004). The myth of separation: America's historical experience with church and state. *Hofstra Law Review*, *33:* 475-500.

Gate, G. & Newport, F. (2012). *Special Report: 3.4% of U.S. Adults Identify as LGBT.* http://www.gallup.com/poll/158066/special-report-adults-identify-lgbt.aspx

Gates, S., Shanefelt, D., & Epstein, R. (2017). On Writ of Certiorari to the Colorado Court of Appeals. https://www.scotusblog.com/wp-content/uploads/2017/09/16-111_tsac_law_and_economics_scholars.pdf

Genovese, E. (1994). The question. *Dissent Magazine*, Summer, 371-376.

Giebler, H., & Merkel, W. (2016). Freedom and equality in democracies: Is there a trade-off? *International Political Science Review*, *37*:594-605.

Gilman, S., Cochran, S., Mays, V., Hughes, M., Ostrow, D., & Kessler, R. (2001). Risk of psychiatric disorders among individuals reporting same-sex sexual partners in the National Comorbidity Survey. *American journal of public health*, *91*:933-939.

Glazov, J. (2009). *United in Hate: The Left's Romance with Tyranny and Terror*. Los Angeles, CA: WND Books.

Gold, S. (2009). *Loving v. Virginia: Lifting the ban against interracial marriage*. New York: Cavendish Square.

Goodrich, L. (2011). The health care and conscience debate. *Engage*, 12:121-127.

Grey, H. et al. (2019). *Brief to the Supreme Court of Oregon in the case of Aaron and Melissa Klein v. Oregon Bureau of Lavor and Industries.* https://firstliberty.org/wp-content/uploads/2019/06/Brief-Supplemental_Redacted.pdf.

Gross, N., & Simmons, S. (2009). The religiosity of American college and university professors. *Sociology of Religion*, 70:101-129.

Hall, C. (1997). The Christian left: Who are they and how are they different from the Christian right? *Review of Religious Research*, 39: 27-45.

Habermas, J. (2006). *Time of transitions*, C. Cronin & M.Pensky (trans.). Cambridge: Polity.

Hallowell, B. (2015). Lawyer for Christian bakers who were forced to pay nearly $137,000 to lesbian couple reveals most shocking element of the case. *The Blaze*, December 31st. http://www.theblaze.com/stories/2015/12/31/lawyer-for-christian-bakers-who-were-forced-to-pay-nearly-137000-to-lesbian-couple-reveals-most-shocking-element-of-the-case/

Hamilton. A. (1775). *The right of revolution: The farmer refuted.* https://founders.archives.gov/documents/Hamilton/01-01-02-0057

Hamilton, A. (1788). *To the people of the State of New York: Federalist Papers # 78.* The Avalon Project. https://avalon.law.yale.edu/18th_century/fed78.asp.

Hannah-Jones, N. (2019). Our founding ideals of liberty and equality were false when they were written. Black Americans fought to make them true. Without this struggle, America would have no democracy at all. *The New York Times Magazine*, August 18th, pp.14-22.

Harty, F. et al. (2014). *Brief before the Iowa Supreme Court in Betty Ann and Richard Odgaard v. Iowa Civil Rights Commission.* https://s3.amazonaws.com/becketpdf/Joint-Appendix-Smallest-Version.pdf.

Harsanyi, D. (2019). Until the Supreme Court acts, Christians will be punished for thought crimes. *The Federalist,* June 10th. https://thefederalist.com/2019/06/10/supreme-court-acts-christians-will-punished-thought-crimes/.

Hawthorn, N. (2003). *The scarlet letter*. New York: Barnes & Noble.

Hitchens, P. (2012). What's socialist about state ownership? Beats me. *Daily Mail*, October 11th.

Holcomb, C. (2016). State's churches must ban sermons on sexual identity; "Not a bona fide religious purpose." *The Family Policy Council of West Virginia.* http://www.familypolicywv.com/new-law-requires-states-churches-censor-sermons-sexuality/.

Horowitz, D. (2019). *Dark agenda: The war to destroy Christian America*. New York: Humanix Books.

House of Representative (2012). *OBAMA Administration's abuse of power: Hearting before the committee on the judiciary.* https://www.govinfo.gov/content/pkg/CHRG-112hhrg75846/html/CHRG-112hhrg75846.htm

Humes, J. C. (2016). *Presidents and Their Pens: The Story of White House Speechwriters*. Lanham, MD: Hamilton Books.

Huxley, A. (1946). *Brave new world*. New York: Harper/Collins.

Ignatiev, N. (1997). The point is not to interpret whiteness but to abolish it. *Talk given at the Conference: The Making and Unmaking of Whiteness. University of California,* Berkeley, April 11-13, 1997.http://racetraitor.org/abolishthepoint.pdf.

Ignative, N. (2002). Abolish the white race. *Harvard Magazine*, September/October. http://harvardmagazine.com/2002/09/abolish-the-white-race.html

Ignatiev, N. & J. Garvey (1996). *Race traitor*. New York: Routledge.

Imbody, J. (2013). Obama 'freedom to worship' assaults First Amendment: Freedom of religion not just for private expression. *Washington Times,* January 28th. https://www.washingtontimes.com/news/2013/jan/28/obama-freedom-to-worship-assaults-first-amendment/.

International Christian Concern (2017). *2016 hall of shame*. Washington, DC: ICC.

Iowa Civil Rights Commission (nd). *Sexual orientation and gender identity*. (Brochure). http://www.adfmedia.org/files/SOGIPublicAccom.pdf

Jal. M. (2010), Interpretation as phantasmagria: Variations on a theme on Marx's Theses on Feuerbach. *Critique,* 38: 117-142.

Jefferson, T. (1784). *Notes on the State of Virginia,* Amendment I: Religion. http://press- pubs.uchicago.edu/founders/documents/amendI_religions40.html.

Jefferson, T. (1804). *From Thomas Jefferson to Ursuline Nuns of New Orleans,* 13 July 1804.

Founders Early Access. http://rotunda.upress.virginia.edu/founders/default.xqy?keys=FOEA-print-04-01-02-0068

Jefferson, T. (1809). *From Thomas Jefferson to Richard Douglas,* 4 February 1809. Founders Online. http://founders.archives.gov/documents/Jefferson/99-01-02-9714

Jefferson, (1819). *From Thomas Jefferson to Spencer Roane*, 6 September. Founders Online. https://founders.archives.gov/documents/Jefferson/98-01-02-0734.

Jefferson, T. (1903-4). *The writings of Thomas Jefferson,* Memorial Edition. A. Lipscomb and A. Bergh (eds). Washington, DC: Library of Congress.

Jefferson, T (1998). *Jefferson's letter to the Danbury Baptists.* The Library of Congress. https://www.loc.gov/loc/lcib/9806/danpre.html.

Jonathan, R. (2015). *Gay baker scolds gay community for acting like Nazis and bullies.* Inquisitr, July 20th. https://www.inquisitr.com/2268740/gay-baker-scolds-gay-community-for-acting-like-nazis-and-bullies-video/#ixzz6f33ckYNP

Jones, J. & Saad, L. (2019). *U.S. support for more government inches up, but not for socialism.* Pew Research Center. https://news.gallup.com/poll/268295/support-government-inches-not-socialism.aspx.

Judicial Watch (2011). *President Obama's Czars. Judicial Watch Special Report.* Washington, DC: Judicial Watch, Inc.

Justia (2017). State laws ruled unconstitutional. *Justia US Law.* https://law.justia.com/constitution/us/state-laws-held-unconstitutional.html

Kainz, H. (2010). *The existence of God and the faith-instinct.* Selinsgove, PA: Susquehanna University Press.

Kalder, D. (2018). *The infernal library: On dictators, the books they wrote, and other catastrophizes of literature*. New York: Macmillan.

Kaminski, J. (2002). Religion and the Founding Fathers. *Annotation: The Newsletter of the National Historic Publications and Records Commission*, 30:1-20.

Kay, B. (2006). Blaming whitey. *National Post.* http://proudtobecanadian.ca/index/writergroup/5436

Keating, J. (2012). Why does Ruth Bader Ginsburg like the South African constitution so much? *Foreign Policy*, February 26th. https://foreignpolicy.com/2012/02/06/why-does-ruth-bader-ginsburg-like-the-south-african-constitution-so-much/.

Kellum, N. & Clark, W. (2017). Amicus brief with the Arizona Court of Appeals in *Brush & Nib v. City of Phoenix.* https://www.azpolicy.org/wp-content/uploads/2018/03/BN-CRE-Amicus-Brief.pdf.

Kersch, K. I. (2006). How conduct became speech and speech became conduct: A political development case study in labor law and the freedom of speech. *Journal of Constitutional Law*, *8*, 255-297.

King, Jr., M. (1986). A knock at midnight. in M. Washington (ed). *A testament of hope: The essential writings of Martin Luther King, Jr.* San Francisco, CA: Harper and Row.

Kiska, R., & Coleman, P. (2012). Freedom of speech and" hate speech"-Unravelling the jurisprudence of the European Court of Human Rights. *International Journal for Religious Freedom*, *5:* 129-142.

Koppelman, A. (2015). Theorists, get over yourselves: A response to Steven D. Smith. *Pepperdine Law Review*, 41:937-942.

Kolakowski, L. (1981). *Main currents of Marxism: Volume III, the breakdown*. Oxford: Oxford University Press.

Krotoszynski Jr, R. (2015). Free speech paternalism and free speech exceptionalism: Pervasive distrust of government and the contemporary First Amendment. *Ohio State Law Journal*, *76:* 659-690.

Le Bon, G. (2001). *The psychology of socialism*. Kitchener, Ontario. Batoche Books.

Lambert, F. (2005). *The Barbary wars: American independence in the Atlantic world*. London: Macmillan.

Laycock, D. (1990). The Supreme Court's assault on Free Exercise, and the amicus brief that was never filed. *Journal of Law and Religion*, *8:* 99-114.

Laycock, D. (2014). Religious liberty and the culture wars. *University of Illinois Law Review*, 14: 839-80.

Laycock, D. (2018). The wedding-vendor cases. *Harvard Journal of Law & Public Policy*, *41:* 49-66.

Leiter, B. (2014). *Why tolerate religion?* Princeton, NJ: Princeton University Press.

Lennox, J. (2009). *God's undertaker: Has science buried God?* Oxford: Lion.

Levin, Y. (2010). The perils of religious liberty. *First Things*, 260: 29-34.

Lewis, C. (2001). *Mere Christianity.* New York: Harper Collins.

Lewis, C. (1970). *God in the Dock: Essays on Theology and Ethics*, W. Hooper (Ed.), London: Wm. B. Eerdmans.

Lincoln, A. (1838). *Address before the young men's Lyceum of Springfield, Illinois.* Lincoln Online. http://www.abrahamlincolnonline.org/lincoln/speeches/lyceum.htm

Lindevaldsen, R. (2010). Fallacy of neutrality from beginning to end: The battle between religious liberties and rights based on homosexual conduct." *Liberty University Law Review*, 4:425-63.

Lipka, M. (2016). *10 facts about atheists.* Washington, DC: Pew Research Center.

Lippman, M. (2020). *Law and society* (3rd ed). Thousand Oaks, CA. Sage.

Lipton, P. (2000). Inference to the best explanation. In W. Newton-Smith (ed.), *A companion to the philosophy of science.* pp. 184.193. Hoboken, NJ: Blackwell.

Loconte, J. (2019). Is liberalism good for religions? *Cato Policy report.* July/August. https://www.cato.org/sites/cato.org/files/serials/files/policy-report/2019/8/cpr-v41n4-5.pdf

Loewy, A. (2002). The positive reality and normative virtues of a neutral establishment clause. *Brandeis Law Journal*, *41*, 533-543.

Lorence, J. et al. (2013). Petition for a Writ of Certiorari: *Elane Photography v. Vanessa Willock.* http://online.wsj.com/public/resources/documents/elane.pdf.

Madison, J. (1776). Madison's Amendments to the Declaration of Rights. Founders Online. https://founders.archives.gov/documents/Madison/01-01-02-0054-0003.

Madison, J. (1785). *Memorial and Remonstrance against Religious Assessments.* http://press- pubs.uchicago.edu/founders/documents/amendI_religions43.html.

Madison, J. (1809). James Madison's first inaugural address. *The Avalon Project at Yale Law School.* https://avalon.law.yale.edu/19th_century/madison1.asp.

Malachi, M. (2008). *Keys of This Blood: Pope John Paul II Versus Russia and the West for Control of the New World Order.* New York: Simon and Schuster.

Malcolm X (1963). Malcolm X speech. *Digital History ID 3619.* https://www.digitalhistory.uh.edu/disp_textbook.cfm?smtid=3&psid=3619

Marcuse, H. (1966). *Eros and Civilization: Philosophical inquiry into Freud*. Boston: Beacon.

Marcuse, H. (1969). *An essay on liberation*. Boston: Beacon Press.

Marcuse, H. (2002). *One dimensional man*. New York: Routledge.

Marks, J. (2012). *Ethics without morals: in defence of amorality*. New York: Routledge.

Matthew, H. (1997). *Gladstone 1809-1898*. Oxford: Oxford University Press.

McGonnigal, J. (2011). Catholic Charities abandons thousands of children instead of adopting to LGBT parents. *Gay voices, Huffington Post.* http://www.huffingtonpost.com/jamie-mcgonnigal/catholic-charities-adoption_b_1095396.html

McConnell, M. (2014). The problem of singling out religion. *DePaul Law Review*, *50:*1-48.

McConnell, M. (2017). Religion Clauses of the First Amendment: Where is the Supreme Court heading? *The Catholic Lawyer, 32:*187-202.

McDowell, J. & Hostetler, B. (1998). *The new tolerance: How a cultural movement threatens to destroy you, your faith, and your children*. Carol Stream, IL: Tyndale House Publishers.

McGurn, W. (2016). A liberal 'gets' religion: A U.S. Civil Rights Commission report on religious liberty is so bad, it's good. *Wall Street Journal*, September 12th. https://www.wsj.com/articles/a-liberal-gets-religion-1473722200.

Miller, M (2010) *The Book and The Right: The Roots of America's Greatness*. Maitland, Fl: Xulon Press.

Miniter, F. (2011). *Saving the Bill of Rights: Exposing the left's campaign to destroy American exceptionalism*. New York: Regnery Publishing.

Morse, S. (2018). HHS announces Conscience and Religious Freedom Division. *Healthcare Finance,* January18th. https://www.healthcarefinancenews.com/news/hhs-announces-conscience-and-religious-freedom-division

Morton, V. (2018). Alexandria Ocasio-Cortez 'represents the future of our party,' DNC Chairman Tom Perez says. *The Washington Times*, July 3. https://apnews.com/857a990003dafa3b12714f3e08108ca0.

Moyer, J. (2015). Indiana Pizza Shop won't cater gay wedding, Gets over $50K from supporters." *Washington Post*, April 2nd. http://www.washingtonpost.com/news/morning-mix/wp/2015/04/02/indianas-memories-pizza-wouldnt-cater-gay-wedding-gets-40k-in-crowdfunding/

Muñoz, V. (2009). *God and the founders: Madison, Washington, and Jefferson*. Cambridge University Press.

Murdock, D. (2016). Why Christians are losing the war over gay-wedding cakes. *New York Post*, April 29th. https://nypost.com/2016/04/29/why-christians-are-losing-the-war-over- gay-wedding-cakes.

Natelson, R. (2005). Original meaning of the Establishment Clause. *The William & Mary Bill Rights Journal*, *14:*73-140.

Nelson, T. (2019). Statement on "telescope" wedding video case. ACLU of Minnesota. https://www.aclu-mn.org/en/press-releases/statement-telescope-wedding-video-case.

Nietzsche, F. & Hollingdale, R. (1990). *Expeditions of an untimely man.* In *Twilight of the Idols; and, The Anti-Christ* (Penguin Classics, London: Penguin Books.

Noll, M. (1988). *One Nation Under God?: Christian Faith and Political Action in America*. New York: HarperCollins.

Novak, M. (2002). ACLU: Atheist Civil Liberties Union. *The Jewish Press*. August 16th.. https://www.jewishpress.com/indepth/opinions/aclu-atheist-civil-liberties-union/2002/08/16/.

Nowlan, R. (2012). *The American Presidents, Washington to Tyler: What they did, what they Said, what was said about them, with full source notes*. Jefferson, NC: McFarland.

NPR Staff (2020). *Understanding The 2020 electorate: AP VoteCast Survey,* November 3rd. https://www.npr.org/2020/11/03/929478378/understanding-the-2020-electorate-ap- votecast-survey.

Ngun, T. & Vilain, E. (2014). The biological basis of human sexual orientation: Is there a role for epigenetics. *Advance in Genetics*, *86:*167-184.

Office of Legal Policy, US Dept. of Justice, Report to the Attorney General. (1986). *Religious Liberty under the Free Exercise Clause.* Washington, DC.

Olson, C. (2012). Cardinal George criticizes Sebelius' declaration of "war on citizens." *The Catholic World Report.* http://www.catholicworldreport.com/Blog/1429/cardinal_george_criticizes_sebelius_declaration_of_war_on_citizens.aspx.

O'Neil, R. (2008). What not to say in class during an election season. *The Chronicle of Higher Education*, September 19th. https://www.chronicle.com/article/What-Not-to-Say-in-Class/33228

Painter, G. (2005). The sensibilities of our Forefathers: The history of sodomy laws in the United States. *Sodomy Laws.* http://www.glapn.org/sodomylaws/sensibilities/introduction.htm.

Paul, D. (1984). Eugenics and the left. *Journal of the History of Ideas*, 45:567-590.

Paulsen, M. (2013). The priority of God: A theory of religious liberty. *Pepperdine Law Review*, *39:*1159-1222.

Paulsen, M. (2014). God is great, Garvey is good: Making sense of religious freedom. *Notre Dame Law Review*, *72*: 1597-1626.

Paulsen, M. (2015) Why the Supreme Court should take up the Bronx Household of Faith case. *National Review*, February 19.

Pedersen, J. (2010). Properties of property: A jurisprudential analysis. *The Commoner*, 14:137-210.

Pepper, S. (1986). Taking the Free Exercise Clause seriously. *Brigham Young University Law Review*, 1986: 299-336.

Peterson, M. (1960). *The Jefferson image in the American mind.* Oxford: Oxford University Press.

Pew Research Center (2016). *Where the public stands on religious liberty vs. nondiscrimination.* https://www.pewforum.org/2016/09/28/where-the-public-stands-on-religious-liberty-vs-nondiscrimination/

Pew Research Center (2019). *Stark partisan divisions in Americans' views of 'socialism,' 'capitalism'.* https://www.pewresearch.org/fact-tank/2019/06/25/stark-partisan-divisions-in-americans-views-of-socialism-capitalism/.

Pilon, R. (2013-2014). Long view: Toward restoring the Constitution. *Cato Supreme Court Review,* vii-xxiii.

Pithouse, R. (2019). South Africa must avoid authoritarian solutions. *Mail & Guardian*, July, 17th. https://mg.co.za/article/2019-07-17-south-africa-must-avoid-authoritarian-solutions/

Planck, M. (1949). *Religion and natural science: Scientific autobiography and other papers.* New York: Philosophical Library.

Pope John Paul II (2000). *Message of the Holy Father John Paul II to the participants in the sixth plenary session of the Pontifical Academy of Social Sciences.* The Vatican, February 22nd. http://www.vatican.va/content/john-paul-ii/en/speeches/2000/jan-mar/documents/hf_jp-ii_spe_20000223_acd-sciences-plenary.html.

Porteous, A. (1934). Platonist or Aristotelian? *The Classical Review*, 48: 97-105.

Powel, S. (2009). Judge Kent reports to prison hospital in Massachusetts. *Houston Chronical*, June 15th. http://www.chron.com/news/houston-texas/article/Judge-Kent-reports-to- prison-hospital-in-1673073.php.

Prager, D. (2018). *Explaining the left: Part II. Townhall Daily,* August 21st. https://townhall.com/columnists/dennisprager/2018/08/21/explaining-the-left-part-ii-n2511543?utm_source=thdaily&utm_medium=email&utm_campaign=nl&newsletterad=&profileid=.

Project Veritas (2015). *Officials at Cornell, Syracuse, and Yale destroy* U.S. Constitution http://www.projectveritas.com/posts/news/officials-cornell-syracuse-and-yale-destroy-us-constitution

Rector, R. & Fagan, P. (2003). The continuing good news about welfare reform. Heritage Foundation. *Backgrounder* No. 1620, February 6. http://www.heritage.org/research/reports/2003/02/the-continuing-good-news.

Reid, T. (2016). Court: Govt bureaucrats have no business deciding whether Iowa church activities are religious. *Alliance Defending Freedom.* http://www.adfmedia.org/News/PRDetail/10098.

Reisman, J. & Eichel, E. (1990). *Kinsey, sex and fraud: The indoctrination of a people*. Lafayette, LA: Lochinvar-Huntington House.

Richardson, B. (2017). Religious people more likely to give to charity, study shows. The *Washington Times*, October 30th. https://www.washingtontimes.com/news/2017/oct/30/religious-people-more-likely-give-charity-study/.

Roediger, D. (1994). *Towards the abolition of whiteness*, London: Verso.

Rogers, A. (2019). A Masterpiece of simplicity: Toward a Yoderian Free Exercise framework for wedding-vendor Cases. *Marquette Law Review*, *103:* 163-216.

Rosen, J. (2020) Commentary: It's time to cancel 'The Star-Spangled Banner.' Here's what should replace it. *LA Times*, July 14th. https://www.latimes.com/entertainment-arts/music/story/2020-07-14/national-anthem-star-spangled-banner-lean-on-me.

Rothenberg, P. (2000). *Invisible privilege: A memoir about race, class, and gender*. Lawrence: University of Kansas Press.

Russell, N. (2020). Transgender lawsuit against Masterpiece Cakeshop's Jack Phillips advances. *Washington Examiner*, May 1st. https://www.washingtonexaminer.com/opinion/transgender-lawsuit-against-masterpiece-cakeshops-jack-phillips-advances.

Rutledge, C. (2008). Caught in the crossfire: How Catholic Charities of Boston was victim to the Clash between Gay Rights and Religious Freedom." *Duke Journal of Gender, Law. & Policy*, *15:* 297-314.

Ryan, C., Huebner, D., Diaz, R. & Sanchez, J. (2009). Family rejection as a predictor of negative health outcomes in white and Latino lesbian, gay, and bisexual young adults. *Pediatrics*, *123:* 346-352.

Saewyc, E., Poon, C., Wang, N., Homma, Y., & Smith, A. (2007). *Not yet equal: The health of lesbian, gay, & bisexual youth in BC.* Vancouver. British Columbia: McCreary Centre Society.

Sampson, R. (2005). *The Heart of Wisdom Teaching Approach: Bible Based Homeschooling.* Merritt Island, FL: Heart of Wisdom Publishing.

Sanburn, J. (2014). Houston's pastors outraged after city subpoenas sermons over transgender bill." *Time Magazine*, Oct. 17. http://time.com/3514166/houston-pastors-sermons-subpoenaed/

Sandfort, T., de Graaf, R., Bijl, R., & Schnabel, P. (2001). Same-sex sexual behavior and psychiatric disorders: Findings from the Netherlands Mental Health Survey and Incidence Study (NEMESIS). *Archives of general psychiatry*, *58:* 85-91.

Scalia, A. & Garner, B, (2012). *Reading law: The interpretation of legal texts* (Vol. 356). St. Paul, MN: Thomson/West.

Schulzke, M. (2013). The politics of new atheism. *Politics and Religion*, 6:778-799.

Schwartzman, M. (2012). What if religion is not special? *The University of Chicago Law Review*, 79: 1351-1427.

Segal, E. (2017). Symposium: Disentangling free speech and freedom of religion in *Masterpiece Cakeshop. Scotus Blog.* https://www.scotusblog.com/2017/09/symposium-disentangling-free-speech-freedom-religion-masterpiece-cakeshop/

Setari, A. & Setari, R. (2016). Trends in Catholic school minority enrollment and higher education entrance over the recession. *Journal of Catholic Education*, *19:* 4-19.

Shackelford, K. (2017). Undeniable: The survey of hostility to religion in America. First Liberty Institute, Plano: TX.

Shalev, B. (2003). *Religion of Nobel Prize winners. 100 years of Nobel prizes.* New Delhi: Atlantic Publishers & Distributors.

Sheen, F. (1948). *Communism and the Conscience of the West*. Indianapolis and NY: Bobbs- Merrill.

Shrader, D. (2005). Thou shalt not: Supreme Court rulings concerning public displays of religious symbols. In *Proceedings of the Fourth Annual Hawaii International Conference on Arts and Humanities* (pp. 5564-5608).

Sioux Center News (2018). *The Odgaards lose all but keep their faith. Sioux Center News*, November 2nd. https://www.nwestiowa.com/scnews/odgaards-lose-all-but-keep-their-faith/article_3b001874-dea6-11e8-b806-7f510f4ebb15.html.

Solzhenitsyn, A. (2006). Templeton Lecture, May 10, 1983," in *The Solzhenitsyn reader: New and essential writings, 1947-2005*, eds. E. Ericson, Jr. and D. Mahoney. Wilmington, DE: Intercollegiate Studies Institute.

Stark, R. (2006). A civil religion: How Christianity created free and prosperous societies. *American Enterprise,* May, 17:16-19.

Starns, T. (2014). Baker forced to make gay wedding cakes, undergo sensitivity training, after losing Lawsuit." *Fox News,* June 3. http://www.foxnews.com/opinion/2014/06/03/baker-forced-to-make-gay-wedding-cakes-undergo-sensitivity-training-after.

Stark, R. (2005). *The Victory of Reason: How Christianity Led to Freedom, Capitalism, and Western Success.* New York: Random House.

Stark, R. (2006). A civil religion: How Christianity created free and prosperous societies. *The American Enterprise,* May: 16-19.

Schulzke, M. (2013). The politics of New Atheism. *Politics & Religion, 6:* 778-799.

Stormer, J. (1964). *None Dare Call It Treason.* New York: Buccaneer Books.

Stychin, C. (2009). Faith in the future: Sexuality, religion and the public sphere. *Oxford Journal of Legal Studies, 29:* 729-755.

Story, J. (1833). *Commentaries on the Constitution of the United States, Volume III.* Boston: Hilliard, Gray and Company

Strossen, N. (2016). Freedom of speech and equality: Do we have to choose. *Journal of Law & Policy, 25:* 185-225.

Stutzman, B. (2019). Christian florist: My longtime customer was a friend, then he sued me over his gay weddings. *USA Today*, October 8th. www.usatoday.com/story/opinion/2019/10/08/supreme-court-florist-gay-marriage-religious-freedom-column/3866964002/

Sweetser, K. (2014). Partisan personality: The psychological differences between Democrats and Republicans, and independents somewhere in between. *American Behavioral Scientist, 58:*1183-1194.

Tatchell, P. (2016). I've changed my mind on the gay cake row. Here's why. *The Guardian,* February 1. https://www.theguardian.com/

commentisfree/2016/feb/01/gay-cake-row-i-changed-my-mind-ashers-bakery-freedom-of-conscience-religion

Taylor, D. (2012). My godless city is full of Christian charity. *Independent*, December 16th. https://www.independent.co.uk/voices/comment/my-godless-city-is-full-of-christian-charity-8420317.html

Thomas, H. (1962). *Understanding the great philosophers*. New York, NY: Doubleday.

Throckmorton, W. (2012). Alan Chambers: 99.9% have not experienced a change in their orientation. *Patheos.* http://www.patheos.com/blogs/warrenthrockmorton/2012/01/09/alan-chambers-99-9-have-not-experienced-a-change-in-their-orientation.

Thucydides (1972). *History of the Peloponnesian Wars*. London: Penguin.

Turley, J. (2020). "All speech is not equal." Biden taps anti free speech figure for transition lead on media agency. *Res ipsa loquitur – The thing itself speaks.* November 17th. https://jonathanturley.org/2020/11/17/all-speech-is-not-equal-biden-taps-anti-free-speech-figure-for-transition-lead-on-media-agency/.

Trigg, R. (2011). Freedom of religion. *Ars Disputandi Supplement Series*, *5:* 109-124.

Tushnet, M. (1988). *Red, white, and blue: a critical analysis of constitutional law.* Cambridge, MA: Harvard University Press.

United Nations (2015). *Universal Declaration of Human Rights.* https://www.un.org/en/udhrbook/pdf/udhr_booklet_en_web.pdf.

United States Conference of Catholic Bishops (2016). *Letter, March 31.* http://www.usccb.org/issues-and-action/religious-liberty/conscience-protection/upload/Conscience-Protection-Act-Dolan-Lori-Ltr-to-Congress-03-31-16.pdf

United States Civil Rights Commission. (2016). *Peaceful Coexistence: Reconciling nondiscrimination Principles with civil liberties.* Washington, DC: U.S. Commission on Civil Rights.

Vermeule, A. (2020). Beyond originalism. *The Atlantic*, March 31st. https://www.theatlantic.com/ideas/archive/2020/03/common-good-constitutionalism/609037/.

Walker, A. & Wester, J. (2017). From Obamacare to *Obergefell*: The Obama administration's troubled legacy on religious liberty. *National Review*, January 18. https://www.nationalreview.com/2017/01/obama-administration-has-troubled-religious-liberty-legacy/.

Walsh, A. (2020). *God, science, and society: The origin of the universe, intelligent life, and free societies.* Wilmington, DE: Vernon Press.

Walsh, A. & Hemmens, C. (2020). Law, Justice, and society: A sociolegal introduction, 5th edition. New York: Oxford University Press.

Washington, G. (1789). *From George Washington to the Society of Quakers, 13 October.* Founders Online. https://founders.archives.gov/documents/Washington/05-04-02-0188.

Washington, G. (1796). Washington's farewell address, 1796. *The Avalon Project*, http://avalon.law.yale.edu/18th_century/washing.asp.

Wehner, P. (2016). Certitude and seeking the truth. *Commentary*, January 26th. https://www.commentarymagazine.com/american-society/why-the-constitution-%e2%80%94-and-what-it-means-%e2%80%94-matters/loutt

West, M. (2005). *The Poverty of Multiculturalism.* London: Civitas.

Wilkins, M., & Moreland, J. (2010). *Jesus under fire: Modern scholarship reinvents the historical Jesus*. Grand Rapids, MI: Zondervan.

Will, G. (2008). Bleeding hearts but tight fists. *Washington Post*, March 27th http://www.washingtonpost.com/wp-dyn/content/article/2008/03/26/AR2008032602916.html

Winthrop, R. (1852). *Addresses and Speeches on Various Occasions.* Boston: Little, Brown.

Zimmermann, A. (2013). A law above the law: Christian roots of the English common law. *Glocal Conversations*, *1*: 85-98.

Zizek, S. (2017). The problem with Venezuela's revolution is that it didn't go far enough. *The Independent*, August 9th. https://www.independent.co.uk/voices/venezuela-socialism- communism-left-didnt-go-far-enough-a7884021.html

Cases Cited

Abington School District v. Schempp, 374 U.S. 203 (1963).

Agency for International Development v. Alliance for Open Society International, Inc., 570 U.S. 205 (2013).

Bailey v. Alabama, 219 U.S. 219 (1911).

Bowers v. Hardwick, 478 U.S. 186 (1986).

Braunfeld v. Brown, 366 U.S. 599 (1961).

Brush & NIB Studio, LC v. City of Phoenix, 448 890, (Ariz. 2019)

Burwell v. Hobby Lobby, 573 U.S. 682 (2014).

Cantwell v. Connecticut, 310 U.S. 296 (1940).

Christian Legal Society v. Martinez, 561 U.S. 661, (2010).

City of Boerne v. Flores, 521 U.S. 507 (1997).

County of *Allegheny v. American Civil Liberties Union*, 492 U.S. 573 (1989).

Dred Scott v. Sandford, 60 U.S. (19 How.) 393 (1857).

Elane Photography, LLC v. Willock, 309.

Employment Division, Department of Human Resources of Oregon v. Smith, 494 U.S. 872 (1990).

Engel v. Vitale, 370 U.S. 421 (1962).

Everson v. Board of Education, 330 U.S. 1 (1947).

Committee for Public Education & Religious Liberty v. Nyquist, 413 U.S. 756, 760 (1973).

Gonzales v. O Centro Espírita Beneficente União do Vegetal, 546 U.S. 418 (2006).

Heart of Atlanta Motel, Inc. v. United States, 379 U.S. 241 (1964).

Holt v. Hobbs, 574 U.S. ___ (2015).

Lawrence v. Texas, 539 U.S. 558 (2003).

Lee v. Weisman, 505 U.S. 577 (1992).

Lemon v. Kurtzman, 403 U.S. 602 (1971).

Lexington-Fayette Urban County Human Rights Commission v. Hands On Originals (2019).

Little Sisters of the Poor v. Burwell, No. 13-1540 (10th Cir. 2015).

Little Sisters of the Poor Saints Peter and Paul Home v. Pennsylvania, 591 U.S. (2020).
Loving v. Virginia, 388 U.S. 1 (1967).
Lynch v. Donnelly, 465 U.S. 668 (1984).
National Institute of Family and Life Advocates v. Becerra, 585 U.S.___ (2018).
Obergefell v. Hodges, 576 U.S. 644 (2015).
Olmstead v. United States, 277 U.S. 479 (1928).
Perez v. Sharp, 32 Cal.2d 711 (1948).
Reynolds v. United States, 98 U.S. (8 Otto.) 145 (1878).
R.G. & G.R. Harris Funeral Homes Inc. v. Equal Employment Opportunity Commission, 590 U.S. __ 2020).
Santa Fe Independent School Dist. v. Doe, 530 U.S. 290 (2000).
Shelley v. Kraemer, 334 U.S. 1 (1948)
Sherbert v. Verner, 374 U.S. 398 (1963).
Spence v. Washington, 418 U.S. 405 (1974).
Stone v. Graham, 449 U.S. 39 (1980).
Telescope Media Group v. Lucero, ___ F.3d ___, *WL. 3979621* (2019).
Texas v. Johnson, 491 U.S. 397 (1989).
Trinity Lutheran Church of Columbia, Inc. v. Comer, 582 U.S. ___ (2017).
United States v. Seeger, 380 U.S. 163 (1965).
United States v. Windsor, 570 U.S. 744 (2913).
Wabaunsee County, Kansas v. Umbehr, 518 U.S. 668, (1996).
Wallace v. Jaffree, 472 U.S. 38 (1985).
Walz v. Tax Commission of the City of New York, 397 U.S. 664 (1970).
West Virginia State *Board of Education v. Barnette*, 319 U.S. 624 (1943).
Widmar v. Vincent, 454 U.S. 263 (1981).
Wisconsin v. Yoder, 406 U.S. 205 (1971).
Wooley v. Maynard, 430 U.S. 705 (1977).
Yacovelli v. Moeser, Aff'd, Case No. 02-1889, 4th Circuit (2002).
Zorach v. Clauson, 343 U.S. 306 (1952).

AUTHOR CONTACT INFORMATION

Anthony Walsh, PhD

Department of Criminal Justice

Boise State University

Boise, Idaho, US

Email: twalsh@boisestate.edu

INDEX

A

Abbott, Greg, 104
Abington v. Schempp, 64
absolutism, 55
Adams, John, 104, 165
Adamson, Blaine, 182, 183
Address Before the Young Men's Lyceum of Springfield, Illinois, 16
Advice to Children, 63
Affordable Care Act (ACA), 159, 176
Aikman, David, 198
Allegheny County v. Greater Pittsburgh ACLU, 31
Alliance Defending Freedom, 131, 134, 183, 220
America the Beautiful, 214
American Civil Liberties Union (ACLU), 31, 42, 43, 64, 125, 126, 127, 130, 131, 132, 186, 207, 220, 221, 222
American Family Association, 204
American Grace, 223
American Humanist Association, 194
American Nazi Party, 205
American Psychiatric Association (APA), 92, 93
American Revolution, 23, 35, 214
amorality, 203
anti-Americanism, 73, 212, 221
Antifa, 205, 213, 214
Approaching the Qu'ran: The Early Revelations, 221
Aristotle, 14, 15, 16
Association of American Physicians and Surgeons, 204
atheism, 30, 36, 51, 65, 68, 75, 192, 202, 203, 207, 218, 219, 222
- and education, 51
- and Establishment Clause, 36
- and moral values, 203
- and socialism, 195, 196
- new, 218

anti-miscegenation law, 81, 81, 82
Atlantic, 112, 151
Avakian, Brad, 149, 150

B

Bacon, Francis, 52
Bailey v. State of Alabama, 115
Bailey, Cynthia, 115, 119
Baldwin, Roger, 42

Barlow, John, 165
Barton, David, 159
Baskerville, Stephen, 74
Bastiat, Frederic, 123, 228
Bean, Tanner, 164
Becerra, Xavier, 60, 61
Becket Fund for Religious Liberty, 158
Benkof, David, 91
Berg, Thomas, 86
Bernstein, David, 111
Berthold, Richard, 215
Bible, 63, 64, 73, 81, 83, 101, 132, 150, 152, 195, 221
  and polygamy, 101
  and slavery, 167
  in school, 63, 64
Biden, Joe, 56, 61, 120, 164, 178, 192, 207
Black Lives Matter (BLM), 192, 204, 213, 214
Black, Hugo, 24
Bleich, David, 200
Bonventre, Vincent, 37, 54
Borgman, Ben, 135, 136, 138
Botham, Fay, 82
Bowers v. Hardwick, 90
Bowman, Laurel, 149
Boy Scouts of America et al. v. Dale, 110
Boyd, Jamar, 211
Brandeis, Louis, 193
Brandenburg v. Ohio, 55
Braunfeld v. Brown, 102
Braunfeld, Abraham, 102
Brave New World, 204
British Fabian Society, 75
British Humanist Association, 223
Browner, Carol, 158
Brush & Nib Studio, 179
Brush & NIB Studio, LC v. City of Phoenix, 180
Buckingham, David, 182, 184
Burger, Warren, 28, 33, 65, 97
Burke, Edmund, 4, 172
Burwell v. Hobby Lobby Stores, Inc., 175
Butler, Paul, 27

C

Cairo Declaration on Human Rights in, 199, 201
Campbell, David, 223
Campbell, Jim, 184
Cantwell v. Connecticut, 39
Cantwell, Newton, 40
Cardozo, Benjamin, 29
Castro, Martin, 165, 166, 168
Catechism of the Catholic Church, 171
Catholic Charities Review, 169
Catholic Charities USA (CCUSA), 168, 169, 170, 222
Catholic Church, 40, 82, 160, 168, 169, 170, 171, 222
  and abortion, 168
  and same-sex adoption, 169, 170
Center for Religious Expression, 179
Chambers, Alan, 95, 231
Charlton, Bruce, 212
Chavez, Hugo, 158
Chesterton, G.K., 201, 205
Christian Brothers Employee Benefit Trust, 161
Christian Legal Society (CLS), 69, 70
Christian Legal Society v. Martinez, 69
Christianity, ix, 21, 63, 65, 67, 71, 75, 76, 82, 92, 137, 166, 171, 172, 186, 194, 197, 198, 200, 202, 203, 207, 209, 211, 215, 224, 227, 229, 239, 247
  a world without, 207, 222
  and freedom, 194, 197, 207
  and LBGTQ activists, 92, 152, 171
  and limited government, 197, 198
  and Marxism, 71, 72
  hostility towards, 32, 44, 172
  in schools, 63, 65, 67

Church of England, 22
Churchill, Ward LeRoy, 215
Churchill, Winston, 7, 193
City of Boerne v. Flores, 49, 143
Civil Rights Act of 1964, 117
clever sillies, 212
Clinton, Bill, 49, 168
coercion test, 31, 67, 154, 155
Coke, Edward, 3
Coleman, Paul, 74
Coleridge, Samuel Taylor, 15
Collinsworth, Misti, 141, 142, 143
Commentaries on the Constitution of the United States, 21
Committee for Public Education & Religious Liberty v. Nyquist, 33
compelled speech, 58, 61, 126, 136, 137, 141, 144, 145
  and Elane Photography, 141, 142, 143, 145
  and Masterpiece Cakeshop, 137
compelling interest, 101, 103, 104, 163
Conkle, Daniel, 62
Conscience and Religious Freedom Division, 162
conscientiousness, 13, 108
conservatism, 10, 14, 16, 191
conspiracy, 75
Constitution, 1, 2, 3, 4, 5, 6, 7, 8, 9, 10, 11, 12, 13, 16, 20, 21, 23, 27, 28, 31, 32, 34, 35, 37, 38, 41, 44, 52, 54, 58, 62, 63, 66, 67, 70, 78, 90, 95, 96, 97, 99, 100, 112, 113, 119, 130, 133, 138, 149, 150, 151, 152, 153, 157, 165, 167, 175, 180, 185, 186, 187, 188, 189, 193, 200, 206, 213, 214, 220, 221, 222
  and LGBTQ, 98
  and Religious Clauses, 26, 35, 37
  and the left, 4, 9
  Article V, 8
  as a living document, 9
Constitutional Convention, 2
constitutional rights, 111, 112, 116, 119, 138, 140, 144, 150, 155, 159, 183, 185, 187, 220
  and CLS, 69
  and laws, 121
  as positive rights, 121, 123
  versus statutory rights, 97
Controlled Substances Act, 103
Coolidge, Calvin, 206, 213
Cooper, Jacquelyn, 83, 84
Corbin, Caroline, 55, 85
Craig, Charles, 126, 127, 128, 129
critical thinking, 73, 75
Crome Yellow, 92
Cruz, Ted, 178
Cryer, Rachel, 149
Cultural Marxism, 71, 72, 73, 74, 75

D

Daily Mail, 195
Danbury Baptist Association of Connecticut, 25
Dawkins, Richard, 218, 219
De Toledano, Ralph, 42, 232
Declaration of Human Rights, 198
Declaration of Independence, 10, 11, 66, 78, 206, 213
Defense of Marriage Act, 77
Dennett, Daniel, 218
Dent, George, 55
Dershowitz, Alan, 221
Dewart, Deborah, 109, 113
DiGeloromo, Diane, 183
discrimination, 13, 31, 41, 42, 60, 82, 83, 84, 85, 90, 91, 98, 107, 108, 109, 110, 111, 117, 118, 126, 128, 129, 130, 133, 134, 135, 140, 145, 148, 149, 150, 165, 166, 175, 181, 182, 186, 189
Donohue, William, 43
Douglas, William O., 56

Dred Scott v. Sandford, 7
Dreher, Rod, 92
Duka, Joanna, 178, 179, 180
Duncan, Richard, 9, 53, 108
Dunn, Anita, 158
Durant, Arial, 192
Durant, Will, 205

E

Eichel, Edward, 94, 245
Eichmann, Adolf, 216
Elane Photography, 141, 142, 143, 145
Elshtain, Jean, 212
Emancipation Proclamation, 8
Employment Division v. Smith, 53
Endean, Steve, 91
Engel v. Vitale, 63
enumerated rights, 13, 96, 97
Episcopal Church, 23
equality, ix, 55, 76, 107, 108, 111, 112, 165, 198, 199
Eros and Civilization, 73, 76
Esbeck, Carl, 37, 38
Establishment Clause, 19, 21, 23, 24, 25, 28, 29, 30, 31, 32, 33, 34, 36, 38, 41, 44, 48, 52, 62, 64, 65, 66, 67, 68, 188
  and coercion test, 31, 67, 154, 155
  and founders, 1, 21, 33, 36, 37, 39, 47, 52, 61, 74, 89, 140, 189, 193
  and Free Exercise Clause, viii, 19, 25, 28, 31, 33, 34, 35, 36, 37, 38, 40, 41, 42, 44, 45, 46, 47, 48, 49, 50, 52, 54, 61, 62, 66, 67, 98, 100, 102, 104, 130, 133, 176, 188, 189
  and Lemon test, 29, 31
Everson v. Board of Education, 23, 24, 39, 42
Exodus International, 95

F

Fawkes, Guy, 75
federalism, 12
Federalist Paper No. 78, 43, 95
Feeding America, 222
First Amendment, viii, ix, 3, 6, 10, 13, 21, 23, 24, 25, 26, 33, 36, 38, 39, 40, 41, 50, 53, 54, 55, 56, 57, 58, 60, 61, 62, 63, 70, 86, 87, 97, 99, 104, 110, 113, 116, 135, 137, 140, 141, 145, 166, 167, 175, 178, 181, 182, 183, 184, 185, 193, 200, 206, 210, 221
First Amendment Defense Act (FADA), 206, 207
First Liberty Institute, 204, 220
Flynn, Taylor, 85
Forms, 15
Franklin, Benjamin, 202
Free Exercise Clause, 19, 25, 28, 31, 33, 34, 35, 36, 37, 38, 40, 41, 42, 44, 45, 46, 47, 48, 49, 50, 52, 54, 61, 62, 66, 67, 98, 100, 102, 104, 130, 133, 176, 188, 189
freedom, 2, 6, 16, 19, 22, 24, 34, 38, 39, 40, 42, 44, 46, 48, 49, 50, 52, 53, 54, 56, 58, 59, 60, 65, 69, 70, 73, 74, 78, 79, 81, 89, 96, 98, 99, 101, 102, 108, 109, 111, 116, 118, 129, 132, 134, 136, 140, 141, 145, 148, 152, 157, 159, 164, 165, 166, 168, 170, 172, 179, 180, 182, 183, 185, 186, 188, 193, 197, 198, 199, 200, 202, 204, 205, 206, 207, 210, 215, 224
  of expression, 54, 59
  of worship, 35, 40, 42, 90, 148, 172
Freedom for all Americans, 179
Freedom in the World Index, 197
French Revolution, 209, 218
Friedersdorf, Connor, 151

G

Gallagher, Maggie, 77
Garry, Patrick, 24
Gay and Lesbian Services Organization (GLSO), 182, 183
general will, viii, 55, 113
Genovese, Eugene, 196
George, Francis, 160
Ginsberg, Ruth, 5
Girouard v. United States, 200
Gladstone, William, 2
Glazov, Jamie, 215, 221
God Bless America, 214
God hypothesis, 219
Gold, Susan, 82
Golden Rule, 10
Gonzales v. O Centro Espírita Beneficente União do Vegetal, 103
Gramsci, Antonio, 71, 152
Great Awokening, 218
Griffiths, Robert, 51

H

Habermas, Jurgen, 199, 235
Hall of Shame Report, 204
Hall, Charles, 210
Hamilton, Alexander, 10, 43, 95
Harris, Sam, 218
Hawthorn, Nathanial, 1, 236
Health and Human Services (HHS), 61, 159, 160, 161, 162, 176, 177, 241
Heart of Atlanta Motel v. United States, 117
Heisenberg, Werner, 52
History of the Peloponnesian Wars, 224
Hitchens, Christopher, 218
Hitchens, Peter, 195
hoasca, 103
Holcomb, Christiana, 148
Holdren, John, 158
Holt v. Hobbs, 103
Horowitz, David, 209
Huguenin, Elaine, 141, 143, 144
Hurley v. Irish American Gay, Lesbian, and Bisexual Group of Boston, 110, 137
Huxley, Aldous, 92, 204
hybrid rights, 54

I

Ignatiev, Noel, 217, 237
Imbody, Jonathan, 157
inalienable rights, 2, 6, 10, 95, 191, 200
individualism, 193, 195
Ingersoll, Robert, 131, 132, 135
International Christian Concern (ICC), 204
interracial marriage, 80, 81, 82
involuntary servitude, 3, 98, 113, 114, 115, 116, 117, 118, 119, 120, 130, 136, 137, 145, 167
Iowa Civil Rights Commission (ICRC), 146, 147, 148, 149
IQ-advertising, 212
Islam, 22, 186, 199, 201, 215, 221

J

Jack, William, 128, 129
Jackson, Robert, 139, 172
Jefferson, Thomas, 8, 24, 25, 26, 27, 28, 29, 32, 34, 39, 41, 48, 117, 161, 170, 201
Jennings, Kevin, 158
Jesus, 68, 82, 84, 100, 102, 121, 160, 167, 199, 204, 211
Jeter, Mildred, 80
Jim Crow laws, 84, 85, 181
Johnson, Gregory, 57
Jones, Van, 158
Judicial Watch, 158
just laws, 122
Justia US Law, 96

K

Kallipolis, 15
Kant, Immanuel, 9
Kennedy, Anthony, 31, 34, 60, 67, 78, 86, 87, 96, 130, 131, 154, 155
Kent, Samuel, 68
King Jr., Martin Luther, 122
Kinsey, Alfred, 93, 94
Kirsanow, Peter, 167
Kiska, Roger, 74
KKK, 70, 205
Klein, Melissa, 149
Koppleman, Andrew, 91
Koski, Breanna, 178, 179, 180
Krotoszynski, Ronald, 55
Kulturbolshewismus, 71, 74

L

LA Times, 214
Larsen, Angel, 184, 185, 186, 187
Lawrence v. Texas, 90
Laycock, Douglas, 43, 77, 83, 91, 98, 129, 139, 165
Lean on Me, 214
least restrictive standard, 99
LeBon, Gustave, 213
Lee v. Weisman, 66, 154
Legal Counsel for Alliance Defending Freedom, 148
Leiter, Brian, 50, 51
Lemon test, 29, 31
Lemon v. Kurtzman, 29
Letters Concerning the English Nation, 48
Lewis, C.S., 113, 202
LGBTQ, 2, 13, 34, 43, 52, 54, 55, 57, 58, 59, 61, 70, 76, 77, 80, 82, 83, 84, 86, 89, 92, 95, 97, 99, 103, 108, 112, 114, 117, 118, 122, 125, 127, 132, 134, 136, 137, 138, 140, 145, 147, 151, 152, 153, 154, 155, 165, 166, 167, 168, 171, 173, 175, 179, 182, 183, 187, 188, 194, 205, 207, 221, 224
  v. religious freedom, 54, 57, 86, 89
liberalism, 14, 72, 160, 165, 210
Lincoln, Abraham, 8, 16, 63
Little Sisters of the Poor, 161, 162, 163, 164, 229
Little Sisters of the Poor Saints Peter and Paul Home v. Pennsylvania, 163
Little Sisters of the Poor v. Burwell, 162, 250
living constitution argument, 9
Lloyd, Mark, 158
locus of control, 13, 14
Loewy, Arnold, 30
Louis XIV, 193
Loving v. Virginia, 80
Loving, Richard, 80
Lutheran World Relief, 222
Lynch v. Donnelly, 28

M

Madison, James, 4, 23, 27, 42, 44, 48, 99, 100, 116, 127, 139, 200
  and auxiliary precautions, 4
  and religious conscience, 23
  on religion, 44, 100, 116, 127
Magna Carta, 191
Malcolm X, 193
Man/Boy Love Association, 221
Marcuse, Herbert, 73, 76, 112, 152, 166, 221, 224
Marks, Joel, 203
Martin, Nicolle, 122, 126, 165, 200
Marx, Karl, 15, 55, 73, 76, 113, 191
Marxism, 71, 73, 75, 76
Masterpiece Cakeshop, 125, 126, 127, 141, 227,
matrimony, 171

McConnell, Michael, 47, 194
McGonnigal, Jamie, 171
McGurn, William, 168
Mein Kampf, 55
Memorial and Remonstrance against Religious Assessments, 27
Memories Pizza, 151, 152
Minnesota's Human Rights Act (MHRA), 184, 185, 186
modern day segregation, 83
moral relativism, 202
morality, 7, 32, 34, 63, 72, 73, 76, 80, 84, 90, 91, 123, 148, 160, 191, 199, 202, 203, 205, 206, 210, 211, 212
  objective, 202, 203, 204
  social, 20
Mullins, David, 126, 127, 128, 129
Murdock, Deroy, 116

N

Natelson, Robert, 25, 32, 38
National Gay Rights Lobby, 91
National Institute of Family and Life Advocates v. Becerra, 60
National Socialist Party, 192
natural law, 3, 9, 10, 111, 122
Nazism, 75, 201
negative rights, 11, 121, 123
Nelson, Teresa, 186
new atheism, 218
New Mexico Human Rights Commission (NMHRC), 141, 145
Nietzsche, Friedrich Wilhelm, 203
Ninth Amendment, 12
Noll, Mark, 39
non-preferentialism, 19
Northwest Ordinance, 63
Novak, Michael, 220

O

Obama, Barack, 11, 12, 34, 42, 75, 120, 130, 157, 158, 159, 160, 161, 164, 165, 168, 172, 178, 206, 212
Obergefell v. Hodges, 76, 77
Ocasio-Cortez, Alexandria, 7
Odgaard, Betty, 146
Odgaard, Richard, 146
Office for Civil Rights (OCR), 162
Office of Legal Policy, 37, 62, 111
Ontario Human Rights Commission, 55
Oregon Bureau of Labor and Industries (BOLI), 149, 150
originalism, 6, 7, 8, 11, 233
Otis, James, 3

P

Paulsen, Michael, 36, 41
Pavan v. Smith, 96
Peaceful Coexistence: Reconciling Nondiscrimination Principles with Civil Liberties, 165
Pearson, Karl, 193
Pepper, Stephen, 37
Perez v. Sharpe, 82
Perez, Tom, 7
Pew Research Center, 207
Phillips, Jack, 125, 126, 127, 128, 129, 130, 131, 136, 137, 138, 139, 183
Pithouse, Richard, 5
Planck, Max, 51
Plato, 14, 15, 16, 113
Pledge of Allegiance, 72, 220
polygamy, 100, 101
Pontifical Council for Pastoral Assistance to Health Care Workers, 222
Pope Francis, 92
Pope John Paul II, 200
Porteous, A.T.D., 15, 16

positive rights, 11
Posner, Richard, 12
Prager, Dennis, 216
precedence, 46, 52, 70, 142, 154
Primer, 63
Project Veritas, 5
proletariat, 113
public accommodation laws, 1, 3, 39, 53, 59, 97, 108, 111, 116, 122, 136, 137
Putnam, Robert, 223

R

R.G. & G.R. Harris Funeral Homes Inc. v. Equal Employment Opportunity Commission, 153
Race Traitor, 217
Rand, Ayn, 112
Raphael, 14
Ratifying Convention on Control of the Military, 42
reason, 5, 15, 27, 36, 37, 47, 50, 51, 54, 57, 77, 85, 95, 100, 117, 118, 120, 131, 197, 198, 203, 206, 210, 222
Rehnquist, William, 28, 66, 68, 110
Reisman, Judith, 94
relativism, 15
religion, 11, 12, 13, 19, 20, 21, 22, 23, 24, 25, 26, 27, 28, 29, 30, 31, 32, 33, 36, 37, 38, 39, 40, 41, 42, 43, 44, 45, 46, 47, 48, 49, 50, 51, 52, 54, 56, 62, 63, 64, 66, 68, 69, 70, 75, 77, 79, 82, 89, 97, 98, 99, 100, 102, 103, 116, 117, 118, 127, 128, 136, 137, 138, 139, 143, 146, 148, 149, 152, 153, 157, 159, 161, 162, 163, 164, 165, 166, 172, 175, 176, 179, 180, 186, 188, 189, 192, 194, 196, 198, 200, 205, 206, 209, 210, 212, 218, 219, 221, 222, 223
  and morality, 205
  establishment of, 6, 19, 20, 21, 22, 24, 26, 33, 37, 65
  hostility towards, 23, 27, 28, 30, 32, 66, 68, 69, 129, 134, 135, 188
  protecting, 46, 47, 165
  public expression of, 26, 39
  subversive, 210
religious clauses, 44, 63, 66
religious conscience, 2, 21, 22, 23, 41, 45, 46, 48, 51, 84, 85, 86, 98, 100, 104, 113, 115, 118, 137, 145, 149, 153, 154, 162, 167, 185, 209
Religious Freedom Restoration Act (RFRA), 49, 53, 103, 143, 151, 160, 175, 176, 178, 207
religious liberty, 2, 3, 21, 23, 26, 27, 28, 34, 36, 37, 42, 43, 45, 49, 52, 53, 54, 62, 66, 79, 83, 86, 87, 89, 90, 91, 95, 97, 98, 99, 100, 104, 105, 125, 127, 129, 141, 143, 144, 157, 158, 159, 164, 165, 166, 167, 175, 178, 186, 189, 200, 204, 210, 220
  and Elane Photography, 141
  and Establishment Clause, 33
  and Free Exercise Clause, v, 189
  and Hobby Lobby, 177, 178
  and Jefferson, 27
  and LGBTQ rights, viii, 90
  and Masterpiece Cakeshop, 141
  and Obama, 157, 168, 172, 206
  and special treatment, 44
  and the state, 98, 99
  Castro on, 165, 166, 168
Reproductive FACT Act (RFA), 60, 61
Republic, 15, 44, 50, 113, 220
Reynolds v. United States, 100
Reynolds, George, 100
Roberts, Owen, 40
Roediger, David, 217
Rogers, Austin, 41
Rolleston, Moreton, 117, 118
Rose, Stephanie, 149
Rosen, Jody, 214

Rost, Thomas, 153
Rothenberg, Paula, 217
Rushton, Phillippe, 55

S

Safe and Drug-Free Schools, 158
Salvation Army, 222
Santa Fe Independent School District v. Doe, 67, 68
Scanlan, Alfred, 27
Scardina, Autumn, 130
Schulzke, Marcus, 218, 219
Schwartzman, Micah, 45, 46
Seattle Post-Intelligencer, 91
self-control, 13, 14, 231
Separation of Church and State, 43
Setari, Renee, 30
Severino, Roger, 162
sexual orientation, 69, 72, 74, 77, 83, 93, 94, 99, 109, 112, 126, 128, 130, 136, 139, 143, 147, 148, 180, 182, 187, 222
Sexual Orientation and Gender Identity, 148
sexual preference, 93, 94
Shabbat, 10
Shapiro, Ilya, 167
Sharia law, 199, 201
Shaw, George Bernard, 75
Sherbert v. Verner, 163
Silva, Marjorie, 128, 129, 136
Sioux Center News, 147
slavery,, 7, 90, 114, 115, 118, 130, 139, 166, 214, 216, 218
Smith, Tyler, 150
Snyder, Larry, 160
socialism, 72, 73, 75, 191, 192, 193, 194, 195, 196, 197, 210, 213, 231, 238, 239, 244, 249
    and big government, 4, 56, 112, 194
Socialist International, 158
Sojourner, 210, 211
Solzhenitsyn, Aleksandr, 196
Southern Poverty Law Center (SPLC), 204
Spence v. Washington, 56
Spence, Harold, 56, 57, 141
spouse, 77
Springsteen, Bruce, 156
Star-Spangled Banner, 64, 214
statutory rights, 95, 97, 112
Steadman, Pat, 77
Stengel, Richard, 56
Stephens, Aimee, 153
Stewart, Potter, 64
Stone v. Graham, 65
Stone, Sydell, 65
Story, Joseph, 21
strict scrutiny standard, 99, 103
Stutzman, Barronelle, 131, 132, 133, 134, 135, 136, 138, 139
Stychin, Carl, 95
subjectivism, 15

T

Talmud, 10, 221
Taney, Roger, 7, 8
Tatchell, Peter, 152
Taylor, D.J., 15, 85, 222
Telescope Media Group, 184
Telescope Media Grp. v. Lucero, 185
Ten Commandments, 65
Tertullian, Quintus, 197
Texas v. Johnson, 96
The Moral Basis of Socialism, 193
The Rights of the British Colonies Asserted and Proved, 3
The Scarlet Letter, 1
The School of Athens, 14
theism, 45
Thirteenth Amendment, 1, 3, 8, 98, 113, 114, 116, 117, 118, 119, 136, 145, 220

Thomas, Norman, 72
Thucydides, 224
Trautvetter, Kathy, 183
Treaty of Tripoli, 165
Trigg, Roger, 40
Trinity Lutheran Church, 188
Trinity Lutheran Church of Columbia, Inc. v. Comer, 18
Trump, Donald, 120, 162
Trump, Ivanka, 156
Turley, Jonathan, 56

U

ubermensch, 203
United States Conference of Catholic Bishops, 161
United States v. Kozminski, 115
United States v. Peters, 96
United States v. Seeger, 47
United States v. Winsor, 77
Universal Declaration of Human Rights, 42
University of Bologna, 197
unjust law, 121, 122
Ursuline Sisters, 161, 169, 170
US Agency for Global Media, 56
US National Gay Task Force, 93

V

Voltaire, 48

W

Waggoner, Kristen, 134, 135
wall of separation, 24, 25, 26, 28, 29, 32, 34, 42, 43
Wall Street Journal, 168
Wallace v. Jaffree, 28, 65
Walz v. Tax Commission of the City of New York, 33
Warren, Earl, 81
Washington Examiner, 131
Washington Times, 157
Washington, George, 35, 66, 68, 205
Webster, Noah, 63
Weisman, Deborah, 67, 154
welfare, 33, 50, 119, 120, 122, 169, 170, 194, 222, 223
West Virginia State Board of Education v. Barnette, 58, 139, 172
West, Michael, 218
White, Byron, 34, 90
whiteness, 216, 217, 218
whiteness studies, 216, 217
Why Tolerate Religion?, 50
Widmar v. Vincent, 70
Will, George, 223
Willock, Vanessa, 141, 142, 143
Wilson, Robin, 164
Windham, Lori, 158
Winthrop, Robert, 195, 202
Wisconsin v. Yoder, 97
Wooley v. Maynard, 58, 145
workfare, 119
World Trade Center, 100

Z

Zedong, Mao, 158
Zizik, Slavoj, 195
Zorach v. Clauson, 28